The Planetary Bargain

The Planetary Bargain
Corporate Social Responsibility Matters

Michael Hopkins

Earthscan Publications Ltd
London • Sterling, VA

First published in the UK and USA in 2003
by Earthscan Publications Ltd

ISBN: 1 85383 978 7 paperback
        1 85383 973 6 hardback

Typesetting by MapSet Ltd, Gateshead, UK
Printed and bound in the UK by Creative Print and Design Wales, Ebbw Vale
Cover design by Declan Buckley

For a full list of publications please contact:

Earthscan Publications Ltd
120 Pentonville Road, London, N1 9JN, UK
Tel: +44 (0)20 7278 0433
Fax: +44 (0)20 7278 1142
Email: earthinfo@earthscan.co.uk
Web: www.earthscan.co.uk

22883 Quicksilver Drive, Sterling, VA 20166-2012, USA

Earthscan is an editorially independent subsidiary of Kogan Page Ltd and publishes
in association with WWF-UK and the International Institute for Environment and
Development

A catalogue record for this book is available from the British Library

Library of Congress Cataloging-in-Publication Data

Hopkins, Michael, 1945 Nov. 16-.

    The planetary bargain : corporate social responsibility matters / Michael
        Hopkins.
        p. cm.

    Includes bibliographical references and index.
    ISBN 1-85383-978-7 (pbk.) — ISBN 1-85383-973-6 (hardback)
    1. Social responsibility of business. I. Title.

    HD60.H67 2003
    658.4'08—dc21

                                                              2003003990

This book is printed on elemental chlorine free paper

To Jawahir and Ivor

'Don't ask what your country can do for you,
ask what your company can do for your country.'
(With apologies to JFK's inaugural speech, January 1961.)

Contents

List of Figures, Boxes and Tables

Figures

Boxes

Tables

Preface

Corporate social responsibility (CSR) now matters and has taken root at an even faster pace than envisaged when the first version of this book was published some five years ago.[1] Encroaching on CSR are other concepts, such as corporate sustainability, corporate citizenship, corporate responsibility, as well as the older concerns with business ethics, business in society and the ethical corporation. I devote sections of the book explaining the main differences and similarities between these concepts. This significantly revised version of the earlier book updates the material with some of the most important developments since that time and also reflects the author's new ideas since these have also evolved with time. It also reflects the change from 'Corporate social responsibility comes of age', the sub-title of the earlier book, to a broader concern with 'Corporate social responsibility matters'.[2]

Many are wondering where it will all end as unemployment remains stubbornly high in most of the richest nations of the world, poverty persists in the developing nations, globalization protests are more and more directed at large transnational corporations (TNCs), and chief executive officers (CEOs) of large corporations are under investigation as never before. The social protection gained for people in Europe over the nearly 60 years since the end of World War II is under continual threat as costs rise. And the richest nation in the world, the US, struggles to keep its more meagre than Europe social-protection provisions. In the face of these mainly economic concerns comes a run of corporate governance scandals from Enron to WorldCom to who knows where it will all end?

Will it all end with the world's production going to the lowest common denominator – that is, the country with the lowest social costs, the most paltry wages, the poorest working conditions, and those with the lowest pensions for the old? The trend seems to be heading this way as inequalities deepen; yet, this is in no one's interest. The perpetrators of the horrible events in New York on 11 September 2001 all died without a clear message and their apologists, of which happily there are few, claim to be beholden to the downtrodden. But most of us do not go out to commit hideous acts in the name of the poor. We have a firm belief that reducing poverty and inequality is right for its own sake, not just because it may reduce terrorism. Indeed, most poor consumers in developing countries would very much like higher living standards, and the sorts of social protection accorded to workers in Germany (say). Transnational corporations need customers for their goods, something not helped by the rising unemployment associated with downsizing or impoverishment in developing countries.

The book's main thesis is that to reverse the negative tendencies of increasing poverty and inequality in the world, there is a need for a worldwide compact, or planetary bargain, between the private and public sectors. In this bargain, the public sector will help private organisms to operate with clear ground rules, and the private sector will pay more attention to longer-term social development issues than ever before. What such a bargain could include, why it is necessary and who should be involved are the themes that run throughout the book.

A planetary bargain will mean more socially responsible enterprises (SREs). In time, it will not be possible to conduct business without being socially responsible. This is inevitable; therefore, contrary to conventional wisdom, the book does not propose a new set of rules for businesses to adhere to – as, for instance, is argued by those pushing for more corporate social accountability or social audits. The book will argue that new rules or corporate laws in this area may well be unnecessary, because corporations will see for themselves – and many have seen this already – the need to behave more responsibly in the social area. The book does argue for a 'level playing field' in which a minimum set of rules for corporate behaviour is required. But it does not argue for new sets of complex rules simply because these would make it even more difficult for corporations to operate and, in turn, would encourage further hopping from one advantageous country to another. If the same rules could be applied universally, many corporations would accept CSR since a level playing field would apply for all. But, despite halting steps in this direction by such bodies as the European Union (EU) and countries such as France, an agreed set of rules for CSR activities is unlikely. Moreover, a world consciousness of stakeholders, such as consumers, employees and local communities, will be better placed to create this level playing field.

Can the private sector do more other than just be good at business? It is the underlying thesis of this book that being a socially responsible enterprise is not only good for business; it is actually better for business in terms of long-term profits and stability. It will not be my job here to suggest areas where the private sector can make profits through helping social development directly – they are their own masters at this. For instance, the private sector has been helpful in housing projects for low-income groups, providing credit through the banking system, promoting education through private educational institutions and so on. But CSR is not just about corporate philanthropy; as the book argues, it is about a new management and strategic philosophy for companies large, medium and small.

The field of CSR, of which this book forms a part, has a burgeoning literature in published form in books, articles, newsprint and, increasingly, on the internet. Where possible, I have indicated the internet web pages that I have used, as well as suggesting others that provide useful reference points.

There have been few attempts at quantification of what is meant by CSR in the literature; what does exist, mainly through the social screens of ethical investment companies, is largely subjective. When I started research in this area in 1992, I had intended to rank the Fortune 500 companies from 1 to 500 on an HDI index (human development index following the United Nations Development Programme's work). This task proved beyond my resources but launched me, nevertheless, some ten years ago into this field. This book captures my efforts at determining a conceptual framework for these indicators and then examines how I calibrated them for the UK. I was fortunate to be able to use the good services of the universities of York and London through my friendship with Professor Roy Carr-Hill to collect the necessary information for the 100 largest companies in the UK – here I only report on the top 25 to keep the book a reasonable length.

However, I could not present indicators without first looking at what others have done in the field of CSR – and there is a lot. So I have critically reviewed this in the first seven chapters. In these, I also develop the elements of an economic theory of socially responsible enterprises when I show, mainly through case studies and anecdotal examples, that social responsibility not only has strong philanthropic undertones, but – as important, if not more so – it has sound economic reasons, too. By this, I mean that it is increasingly in the economic interest of business and, consequently, of societies to engage in socially responsible activities. If it is not in the fabric of companies today, then these companies, more than likely, will not exist tomorrow. This is why, in the book, I argue the need for a planetary bargain.

The main work in the area of CSR has been in the US and, more recently, in the UK. The book draws most of its examples from these two countries. Many other countries in both the so-called 'developed' and 'developing' worlds are starting to take the concepts, ideas and practices seriously, too. I cover some of these experiences in Chapters 6 and 10 of the book.

Thus, the book covers CSR matters and, more particularly, it:

■ defines what is meant by CSR;
■ reviews the historical roots of CSR;
■ provides the elements of a theory of CSR;
■ suggests a number of precise indicators that can be used to measure CSR based upon a clear conceptual framework;
■ shows how these indicators can be applied in practice;
■ provides a number of case studies, including some evidence from developing countries; and
■ reviews how CSR is being implemented, audited and reported upon by leading groups in the area.

The central theme is: What sort of planetary bargain could help increase corporate profitability while not resorting to the bargain basement? Gradually, the United Nations (UN), World Bank, International Labour Organization (ILO), Organisation for Economic Co-operation and Development (OECD), International Development Bank (IDB), Asian Development Bank (AsDB), African Development Bank (AfDB), United Nations Conference on Trade and Development (UNCTAD), United Nations Educational, Scientific and Cultural Organization (UNESCO), United Nations Development Programme (UNDP), United Nations Children's Fund (UNICEF), United Nations Research Institute for Social Development (UNRISD), United Nations Environment Programme (UNEP), the UN's Global Compact and the World Trade Organization (WTO), as well as the burgeoning number of private networks of enterprises and non-governmental organizations (NGOs), such as the Social Venture Network (SVN), the European Business Ethical Network (EBEN), AccountAbility, Business for Social Responsibility (BSR), Business in the Community, the Global Reporting Initiative (GRI), the World Economic Forum (WEF), the World Business Council on Social Development (WBCSD), the International Business Leaders Forum (IBLF) and the Caux Principles, are coming to grips with the global issue but, as yet, have not seen this as a planetary bargain. It is my hope that this book will contribute to this process, and that beggar-thy-neighbour polices, of countries and enterprises, will be a thing of the past as the peoples of the world move toward a global agreement with the private sector. The next millennium will have to be the age of CSR.

List of Acronyms and Abbreviations

AA1000	AccountAbility 1000
ABB	Asea Brown Boveri
ABSA	Association for Business Sponsorship of the Arts
ACCA	Association of Chartered Certified Accountants
ACP	African, Caribbean and Pacific countries
AfDB	African Development Bank
AGM	annual general meeting
ANSALDO	Italian electromechanical company
APO	Asian Productivity Organization
ASA	Advertising Standards Authority
AsDB	Asian Development Bank
BA	British Airways
BBC	Bishops Businessmen's Conference for Human Development
BIE	Business in the Environment
BitC	Business in the Community
BP	British Petroleum
BT	British Telecom
BSI	British Standards Institute
BSR	Business for Social Responsibility
BT	British Telecommunications
CalPERS	Californian Public Employees Retirement System
CACG	Commonwealth Association for Corporate Governance
CAR	Central African Republic
CBI	Confederation of British Industries
CEE	Corporate Environmental Engagement
CEO	chief executive officer
CEP	Council on Economic Priorities (US)
CEPAA	Council on Economic Priorities Accreditation Agency (now SAI)
CERES	Coalition for Environmentally Responsible Economies
CFC	chlorofluorocarbon
CIA	Central Intelligence Agency (US)
CNN	Cable News Network (US)
CO_2	carbon dioxide

CONAR	Conselho Nacional de Auto-Regulamentação Publicitária (Brazil)
CORE	Child Survival Collaborations and Resources Group (The CORE Group)
CR	corporate responsibility
CRITICS	Corporate Responsibility Index through Internet Consultation of Stakeholders
CRM	cause-related marketing
CRSP	Center for Research in Security Prices (US)
CSM	Centre for Social Markets
CSP	corporate social performance
CSR	corporate social responsibility
CSR_2	corporate social responsiveness
CSu	corporate sustainability
DFID	Department for International Development (UK) (*formerly* ODA)
DG	director general
DJSI	Dow Jones Sustainability Index
DJSI STOXX	Dow Jones STOXX Sustainability Indexes
DOL	Department of Labor (US)
DOM-TOM	départements et territoires d'outre-mer
DSI	Domini 400 Social Index
EAS	ethical accounting statement
EBEN	European Business Ethics Network
EBIT	earnings before interest and taxes
EBNSC	European Business Network for Social Cohesion
EC	European Commission
EDF	Electricité de France
EEOs	equal employment opportunities
EEOC	Equal Employment Opportunities Commission
EIP	Employment Intensive Programme
Eiris	Ethical Investment Research Service
EMAS	Eco-Management and Audit Scheme
ENEL	Italian electricity company
ENI	Ente Nazionale Idrocarburi
EPA	Environmental Protection Agency (US)
ERM	Environmental Resources Management
ETI	Ethical Trading Initiative
EU	European Union
EVA	economic value added
FIDES	Fundação Instituto de Desenvovimento Empresarial e Social
FS	Italian railways
FSC	Forest Stewardship Council (UK)
FT	Financial Times
FTSE	Financial Times Stock Exchange

GATT	General Agreement on Tariffs and Trade
GDP	gross domestic product
GE	General Electric
GM	General Motors
GRI	Global Reporting Initiative
GSM	Global System for Mobile Communications
HD	human development
HDE	human development enterprise
HDI	human development index
HR	human resources
HRE	human resource enterprise
HSBC	Hong Kong and Shanghai Banking Corporation
IBLF	International Business Leaders Forum
ICC	International Chamber of Commerce
ICFTU	International Confederation of Free Trade Unions
ICI	Imperial Chemical Industries
ICRBP	International Centre for Business Performance and Corporate Responsibility
IDB	International Development Bank
IES	Institute of Employment Studies (UK)
ILO	International Labour Organization
IMD	International Institute for Management and Development (business school in Lausanne, Switzerland)
IMF	International Monetary Fund
INPS	Italian national institute for pension funds
INSEAD	Institut Européen d'Administration des Affaires (business school in Fontainebleau, France)
IRI-STET	Italian telecommunications company
IRRC	Investor Responsibility Research Center (US)
ISEA	Institute for Social and Ethical Accountability
ISO	International Organization for Standardization
ITC	Independent Television Commission
ITGLWF	International Textile, Garment and Leather Workers' Federation
IUF	International Union of Food Workers
JSI	Jantsi Social Investment Index
KLD	Kinder, Lydenberg & Domini
KPMG	one of the 'Big Four' accounting firms (with Deloitte & Touche, Ernst & Young and PriceWaterhouseCoopers)
LDC	less developed country
LSE	London Stock Exchange
MCCR	Minnesota Centre for Corporate Responsibility
MIBA	Société Minière de Makwanga (the Congo)
MNE	multinational enterprise
MORI	Market and Opinion Research International
NAFTA	North American Free Trade Association

NEF	New Economics Foundation (UK)
NESC	National and Economic Social Council (Ireland)
NGO	non-governmental organization
NIC	newly industrialized country
NLC	National Labour Committee (US)
ODA	Overseas Development Administration (UK) (*now* DFID)
OEBU	Schweizerische Vereinigung für ökologisch bewusste Unternehmensführung (Swiss association for ecological awareness in management)
OECD	Organisation for Economic Co-operation and Development
OFT	Office of Fair Trading (UK)
ORSE	Observatoire sur la Responsabilité Sociétale des Entreprises
PBSP	Philippine Business for Social Progress
PE	price earnings
PfG	Partners for Growth (Zimbabwe)
PIMS	Profit Impact of Market Strategy Group (UK)
PNG	Papua New Guinea
PR	public relations
Q-RES	Quality of Social and Ethical Responsibility of Corporations Project
QSF	Quality Scoring Framework (of the ISEA)
QUEST	QUality, Ethics and SafeTy (B&Q assessment process)
R&D	research and development
RTZ	Rio Tinto Zinc
S&P	Standard & Poor's
SA	social auditing
SA8000	Social Accountability 8000
SAI	Social Accountability International
SAM	Sustainability Asset Management Group
SAS	Special Air Service
SEC	Securities and Exchange Commission (US)
SIGMA	Sustainability: Integrated Guidelines for Management
SIM	social issues in management
SIP	statement of investment principles
SMART	specific, measurable, achievable, realistic and timely
SR	social responsibility
SRE	socially responsible enterprise
SREI	socially responsible enterprise index
SRI	socially responsible investment
SRIE	socially responsible indigenous enterprise
ST	stakeholder theory
STEP	Shell Technology Enterprise Programme
SVN	Social Venture Network
TBL	triple bottom line

TCC	Copenhagen Centre
TERI	Tata Energy Research Institute
TIAA-CREF	Teachers Insurance and Annuity Association – College Retirement Equities Fund (US)
TNC	transnational corporation
TSE	Toronto Stock Exchange
TSRDS	Tata Iron and Steel Rural Development Society
TUC	Trades Union Congress
UK	United Kingdom
UN	United Nations
UNAIDS	Joint United Nations Programme on HIV/AIDS
UNCED	United Nations Conference on Environment and Development (*also known as* the Earth Summit)
UNCTAD	United Nations Conference on Trade and Development
UNDP	United Nations Development Programme
UNEP	United Nations Environment Programme
UNESCO	United Nations Educational, Scientific and Cultural Organization
UNIAPAC	International Union of Christian Business Executives
UNICEF	United Nations Children's Fund
UNRISD	United Nations Research Institute for Social Development
UPS	United Parcel Service
US	United States
USM	Unlisted Securities Market
VW	Volkswagen
WBCSD	World Business Council for Sustainable Development
WCED	World Commission on Environment and Development
WEF	World Economic Forum
WTO	World Trade Organization
WWF	*formerly known as* World Wide Fund For Nature

Chapter 1

Why Corporate Social Responsibility?

This chapter introduces the notion of corporate social responsibility (CSR), from its historical roots to what is happening today, particularly in the US and UK, where ideas about social responsibility have made their biggest impact to date. The key issue for a business is its bottom line, and how social responsibility either contributes to or weighs against this. I look at this under the heading: 'Is business's only job to make a profit?' Linked to this important question are three further areas that have dominated the CSR debate in recent times: stakeholder theory, the notion of trust and business ethics. I examine each of these areas in this chapter in relation to how they fit within the framework of a socially responsible enterprise. There are a variety of definitions of CSR and no overall agreement. My own definition, which I elaborate in various sections throughout this book, is:

> CSR is concerned with treating the stakeholders of the firm ethically or in a responsible manner.

'Ethically or responsible' means treating stakeholders in a manner deemed acceptable by society. Social includes economic responsibility. Stakeholders exist both within a firm and outside – the natural environment is a stakeholder. The wider aim of social responsibility is to create higher and higher standards of living, while preserving the profitability of the corporation, for peoples both within and outside of the corporation.

Introduction

Historical roots

CSR is not a new issue. The social responsibility of business was not widely considered to be a significant problem from the time of the 18th-century Scottish social philosopher and classical economist Adam Smith to the Great Depression in the 1930s. But since the 1930s and, increasingly, the 1960s, social responsibility has become 'an important issue not only for business but in the theory and practice of law, politics and economics'.[1]

During the early 1930s, Merrick Dodd of Harvard Law School and Adolf Berle of Columbia Law School debated the question: 'For whom are corporate managers trustees?'[2] Dodd advocated that corporations served a social service as well as a profit-making function, a view repudiated by Berle. This debate simmered for the next 50 years, according to Gary von Stange, before it once again sprang into prominence during the 1980s, in the wake of the 'feeding frenzy atmosphere of numerous hostile take-overs'. This concern for the social responsibility of business has even accelerated since the fall of the Berlin Wall, which symbolized the collapse of communism and (more importantly) has turbo-charged globalization.

Further acceleration has occurred in the past few years. Global concerns were given an additional edge by the awful events of 11 September 2001. The collapse of Enron and WorldCom and their auditor Andersen due to dubious accounting practices has raised the level of examination of large companies, as well as their auditors. At the time of writing, this occurs in spite of the most friendly-to-companies US president known in modern times, George Bush – with a dubious past in share dealings and in 'sailing close to the wind' in business transactions as Paul Krugman's 'Op-Ed' columns in *The New York Times* have carefully analysed. Even the president has broached, albeit tamely, the notion of the responsibility of corporations.[3] Moreover, previously quiet chief executive officers (CEOs) have begun to note the pressure. For instance, in a rare public appearance in June 2002, the chairman and chief executive of Goldman Sachs, Henry M Paulson Jr, noted, after the collapse of the Enron Corporation in late 2001, that 'I cannot think of a time when business overall has been held in less repute'.[4]

Moreover, the need to address questions of low living standards, exploitation, poverty, unemployment, and how to promote social development in general, has been almost entirely the preserve of governments. Clearly, they will continue to have *a*, if not *the*, major role to play. But in the future, the promotion of social development issues must increasingly also be one of partnership between the government and private and non-governmental actors, as well as – in particular – the corporate sector. The importance of this is brought home by their size. When companies' turnover is compared with the gross domestic product (GDP) of countries, then, of the world's largest 100 economies, 50 turn out to be corporations![5]

Up until the 1970s, despite regulation and legislation, business continued largely along an autonomous path from which it ignored its critics and listened only to its shareholders, to whom it felt somewhat responsible. But the decade of the 1960s was to be a period of enlightenment for many. The Korean War had ended indecisively, and new conflicts in South-East Asia seemed destined to follow the same pattern. Citizens were distrustful of government, of business and of the undefined 'establishment'. Consumers had grown suspicious of adulterants in their food and dangerous defects in the products they bought. People were becoming aware of the

/ sustainability

fragile nature of the Earth's ecology, while simultaneously becoming more cognisant of human rights.

However, the drive during the 1970s to set every nation to contribute 1 per cent of its GDP to socio-economic development failed miserably, with only small countries such as the Netherlands and Sweden getting anywhere near that figure. The largest economy, the US, gives only a meagre 0.1 per cent, and most of that goes to only two countries – Egypt and Israel. Now, should we expect those companies with turnovers larger than that of Holland to contribute 1 per cent of turnover to compensate – that is, to fill – this gap where nation states have failed? Is this excessively naive, or is it crucial that they do so to secure future sustainable development? The fact that over 300 UK companies already belong to a Per Cent Club, with an aim of contributing 1 per cent of pre-tax profits to the community, is both a step in the right direction and an indication that many firms are beginning to take their social responsibilities seriously.

The focus, in this book, is on the largest companies – the transnational corporation (TNCs). By the early 1980s, trade between the 350 largest TNCs contributed about 40 per cent of global trade; today, the TNCs account for 70 per cent of the world's trade. In addition, foreign direct investment from TNCs doubled from the early 1980s to the early 1990s, from US$910 billion to US$1.7 trillion. Because of the often immense size of TNCs, decisions about the location of their investments, production and technology not only influence the distribution of factor endowments – notably of capital, skilled labour and knowledge – between the countries in which they run their activities, but also assume a crucial importance for their political and social consequences.

Today

Today we see consumers avoiding what they see (rightly or wrongly) as socially irresponsibly made products or products of companies that have allegedly not acted in society's best interest. It is inevitable, as I shall argue in this book, that, more than ever before, companies in the private sector will be expected to behave socially responsibly. Already, many enterprises across the world have taken this as part of their business plan, and, one may note, they are doing this because they feel it is good for business.

Enterprises have noted that social responsibility is good for business for, and from, each part of the *seven main azimuths* within which they trade and operate. These parts are their shareholders and potential investors; managers; employees; customers; business partners and contractors or suppliers; the natural environment; and the communities within which they operate, including national governments (discussed in Chapter 3). These azimuths are now commonly known as an enterprise's stakeholders. I will show with anecdotal and statistical evidence throughout this book – and, in particular, in Chapter 9 – using data for the largest enterprises in the UK, that an emphasis on stakeholders does not hinder profitability. On the other hand, negative social events, such as a poor internal human-resource policy, cavalier downsizing, and an industrially caused environmental disaster or conviction for a corporate crime, are likely to have harmful effects on profitability and return on investment.

On the plus side, according to the US Social Investment Forum, for the first time ever, more than US$1 trillion in assets are under management in the US in socially and environmentally responsible portfolios.[6] Estimates vary, since it all depends upon definition; but this latter figure has been backed up in the September issue of *The Cerulli Edge-Global Edition* published by Cerulli Associates, a well-regarded Boston- and London-based research consultancy who estimated, in September 2001, the value of the *world's* ethical investment portfolio to be US$1.42 trillion.[7]

In the UK pension fund, trustees are required to incorporate their policy on socially responsible investment (SRI) in their statement of investment principles (SIP) – the document that sets out the aims, scope and restrictions for the investment of the pension fund. Concomitantly, there has been a rapid expansion of firms that screen companies for socially responsible performance, which is having a positive effect on the redirection of investors toward those companies that are top performers in this area. According to Eiris, in the UK about US$49.3 billion was invested in SRI funds in 2001, less than 1 per cent of total funds under management, although this figure has been doubling every two years.[8] Across Europe, about US$9.38 billion was under SRI management in 2001, again according to the SRI monitoring firm Eiris.

Pension funds and other financial vehicles have billions of dollars available, and speak with a loud voice as their members become increasingly concerned about where and how their money is invested. Indeed, appalled at being implicated in antisocial practices, thousands of investors are placing ethics on a par with personal gain in choosing where to put their money. In response, a number of money managers are tailoring portfolios to allay their clients' qualms. By now, the managers of billions of dollars of investment funds have channelled their cash into companies that pass one test or another for ethical or social responsibility. For people investing their own money, several investment management companies maintain blacklists of ethically or socially *ir*responsible companies.

Moreover, poor social performance will drive away potential investors. The increase in litigation, especially in the US (arising from corporate lawbreaking), has strengthened the penalties on professionals and has made the conduct of business a hazardous occupation. Because of the litigation explosion, business now faces a two-front battle: increases in both the number of multi-million dollar verdicts and the number of actions actually filed. Expanded third-party liability means that many more professional groups are being held liable, including underwriters, accountants and lawyers. The year 1992 was the first in which substantial awards were given to corporate whistle-blowers; since then, the increased focus on business conduct has coincided with the growing public perception that business should be more socially responsible.

As the public becomes aware of the negative consequences of the social irresponsibility of some businesses, so too has it become aware of good products and socially responsible activities. In parallel, business has also become equally aware of the informed consumer and/or investor. Yet, although TNCs could potentially play an important role in social development, their current impact on this process is moderate, according to some commentators.[9]

Corporate wrongdoers

Alice Tepper Marlin, the founder of the US Council on Economic Priorities (CEP), was the original promoter of a report that has since sold 600,000 copies with the title *Shopping for a Better World: A Quick and Easy Guide to Socially Responsible Supermarket Shopping*. The book rated 168 companies behind 1800 products in such areas as charitable giving, community outreach, information disclosure, environmental impact and family benefits. So many people contacted companies after the 1989 guide was published that the 1990 issue included an appendix with the names and addresses of all the listed companies' chief executive officers. A CEP study of buyers of the guide found that 78 per cent said they had switched brands as a result of using it, and that 64 per cent refer to it regularly. The seeds of CEP were planted when Tepper Marlin was a Wall Street securities analyst with a client who did not want to invest in companies that supplied arms for use in Vietnam. Since its beginning, CEP had an impact far in excess of its size, now at 6500 individual members.[10] CEP has since evolved into Social Accountability International (SAI) and promotes labour standards and rights with its instrument known as SA8000 (Social Accountability 8000 – see Chapter 7).

Responsible corporations

There are many attempts nowadays to reward good corporate social performance (CSP). It seems that not a month goes by without some publication announcing winners of a corporate award, and these have more than doubled since 1979. According to Gita Siegman, editor of the tenth edition of *Awards, Honors and Prizes*, there were 6000 listings of awards in the US; in the latest edition, there will be 15,500 listings.[11] Besides the normal complement of prizes in arts, sciences and letters, corporate awards can be given and received in such diverse categories as women's achievement, human rights and environmental correctness. Many of the significant honours – including the Baldridge – were created in the mid to late 1980s.[12] Most were established to honour corporate responsibility, initiative, environmental sensitivity or other exemplary behaviour. A good corporate award should be clearly defined and relevant. It should illuminate exemplary behaviour, even corporate heroism, and it should spawn imitative actions. It should also be well publicized, so that there is an air of expectation.[13]

More and more, we are seeing awards going to ethical businesses; the best known in the US are the top 100 corporate citizens of the magazine *Business Ethics*, and in the UK the Association of Chartered Certified Accountants (ACCA) business ethics awards and the awards for excellence of Business in the Community (BitC).[14,15,16] A problem with all of these rewards is either that they tend to acclaim a specific programme or policy, without regard to other factors, or that each awarding agency has its own, often unpublished, criteria for the awards. Thus, each of the awards may carry some motivational impact, but the totality lacks impact due to the absence of comparability. *Business Ethics* publishes, to a certain extent, its criteria for selection using work by Samuel Graves and Sandra Waddock of Boston College.[17] Their 2002 list ranked IBM as the leader, followed by Hewlett Packard and Fannie Mae. Their criteria are based upon five areas:

1 *Environment* looks at positive programmes in place, such as pollution reduction, recycling and energy-saving measures, as well as negative measures, such as level of pollutants, US Environmental Protection Agency (EPA) citations, fines, lawsuits, and other measures.
2 *Community relations* looks at philanthropy, any foundation the company has, community service projects, educational outreach, scholarships, employee volunteerism, etc.
3 *Employee relations* looks at wages relative to the industry, benefits paid, family-friendly policies, parental leave, team management, employee empowerment, etc.
4 *Diversity* looks at per cent of minority and women among employees, managers and board members; any Equal Employment Opportunities Commission (EEOC) complaints; diversity programmes in place; lawsuits, etc.
5 *Customer relations* might include quality management programmes, quality awards won, customer satisfaction measures, lawsuits, etc.

What is comforting in the *Business Ethics* list is that neither Enron nor WorldCom – the bad boys of 2001 and 2002 – appear. However, the absence of comment on either company illustrates yet another limitation of awards – bad boys don't get punished nor, in fact, do award examinations allow the sort of early warning of poor behaviour that the public craves.

For its part, the business community has recognized the power of both its friends and critics in abandoning its earlier defensive stance. Now the literature and media are awash with examples of CEOs presenting their personal and corporate ethics through various fora – the views of Goldman Sachs CEO were noted above. Even during the early 1990s, several CEOs addressed social responsibility.[18] Robert A Schoellhorn, chairman and CEO of Abbott Laboratories, stated that private enterprise has a role in addressing social problems, but that role is primarily through the conduct of its business. On an even higher plane, Alcoa Chairman and CEO Charles W Parry said that an organization cannot operate successfully if its sole goal is profit, and Navistar's Donald D Lennox feels it is his job to be responsible in an ethical manner that relates to all of the firm's stakeholders, including lenders, vendors, employees and stockholders. The examples in which corporate leaders insist on a high standard of fair play in their organizations shows that fair-minded competition is viewed as being more important than immediate, tangible gains. Nevertheless, the continuing pressure on corporations to behave socially responsibly has yet to result in accounting practices and behaviour that do not smack of corruption and shady dealing. There is still a long way to go. Should this way be regulated? Chapter 2 examines this issue.

Corporate governance and CSR

With the publication of the Organisation for Economic Co-operation and Development (OECD) Principles of Corporate Governance in 1999, added impetus has been given to improving corporate governance of firms.[19] The OECD report, which did not say an awful lot about CSR – it only covered a few stakeholders – covered the rights of shareholders, the equitable treatment of shareholders, the role of stakeholders in corporate governance, disclosure and transparency and the responsibilities of the board. It was followed by the King report on guidelines on corporate governance for the 56 Commonwealth countries.[20] In the Commonwealth Association for Corporate Governance (CACG) guidelines, good corporate governance requires that the board must govern the corporation with integrity and enterprise in a manner that entrenches and enhances the licence it has to operate. Stakeholder and ethical issues are discussed within the CACG report, leading to the question of whether CSR and corporate governance issues are covering the same ground?

The World Bank notes, however, that there is no single model of corporate governance with systems varying by country, sector and even in the same corporation over time. Among the most prominent systems are the US and UK models, which focus on dispersed controls, as well as the German and Japanese models, which reflect a more concentrated ownership structure. My definition of CSR, stated above, is much wider than the corporate governance definitions used to date, for instance, by the OECD and the World Bank. The OECD principles imply that a key role for stakeholders is concerned with ensuring the flow of external capital to firms and that stakeholders are protected by law and have access to disclosure. The World Bank has been intrigued by a June 2000 Investor Opinion Survey, conducted by the consultancy McKinsey, that finds that investors say that board governance is as important as financial performance in their investment decisions. The survey finds that across Latin America, Europe, the US and Asia, investors (over 80 per cent of those interviewed) would be willing to pay more for a company with good board governance practices.

'Poor governance' was defined by McKinsey as a company that has:

- a minority of outside directors;
- outside directors who have financial ties with management;
- directors who own little or no stock;
- directors who are compensated only with cash;
- no formal director evaluation process;
- high unresponsiveness to investor requests for information on governance issues.

'Good governance' was defined by McKinsey as:
- a majority of outside directors;
- outside directors who are truly independent, with no management ties;
- directors who have significant stockholdings;
- a large proportion of director pay that is stock/options;
- a formal director of evaluation who is in place;
- high responsiveness to investor requests for information on governance issues.

Given the questions, it is not surprising that the figure of 80 per cent was arrived at; but the point is that 'good governance' has a very narrow fit with the OECD principles, and even narrower when compared with CSR sentiments. Nevertheless, there is increasing advocacy of a broader and more inclusive concept of corporate governance that extends to corporate responsibility and has a wider concept of 'stakeholder' than that used by the OECD. These ideas are reflected in the *King Report for South Africa*, the Commonwealth principles of business practice and the UK's Tomorrow's Company.

In conclusion, the notion of corporate governance fits well with current concerns of management structure at the top of corporations and is becoming increasingly better defined thanks to the work of the World Bank and the OECD; but it hardly encompasses the concerns of CSR notions. On the other hand, notions of CSR have not advanced as far as the corporate governance school, with its agreed set of principles. There is light on the horizon thanks to work by King and others, and also in the Cadbury Code of Ethics definition that notes that the aim of corporate governance is to align as nearly as possible the interests of individuals, corporations and society. Indeed, while thinking about corporate governance issues is becoming more popular, so are codes of ethics that are developed by individual companies and associations.[21]

...so what is corporate social responsibility (CSR)?

In this book, I talk about CSR as the ethical behaviour of business towards its constituencies or stakeholders (I discuss ethics, briefly, later in this chapter). I define stakeholders as consisting of seven azimuths or major groups (see Chapter 3), which form the core of the discussions and measurement in this book – the theoretical framework.

Numerous concepts and definitions are associated with the term 'corporate social responsibility', but there is no general agreement of terms. To provide some guidance to readers in this area, I have included a 'Glossary of terms' (see Box 1.1) that provides a number of definitions. Alert readers will notice, however, a fluidity of concepts that really requires more extensive research and consideration than has been done so far. Without a common language, we don't really know that our dialogue with companies is being heard and interpreted in a consistent way. To date, I believe that the dialogue has been highly flawed. Some companies use the term 'corporate citizenship', some the 'ethical corporation', while others use 'good corporate governance'. These flaws lead some companies to consider CSR as purely corporate philanthropy, others – such as the Royal Dutch/Shell Group of Companies – as a new corporate strategic framework, while others dismiss the notion entirely.

In this context, a lively debate has led some authors, mainly US-based academics, to prefer to use the concept of 'corporate social responsiveness' (CSR_2), rather than CSR per se. They argue (Ackerman and Bauer among them, for instance) that the connotation of 'responsibility' is the process merely of assuming an obligation.[22] It places an emphasis on motivation rather than performance; but, they believe, this motivation is not enough, because responding to social demands is much *more* than deciding what to do. Thus, there remains the management task of *doing* what one has decided to do: *this* is social responsiveness. However, I believe that managers must accept the notion of social responsibility *before* they work out what to do. There is no argument about the fact that once this has been accepted, the next step is the response – in other words, acceptance of the motivation to be socially responsible *immediately leads* the manager into what should be done next: social responsiveness. Acceptance, of course, does not come easily, and the point of this book is to show that CSR makes sound economic as well as social, ethical, political and philosophical sense. Being socially responsible and applying the main principles of this will result in a good business – that is, one that is long-lived and profitable.

In my definition of CSR, I include economic aspects simply because the study of economics is a 'social' science that also encompasses financial aspects. Triple bottom line is also implicit since the third part of the triple

Box 1.1 Glossary of terms[23]

Corporate social responsibility is concerned with treating the stakeholders of the firm ethically or in a responsible manner. 'Ethically or responsible' means treating stakeholders in a manner deemed acceptable in civilized societies. Social includes economic responsibility. Stakeholders exist both within a firm and outside – for example, the natural environment is a stakeholder. The wider aim of social responsibility is to create higher and higher standards of living, while preserving the profitability of the corporation, for peoples both within and outside of the corporation.

(Michael Hopkins.)

Corporate citizenship implies a strategy that moves from a focus on short-term transaction to longer-term, values-based relationships with these stakeholders. Loyalty will be based on a company's ability to build a sense of shared values and mission with key stakeholders.

(Zadek et al, 2000.)

A socially responsible company will seek and identify the concerns of its stakeholders and endeavour to treat those stakeholders fairly.

(Draper, 2000.)

Corporate social responsiveness is the management task of *doing* what one has decided to do to become socially responsible.

(Ackerman and Bauer, 1976.)

Corporate governance is concerned with holding the balance between economic and social goals and between individual and communal goals. The corporate governance framework is there to encourage the efficient use of resources and, equally, to require accountability for the stewardship of those resources. The aim is to align as nearly as possible, the interests of individuals, corporations and society.

(Cadbury, 2000.)

Corporate sustainability aligns an organization's products and services with stakeholder expectations, thereby adding economic, environmental and social value.

(PriceWaterhouseCoopers.)

Ethics is the science of morals in human conduct.

(Oxford English Dictionary.)

Ethical accounting is the process through which the company takes up a dialogue with major stakeholders to report on past activities with a view to shaping future ones.

(Rosthorn, 2000.)

Ethical auditing is regular, complete and documented measurements of compliance with the company's published policies and procedures.

(Rosthorn, 2000.)

Ethical book-keeping is systematic, reliable maintaining of accessible records for corporate activities that reflect on its conduct and behaviour.

(Rosthorn, 2000.)

Reputation assurance comprises a number of common global principles for the business environment, assembled to provide quantitative and trend information.

(Rosthorn, 2000.)

Social reporting is non-financial data that covers staff issues, community economic developments and stakeholder involvement, and can include voluntarism and environmental performance.

(Michael Hopkins.)

Sustainable development involves environmental impact measurement, improvements, monitoring and reporting.

(Rosthorn, 2000.)

is the environment, and I have always considered the environment to be one of the stakeholders of a company. Nevertheless, many prefer the term 'corporate responsibility', and in a correspondence with the journal *Ethical Corporation*, I took issue with the editor's wish to drop the word 'social'. The journal's argument was that 'CSR is confusing, not only to those who do not yet know what these three letters stand for, but also to those who do, and yet see it used in contexts in which corporate environmental or financial performance is the issue...we prefer the simple "corporate responsibility" because it's not at all confusing, does not exclude environmental and financial aspects of corporate performance and does not represent too great a departure from the current, unsatisfactory "CSR."'[24]

My own view, reproduced in *Ethical Corporation* is that using the term corporate responsibility (CR) instead of CSR changes the nature of the publication and its conferences.[25] The term 'social' is included by many practitioners to encourage corporations to look at their social responsibilities, as well as their usual responsibilities. To date, the main responsibility of a corporation has been to make profits for its shareholders. Hence, 'corporate responsibility' describes this very well. However, including 'social' means, and emphasizes, the inclusion of other aspects, such as the wider economy, other stakeholders than shareholders and the environment. I noted that the International Business Leaders Forum (IBLF) fell into the CR trap when it announced, in one of its recent press releases, that 'President Bush addresses corporate responsibility' and then went on to say: 'US President George W Bush has outlined a ten-point plan to "improve corporate responsibility and protect America's shareholders".' The proposals are guided by the following core principles:

- provide better information to investors;
- make corporate officers more accountable; and
- develop a stronger, more independent audit system.

Critics slam Bush's ten-pointer for lacking specifics, penalties, budget support and consideration of CSR. But a closer look at those ten points would reveal that the nearest Bush got to CR was when he announced:

> *Proposal number 8: an independent regulatory board should ensure that the accounting profession is held to the highest ethical standards. Under this proposal, an independent regulatory board would be established, under the supervision of the SEC [Securities and Exchange Commission], to develop standards of professional conduct and competence. This board would have the ability to monitor, investigate and, where needed, enforce its ethics principles by punishing individual offenders.*

This is hardly what *Ethical Corporation* meant by its definition of corporate responsibility! It is just that much harder to avoid giving short shrift to the social part of corporate responsibility if you include the word 'social'.

The focus of this book, then, is to address both existing and new ways in which social responsibility and, consequently, social development can be pursued by the private sector (with emphasis mainly on the large TNCs) and by government itself. Companies that are socially responsible in making profits also contribute to some aspects of social development, although obviously not all. One should not expect *every* company to be involved in *every* aspect of social development; this would be ludicrous and unnecessarily restrictive. But for a firm to be involved in some aspects both within and outside itself will, so the argument goes in this book, make its products and services (for example, financial services) more attractive to consumers as a whole and, therefore, will make the company more profitable. There will be increased costs to implement CSR. However, as argued in this book, the benefits will far outweigh the costs. The link to profits is discussed next.

Is business's only job to make a profit?

Milton's Friedman's oft-cited pronouncement that the social responsibility of business begins and ends with increasing profits plays less well, according to John Plender, today than in the heyday of Reaganomics or Margaret Thatcher's Conservative government.[26,27] Plender cited a MORI poll that showed that 87 per cent of people in the UK believed, in 1996, that large companies should have a wider responsibility to the community than profit making per se. When Dwight Eisenhower was president of the US, there was a widespread acceptance of the oft-quoted statement of its CEO that 'What's good for General Motors is good for the USA.' Business practices were rooted in the 19th-century operations of US and European industry.

The practices of the oil industry and its many companies, however, began to bring about an awareness of the role and power of business in society. Theodore Roosevelt and his trustbusters attacked many of the monopolistic practices of the largest of US businesses. The determination of the federal and state governments to regulate the oil industry prompted the industry to examine itself and to move towards practices that would better conserve what was rapidly becoming the world's most important non-renewable resource. Even under President Bush's obvious affinity for the oil companies, the withdrawal of the US from the Kyoto Protocol in 2001, and the struggle to explore for oil in virgin lands in Alaska, the environmental lobby for sustainable development is an important damper on any excesses in the oil industry.

Nevertheless, many private enterprises continued to treat certain resources such as air and water as 'free', and ignored the effects of using or damaging common resources and releasing waste into what many thought was a bottomless rubbish bin. During the 1950s, business practice in this area consisted largely of obeying the law in a minimal way, lobbying to defeat regulatory action and retaining good corporate lawyers. Business was seen as an 'economic' institution, quite separate from 'social institutions' and in no way under the control of society, nor responsible to it.

Not all observers were willing to grant such a broad autonomy to business. During the 1950s, a field of scholarship developed that questioned the roles and obligations of business in a capitalist democratic society. Early writers in business and society such as Bowen, Elbing and Elbing and Healt were concerned with what they saw as an excessive autonomy and degree of power for business, apparently unconnected to any responsibility for the negative consequences of business activities.[28]

The literature of the early 1970s was concerned with the impact of social responsibility on profits. For instance, much like Friedman, Linowes insisted in 1974 that the touchstone of 'responsibility' was costs or foregone profits.[29] He provided a measurement system of social responsibility based on the marginal costs of activities beyond the regular costs of doing business. It is obviously necessary to understand the exact costs of social responsibility. But with costs come benefits that were not quantified by Linowes. Such a 'hard-nosed' approach is rarely taken by the more romantic social reformers. As Ackerman and Bauer of the Harvard Business School say, the slogan of many reformers is that business must forego some of its (presumably swollen) profits to serve social goals.[30] Conservative economists go even further and argue that it is 'unethical' to forego profits. Ackerman and Bauer continue: 'most activist reformers seem to vastly overestimate the amount of profits available for diversion to good causes'.

These notions were backed up to a certain extent by the findings of the Opinion Research Corporation in the US during the mid 1970s that the public believed that business earned 28 per cent profits after taxes on the sales dollar, whereas the correct figure was a little over 4 per cent after taxes. Furthermore, there was little awareness of the uses to which profits were put, and the dangers of a take-over to which a firm would expose itself if, as 'seems certain', its stock price were depressed because it diluted its profits substantially.[31]

However, social responsibility, as argued in this book, is not solely about using profits for good causes. It is about the whole fabric of the enterprise being involved in socially responsible processes and procedures. Ackerman and Bauer realize this, later saying in their book that only 'assessing marginal costs for social investments, as Linowes proposes, could produce anomalies'.[32] They cite the case of a bank that wrestled for seven years to develop a programme for lending to minority entrepreneurs. At the end of that time, the bank had a smoothly running programme. The officers had learned how to manage that type of loan and had reduced losses. Furthermore, the handling of these loans had been transferred to regular loan offices; as a result, the assignment of overhead costs to the programme would have been very difficult and scarcely worth the accounting costs. In other words, precisely when the programme was institutionalized within the regular operations of the bank, the measured 'social responsibility' of the bank would have approached zero.

Thus, linking costs with social responsibility too closely muddies as much as it clarifies. As Ackerman and Bauer say, no business investment pays off instantaneously. If future benefits can be anticipated, then whether an expense is seen as a cost or investment is arbitrary. They continue that they have 'liquidated the apparently neat argument of the conservative economist such as Milton Friedman, who argues against the propriety of business expenses that do not contribute to profitability'. The question is of long-range profitability based on investments of today. Consequently, a short-time horizon and no imagination will allow expenditures with no direct, immediate business benefit to be eliminated. Managers of today are increasingly recognizing the staying power of positive social acts that may not, in the short term, offer any immediate benefits.

The 1980s also saw business and profits in a different light. The fall of the Berlin Wall and the subsequent collapse of the Soviet Union and communism were landmarks. At first, the West thought that the score was unbridled market capitalism 1, socialism 0. But the rules of the game were quickly revised (and the teams changed) as it became clear that the winners could not ignore social questions such as unemployment in the developed world and poverty in the developing world. Instead, business began bringing about its own scrutiny by society as a result of a series of environmental disasters and corporate crimes. Consumer activist groups successfully attacked products that were dangerous or of poor quality, and groups such as Friends of the Earth and Greenpeace challenged conventional wisdom that had allowed the trashing of the seas and the atmosphere for so many generations. Society's growing awareness of the faults of some businesses, combined with business's own errors, became the motivation behind the further development of the field of CSR and the notion of ethics in business.

The word 'business' assumes some common understanding of a set of social phenomena. A business is certainly a social organization, and by its nature interacts with other social organizations. This interaction is not confined to its customers, suppliers, and stockholders and owners, but spreads widely through many different social groups. Neither is a business internally simple. Even the smallest of businesses have employees, regulations and policies, communications needs, and a myriad of other concerns, mechanisms and day-to-day operational principles.

When we examine the interaction of one or more businesses with society, these relationships become more complex. Some aspects of a business deal directly with the external world – sales staff, buyers and so on. Others may appear to deal only with the direct staff of the business. But even internal staff operate under regulations and assumptions that relate their activities to the larger society. It is no easier to classify and understand business in society than to classify and understand how one person, and his or her constituent personality, interacts with another.

One of the confusions over defining and acting upon CSR results, according to Young-Chul Kang and Donna Wood, from a flawed assumption that CSR is an *after-profit* obligation.[33] This means, they say, that if companies are not profitable, they do not have to behave responsibly – 'in the extreme, if all firms are affected by severe economic turmoil or are run by lazy, short-sighted managers, then societies would have no choice but to accept pollution, discrimination, dangerous working conditions, child labour, etc.' Embedding socially responsible principles within corporate management is what the two authors call a '*before-profit*' obligation. They cite corporations who embody these ideas and see the trend accelerating. For instance, in 1950 Sears's CEO listed four parties to any business in order of importance as 'customers, employees, community and stockholders'.[34] For him, profit was a 'by-product of success in satisfying responsibly the legitimate needs and expectations of the corporation's primary stakeholder group'. By the 1980s, Levi's even repurchased its stock in the public market under the rationale that stockholders' interests might limit the firm's effort to be a socially responsible organization. And, in the 1990s, both Rhino records in the US and NatWest in the UK recommended that employees be actively involved in charitable community service performed in company time. Migros, of Switzerland, funds its cultural and social programmes not by profits, but by gross sales, so that profitability does not influence the firm's level of involvement.

Nevertheless, the debate on profits and CSR has not gone away. On 16 May 2001, Martin Wolf of the *Financial Times* (FT) wrote a provocative article 'Sleepwalking with the Enemy' criticizing CSR and argued, based on a pamphlet by David Henderson – former chief economist of the OECD – that social responsibility distorts the market by deflecting business from its primary role of profit generation.[35] Wolf argued that CSR is conducted by activist groups who are 'with few exceptions...hostile to, or highly critical of, multinational enterprises, capitalism, freedom of cross-border trade and capital flows and the idea of a market economy. One might expect, and indeed hope, that the business community would effectively contest such anti-business views. But the emphasis is on concessions and accommodation'. Wolf believes that powerful objections can be made to such a radical redefinition of corporate objectives: it accepts a false critique of the market economy; it endorses an equally mistaken view of the powers of multinational businesses; it risks spreading costly regulations worldwide; it is more likely to slow the reduction of global poverty than to accelerate it; it requires companies to make highly debatable political judgements; and it threatens a form of global neo-corporatism, in which unaccountable power is shared between companies, activist groups, some international organizations and a few governments. Wolf's article concludes with the statement that 'the role of well-run companies is to make profits, not save the planet. Let them not make the error of confusing the two.'

One problem with Wolf was that he did not start with a definition of CSR. My definition above, remember, was that CSR is concerned with treating the stakeholders of the firm ethically or in a responsible manner, and that stakeholders exist both within a firm and outside. Wolf apparently believes that this will lead to the distortion of the market and reduce profits. This is the heart of the matter. Does Wolf imply profits at any cost? Does not Wolf realize that treating stakeholders well will actually lead to improved profits? For instance, those companies that treat one stakeholder well – its employees – tend to perform better than those who do not.[36] Yet, other stakeholders comprise a company's shareholders and management.

Wolf's straw CSR man is then turned into a diatribe of those who are against markets and profits (he equated those who see merit in CSR as anti-market). He said 'hostility to markets is sour old wine' and cited Henderson, who says many activist groups 'with few exceptions...are hostile to...the idea of a market economy'. But Wolf is correct in saying that the 'aim is not to eliminate private business but to transform the way it behaves'. He qualifies his previous statements by arguing that profits should be pursued within 'the constraints of law and the principles of honest dealing'. This is exactly what the more serious proponents of CSR are examining (that is, what aspects of law need to be improved and what is meant by honest dealing and the ethical treatment of stakeholders).

Wolf continued in the vein that CSR is against the market when he equated CSR to a notion of the 'triple bottom line...economic, social and environmental' and then said that this 'accepts a false critique of the market economy'. In fact, there are many instance where economic aspects alone produce profits, but to the detriment of the environment and social welfare. There is an increasing body of evidence that positive environmental action by firms leads to increased profits and longer-term sustainability. The evidence linking social aspects to increased profits is still the subject of research; but preliminary results are positive and companies such as The Co-operative Bank in the UK, as stated in their 2001 social report, are very happy with their results based on improved levels of CSR.

Will CSR increase costs to businesses? The short answer is, probably, yes. But to say that this will be imposed on companies, as Wolf argued, by Greenpeace is only partly true. Unless Greenpeace makes a solid case, they will be ignored – to whit their confusion over the *Brent Spar*. But the balance is on both sides of the equation – costs will increase but so will profits and longevity. I illustrate this point later in a matrix of costs and benefits in Chapter 7. Wolf also argued that a company that follows CSR policies will harm the development of poorer countries. This issue is discussed in Chapter 10.

The list of enterprises that believe in CSR, or 'before-profit obligation', in Kang and Wood's words, is expanding. More and more, the above arguments affirm, and this will be seen by the examples and case studies throughout this book, that businesses are realizing that gaining short-term profits at the expense of social responsibility is not likely to lead to longer-term viability. Consequently, I believe that it is appropriate to revise Friedman's aphorism from one of social responsibility *or* profits to one of social responsibility *and* profits. This is the new bottom line!

Social responsibility and stakeholder theory

Is the notion of a socially responsible enterprise just another side of stakeholder theory (ST)? There are some similarities and some differences. First, let us look at what is meant by ST. Preston traced the origins of the stakeholder approach, if not the actual use of the term, to the Great Depression in the US, when the General Electric Company identified four major stakeholder groups: shareholders, employees, customers and the general public.[37] The publication of Freeman's book *Strategic Management – A Stakeholder Approach* saw the concept of stakeholder become embedded in management scholarship and managers' thinking.[38] Stakeholders, according to Max Clarkson, are persons or groups who have, or claim, ownership, rights or interests in a corporation and its activities, past, present or future. He divides these into two. *Primary* stakeholders are those without whose continuing participation the corporation cannot survive as a going concern – typically shareholders, investors, employees, customers and suppliers, together with what is defined as the public stakeholder group: governments and communities who provide the infrastructure, markets, laws and regulations. *Secondary* stakeholder groups are defined as those who influence or affect the corporation but are not engaged in transactions with the corporation and are not essential for its survival. The media and a wide range of special-interest groups are such people. When Clarkson studied and collected data from 70 of the largest companies in Canada, he found that it was necessary to distinguish between *stakeholder* issues and *social* issues, because corporations and their managers manage relationships with their stakeholders and not with society.[39] In Chapter 3, where I list the stakeholders, I take note of Clarkson's list; but, as will be seen, I argue that corporations must also manage their relationships with society.

In the UK, to date, ST has hardly been adequately defined. The influential publication of the Royal Society of Arts (RSA), *Tomorrow's Company*, tackled what it considered to be the 'sterile debate over shareholder versus stakeholder' head on.[40] It stated that only by giving due weight to the interests of all key stakeholders can shareholders' continuing value be assured; it described this as the inclusive approach. This was taken further by David Wheeler and Maria Sillanpää in their book *The Stakeholder Corporation*, which was greatly influenced by their experiences at The Body Shop, in which they argue that: 'It is our belief that in the future the development of loyal, inclusive stakeholder relationships will become one of the most important determinants of commercial viability and business success.'[41]

John Plender's book on stakeholder theory, *A Stake in the Future*, is full of anecdotes; but the path he suggests is vague.[42] He begins by claiming success for the notion of ST on the grounds that Tony Blair made a much-publicized speech about it in Singapore in early 1996, a year before he was elected UK prime minister for the first time. In the speech, Blair described a stakeholder economy as one in which opportunity is available to all, advancement is through merit, and from which no group or class is set apart or excluded; people have a stake in society, so that they feel a responsibility toward it and an inclination to work for its success.

Blair also put his weight behind the notion of a voluntary bargain when he said that 'legislation could not guarantee that a company will behave in a way conducive to trust and long-term commitment'. However, he thought that it was time to assess how to shift the corporate ethos from one in which the company is a mere vehicle for the capital market to be traded, bought and sold as a commodity, toward one where a company is a community or partnership in which each employee has a stake, and where a company's responsibilities are more clearly delineated.

According to Plender, the stakeholder idea was eventually shelved by Blair, partly as a reaction to a powerful book by Will Hutton, *The State We're In*.[43] Hutton's negative assessment of the UK's economic prospects, coupled with his advocacy of a reformed constitution and a stakeholder economy, smacked of 'Old Labour' interventionism, and was something Blair was keen to avoid in the run-up to the May 1997 election.

Plender argued that ST offers a means of 'legitimizing the tempestuous mechanics of capitalism and of preserving human and social capital in the interests of competitive advantage'.[44] To define ST, Plender offered four basic tenets. First comes the concept of inclusion, whether at the level of society or of the company. By this he presumably meant that a poor distribution of income, where those who work earn great rewards while the increasingly unemployed are penalized, is something that must be avoided. Second, behaviour in markets must be tempered by self-imposed *social* and *ethical* constraints – that is, the exercise of property rights entails obligations that do not begin and end with the property owner, but extend to the wider community. This, clearly, falls within the ambit of a voluntary planetary bargain for socially responsible enterprises as advocated in this book. Third, ST is an efficient *alternative to market liberalism* and its individualistic excesses. What is meant by this is not clear. Plender is against global Keynesianism (a plank of our planetary bargain argument). He cites several UK companies to support his argument, such as Marks & Spencer, Unipart and the John Lewis Partnership, which are all run as profitable companies with strong paternalistic characteristics in the Quaker tradition. Fourth, ST views firms as social institutions in which people aspire to *self-respect*, as well as to a higher standard of living. This reflects the notion that values of loyalty and trust within the organization foster wealth creation and contribute to competitive advantage, so that, in the long run, the stake-holding ethos is more conducive to corporate success than is a culture in which fear is the main motivator.

Hutton's negative book on the UK was written in 1995, when prospects for Britain looked bleak under the 'everything for sale' Conservative government and in the face of persistent unemployment and rising poverty. Conditions have improved since then, but did not prevent Hutton, in his later book, *The State to Come*, from continuing his diatribe against the tendencies in British society towards more government by contract, in which, seemingly, every service from transport through water to the provision of health services was open to private-sector contracts.[45] This was leading to a society in which the imbalance of power, knowledge and financial muscle was forgotten, as were the wider social consequences that make contracting unstable and inefficient.

In a revised defence of stake-holding, Hutton argued that stake-holding is not a call for the socialization of capitalism, big government or a new corporatism; rather, it requires institutions, systems and a wider architecture, which creates a better economic balance, and with it a culture in which common humanity and the instinct to collaborate are allowed to flower.

In fact, Hutton contradicts himself here, because he is, even if implicitly, calling for the socialization of capital. He later notes that 'Britain could develop a new capitalist model in which market flexibilities are integrated with webs of trust and commitment, and where society acknowledges the imperative of sharing risk and income as fairly as possible.' He rightly notes that the owners of most UK companies are professional investment-fund managers, who can switch billions of pounds at the press of a button. They, therefore, take a short-term perspective, which is harmful for any company that wishes to take a longer-term view. Hutton advocates that government should prevent funds from being transferred from one investment manager to another for at least five years for funds over a certain size – those more than £100 million, he suggests. This is obviously unworkable in practice. A bad investment manager would be rewarded by being unable to lose invested funds for five years. What I think Hutton should have said is that the stake-holding idea holds the seeds of the solution, which is to convince stakeholders that their company must become socially responsible, to define what this means in practice and to identify, clearly, the roles of the state and the private sector. But it cannot be that corporations should be responsible to all stakeholders in the sense that any or *all* stakeholders can tell a company what to do. This would make a nonsense of CSR. A company should treat its stakeholders in an ethically responsible way and should take account of their views, but not be dictated to as such.

Samuel Brittan is scathing of ST.[46] He argues that it is the *role of markets* to make use of the dispersed knowledge not available either to boards of directors or to governments. The knowledge problem is something he believes is overlooked by so-called ethical economists. A simple profit-maximization model provides subsidiary performance indicators for decentralized managers within a corporation, but not the much vaguer, he says, stakeholder objectives. The market liberal, whose position is what Brittan defends, believes that ST will give business leaders new responsibilities for the role of shaping society for which they are ill-suited, and that they would serve us and themselves better if they stuck to limited aims. Brittan, as is so often the case, uses the phrase 'role of markets' as though markets will make use of dispersed knowledge in society's best interest. Presumably, he expects the analysts and soothsayers who are involved in buying and selling shares in London, Wall Street, Frankfurt, Singapore or Tokyo to inject concerns of social responsibility within the affairs of companies. However, traders of this kind are not the people to do this – hence the rise of social investment funds such as

FTSE4good. Consequently, the simple profit-maximization model of the boardroom has to be extended. This does not mean further complications; but it does mean that clear benchmarks and indicators are required. This subject is discussed in Chapters 7 and 8.

ST is backed up by a recent work that has proved very popular in the US – the book *Built to Last* by James Collins and Jerry Porras.[47] The core argument is based on the premise that managers who reflect a genuine concern for the interests of all of their stakeholders are those who produce superior results for their shareholders (as well as for other stakeholders) over the longer term.[48] One of the most fundamental conclusions of the study is that successful companies do not resemble the centrally controlled machines upon which so much management theory, language and practice are still based. Instead, they are more like biological organisms, which adapt mainly through what the authors call 'undirected variation', or what Darwin termed 'random genetic mutation'.[49] That has untold implications for the way in which companies are organized and run – or, rather, steered. The book gives little direct advice about the vital question of how an average company can become a great one. But, by comparing each of its study companies with the evolution of a less successful rival, the authors help to show just why Ford compares favourably with General Motors (GM), as Disney has for years with Columbia, General Electric (GE) with Westinghouse, Motorola with Zenith and Citicorp with Chase Manhattan.

Moreover, citing the same study, Bruce Lloyd of South Bank University adds that where any organization is driven primarily by the interests of one stakeholder, this will invariably result in conflict that will have a negative effect on its bottom-line performance over the longer term.[50] Of course, it is possible for organizations to get away with operating on the basis of a narrow set of priorities in the short term, and sometimes that is even necessary for sheer survival. But this is the exception rather than the rule. For the best results, says Lloyd, a stakeholder philosophy should be incorporated within an overall responsibility-driven approach that avoids a bureaucratic or legalistic attitude. This also needs to be believed in by all those responsible for the performance of the organization. In other words, put people first!

These findings are backed up by Arie de Geus, writing in the *Harvard Business Review*.[51] He asks: why do so many companies die young? He found from an analysis of companies across the Northern Hemisphere that average corporate life expectancy was below 20 years. Yet, he also found 27 companies that ranged in age from 100 to 700 years – including DuPont, Kodak, Mitsui, Sumitomo and Siemens. Within these 27 long-term survivors, he found that the group shared four personality traits: conservatism in financing; sensitivity to the world around them; awareness of their identity; and tolerance of new ideas. One of the most surprising finding was that each of the 27 companies had changed their business portfolio completely at least once. DuPont, which is approximately 200 years old, started out as a gunpowder company. During the 1920s, it was the major shareholder of GM, and now is a speciality chemical company. These companies had valued people, not assets, concluded de Geus. Scuttling people to preserve plant and equipment is tantamount to suicide.

So, returning to the question phrased initially: is CSR just another face of ST? To a certain extent it is, because both are interested in the social responsibility of corporations, and this is best tackled by breaking down the corporation into specific stakeholder groups and analysing what is meant by social responsibility among each group. However, CSR, as envisaged here, goes further, in one sense, than ST because it advocates social responsibility, not only at the enterprise level but also at the world or planetary level. This is described in what I call the planetary bargain, and takes a more global view than ST, as I argue in the next chapter. But corporations should not be responsible to *all* stakeholders in the sense of control. The idea is to take account of stakeholder interests in an ethically responsible manner since stakeholders, as defined in the next chapter, are the fundamental building blocks for a company that is to be considered a socially responsible enterprise (SRE).

Trust, social capital and CSR

A gentleman's or lady's word is their honour, and the contract is sealed by their handshake. Such was the maxim behind the UK's rise as the industrial power during the 18th and 19th centuries. If trust does not exist in business behaviour, then the transaction costs of doing business are much higher than they need be. This is because trust lowers the need for costly information-gathering and avoids elaborate contracts that are produced by expensive lawyers.[52] Trust and CSR are closely linked. A company practising CSR will have provided the data and the sort of track record that increase the level of trust of all its stakeholders in its activities. The costs of breaking this trust are high. Indeed, in the US, litigation has got out of hand as consumers take the meaning of corporate responsibility to new and often absurd heights.

Francis Fukuyama, the author of the book on the 'end of history and the last man', in his book on the subject of trust, linked the latter to the notion of social capital.[53] This, he says, arises from the prevalence of trust in a society or in certain parts of it. It can be embodied in the smallest and most basic social entity (the individual or the family), as well as the largest of all entities (the nation), and all the other entities in between. At the individual level, clearly it is socially responsible to put one's litter in a provided receptacle. A person who carries his or her (and 'she' normally has more social capital than 'he', in general) waste despite ample opportunities to throw it away in a secluded spot is certainly the type of person one can trust. If all people in a society could be trusted on small things like this, then bigger things would follow, and the social capital of the society would increase.

A nation such as Iraq, which surreptitiously fabricated nerve gas even under international scrutiny, is a nation whom no one is ready to trust. Now that Iraq has escaped rule by a clique of thugs, it will nevertheless take generations to rebuild its social capital and thereby raise the living standards of its people. A different story could have emerged if Iraq had had the notion of social responsibility during the 1980s and had then invested in the human capital of its people using its oil wealth. It would have had no need to invade Kuwait. Such a socially responsible strategy would have earned it enormous respect internationally, leading to greater wealth; who knows, maybe Kuwait would have clamoured to be part of it.

Clearly, the West is not without its skeletons. The US Central Intelligence Agency (CIA) activities of the US in Latin America in recent times (in Chile, Guatemala and Honduras) have led to fewer developing nations who trust the US as a partner. When the station chief of the CIA was asked in mid 1997 to mediate between Israel and the Palestinians to find the perpetrators of recent outrages in Israel, the attempt was doomed to failure because there was no trust. Who can trust the US to act independently when its own interests are at stake and it uses a body (the CIA) with a terrible reputation for trust?

This extends to corporate life. On a larger scale, the litter that Shell wished to dispose of in the Atlantic Ocean (the obsolete *Brent Spar* oil rig), led to an international outcry. Whatever social capital and trust Shell had built up over the years (and it was known at one time as a particularly altruistic enterprise) was destroyed very rapidly, and has taken years to replenish. Cor Herkstroter, chairman of Shell's committee of managing directors, admitted at that time that Shell had been 'slow to appreciate the growing authority and importance of environmental and consumer groups' and had 'failed to engage in serious dialogue' with them.[54] In recent years, though, Shell's series of social reports has led to Shell being one of the leaders in the CSR stakes.[55] As its chairman, Mark Moody-Stuart, stated in the 2000 report: 'My colleagues and I are totally committed to a business strategy that generates profits while contributing to the well-being of the planet and its people. We see no alternative.'

Already, these changes have translated into measurable outcomes to the extent that Shell (UK) comes fairly high on a set of indicators of social responsibility, as can be seen in Chapter 9. In a list of the 25 largest UK companies, it ranks eighth because it has one of the highest scores in terms of a battery of environmental indicators; is very keen that its suppliers adopt a code of good practice; is one of the best contributors to charitable causes; and has one of the best records in recent years in terms of advertising complaints against it.

Turning back to Fukuyama, who noted that social capital is like a ratchet that is more easily turned in one direction than another, social capital can be dissipated by the actions of governments more readily than those governments can build it up again.[56] Now that the question of ideology and institutions has been settled, the preservation and accumulation of social capital will occupy centre stage. A socially responsible enterprise will fight to preserve that and to create even more social capital in the future.

Ethics and CSR

Towards the end of the 19th century, an Oxford tradesman observed how his competitors were cheating and swindling at every opportunity. He agonized about how he could avoid doing the same without going out of business. Eventually, the tradesman screwed up his courage and took his problem to the formidable Benjamin Jowett, the master of Balliol College. Jowett paused only for a moment before replying: 'Cheat as little as you can.'[57] The moral of the story is that there are no hard and fast rules for ethical good practice. In fact, most university business schools that teach ethics, such as the top-rated Darden School of Business in Charlottesville, Virginia, US, recognize the difficulties and use case studies to illustrate how ethics can be treated in business.

The idea of ethics in business is not new. It can be traced back to 19th-century philanthropists, such as the early socialist entrepreneur Robert Owen and various Quaker-owned businesses. But by the 1950s, governments had introduced laws and regulations to prohibit many unethical practices.[58] In more recent times, especially in the US business schools, ethics has been a growth area although, as the collapse of Enron and WorldCom illustrated, it is still not part of general business practice.

Ethics comprises a set of values and principles that influence how individuals, groups and society behave. Business ethics are concerned with how such values and principles operate in business. According to Chryssides and Kaler, ethics has two aspects: one involves the specific situations in which ethical controversy arises; the other aspect concerns the principle of behaviour by which it is appropriate to abide.[59]

What is the relation between business ethics and social responsibility? The latter goes much further. CSR is part and parcel of the management strategy of a company, and thus social responsibility encompasses good business ethics. This is because one normally thinks of business ethics applying to what business does within its walls – that is, to four of the seven stakeholders that I focus upon in this book: managers, consumers, investors/owners and employees. Less concern is placed on the natural environment, the community and its suppliers and their conditions of work. Social responsibility encompasses good ethics, both within the walls of the company and without. It encourages enterprises to be involved in social issues – such as community involvement, improving working conditions in the developing world and so on – that are outside of the walls of the enterprise. The consideration of all seven stakeholders is encouraged for two main reasons. First, it is good for business – that is, for longevity and profitability. Second, the private sector has won the battle to keep government out of business; but this still leaves many areas of the world where the private sector can either replace or assist the public sector in improving living standards. Both of these reasons take the issue further than confining the study of ethics to a 'not-for-profit' course, as it was at one time at Harvard Business School.[60]

Chapter 2

The Need for a Planetary Bargain

Those who engage in social cooperation choose together, in one joint act, the principles which are to assign basic rights and duties and to determine the division of social benefits (John Rawls).[1]

Introduction

This chapter outlines the elements of what could be in a planetary bargain to promote corporate social responsibility (CSR). The two main actors in such a bargain are governments and business. There are, of course, many actors on the world stage, and governments do not always best represent their own societies, especially in some developing countries. Yet, if a planetary bargain is to come about to promote CSR, then the lead will have to come jointly from governments (including international organizations) and business itself. Therefore, the first two sections in this chapter set the parameters of what each could expect from the other. I then discuss the link between a planetary bargain and globalization before entering into some detail of what a planetary bargain could consist of. Whether a planetary bargain should be voluntary or enter into the legal framework of nations is an issue I cover before ending the chapter with a link to theory, when I ask: is a planetary bargain simply another version of global Keynesianism?

What could governments (and people, in general) expect from business in the area of social responsibility and social development?

Before 1991, relatively little literature or research existed in the area of *corporate social responsibility*, particularly outside the US. Since that date, however, social responsibility has not only entered corporate acceptability, but has also blossomed into a large number of activities. Nevertheless, no single objective method has emerged by which corporations might be judged against some sort of international standard, although many are trying to do this (see Chapter 7). Businesses, non-governmental organizations (NGOs) and scholars in Europe, the US and elsewhere have approached this problem in a variety of ways; but a single set of agreed indicators is still being researched.[2]

Broadly speaking, what can people and governments expect of large transnational corporations (TNCs) in the future? A list of items might comprise:

- profitability;
- adherence to an appropriate set of good corporate governance principles (for example, the Organisation for Economic Co-operation and Development's (OECD's) Principles of Corporate Governance);
- tax contributions;
- long-term view of investment and profitability;
- environmentally friendly production processes;
- socially responsible products;
- code of ethics of company operations;
- comprehensive CSR policy:
  - does the company have a social responsibility policy?
  - is the policy backed by suitable resources and organization (for example, does it perform a social audit)?
  - does the company have a management system for social responsibility?
  - what is the social responsibility network in the company?
  - is there someone to implement the policy?
  - what social responsibility communications does the company have?
  - what social responsibility training does the company have?
- local community support where plants are located;
- philanthropic contributions;
- abstention from corrupt practices;
- abstention from transfer pricing;
- good conditions of work for employees;
- high proportion of workforce in regular protected employment;
- internally flexible labour practices;
- non-discriminatory recruitment and advancement policy;
- skill upgrading programmes conducted either internally or externally;
- labour involved in discussions of structural change, plant relocations and closures through labour-management councils;
- explicit procedures to help employees retrain and relocate in the case of downsizing;
- open accounting procedures for shareholders and disclosure of relevant information for the public at large;
- support for social investment funds;

- support to enhance small-scale savings and credit; and
- transfer of technology (for example, management skills).

Moves are afoot to bring these ideas into practice. For instance, the UK government has called for a 'new partnership' between the government and the private sector to eliminate world poverty, and has warned companies that they cannot afford to ignore increasing consumer interest in the production of goods.[3] It believes that boycotting retailers who sell products made in developing world sweatshops is outdated. Work in tandem, the government believes, between the public and private sector, is the main way for poverty to be eliminated.[4] Claire Short, the UK Labour government's chief international development minister, has called for ethical codes of conduct to govern the relationship between big companies and poor countries. She has pointed out that TNCs have realized that the bulk of economic growth, as well as the bulk of population, will in future be in developing countries and that they have to be seen to be fair.[5]

Sainsbury's, a supermarket chain in the UK, for instance, has embraced these ideas, and the government has praised its initiatives. The firm has completed four pilot schemes in Africa and Asia to establish a code of ethics for all of its own-brand suppliers, and has issued questionnaires to its suppliers that will, eventually, be monitored independently. Sainsbury's says that 'consumers are very interested in ethics now and we get many letters from people saying they shop with us and want to know what our policy is so they can continue to shop with us.'[6]

But what are the limits? Where do state social obligations end and corporate obligations begin? This subject has received an enormous amount of attention – the World Bank's 1997 *World Development Report*, for example, was concerned with this question. There is no easy answer, particularly because the relative roles are changing, rapidly in some cases. What is becoming clear is that business is assuming the mantle of social programmes that only in rare cases it would have previously considered. The main difference at the conceptual level, of course, is that government is nationwide. A government, for instance, is committed to provide old-age pensions, which applies to all over 65 years of age; but a company's commitment extends only as far as its stakeholders. It is difficult to imagine, for instance, a company located in California being responsible for *all* of the pensions of over 65-year-olds in Kansas or Kenya. On the other hand, it is difficult to imagine that government should be responsible for all telecommunication services as, until recently in Europe at least, it has been.

The authorities at both the United Nations Development Programme (UNDP), in its 'umbrella programme for engaging the private sector' and its Money Matters initiative, and the World Bank, in its Corporate Citizenship programme, have already started to think how they could engage the private sector more than before.[7] This is because they have seen that public assistance to developing countries has been overwhelmed by the huge private capital flows, at least to the richer developing nations. In parallel with this, the largest donor, the US, prompted by arch-conservative Senator Helms, withheld its contributions to the United Nations (UN) for almost a decade, and still has an uneasy relationship with the UN (and international agreements, in general).[8]

However, the efforts of the UN in humanitarian and human rights has not gone unnoticed in the private sector, as is evidenced by the path-breaking personal gift of US$1 billion by Cable News Network (CNN) founder Ted Turner. Undoubtedly this will herald an even greater reflection among both wealthy individuals and large private corporations on the sorts of things that they can do to promote social responsibility, either through existing organizations or through new ones.

What I have considered in this book is the need for more social responsibility on the part of enterprises. What I have not considered, in any detail, is where it should stop. What are the limits? This will be for the stakeholders of companies to decide in the future. It is especially the case as the nation state itself continues to lose the power to decide on the future of its citizens. This power is being redistributed not only to regional groupings such as the European Union (EU), to smaller regions within a country (for example Scotland and Wales in the UK) and to local communities, but also, even more (and worryingly, given their lack of democracy) to the larger private corporations themselves.

What should businesses expect from government in return for greater social responsibility?

As the balancing part of a planetary social bargain, what can businesses reasonably expect from government in return for their own best practices in social responsibility? Clearly, this will vary from one type of enterprise to another – for instance, a financial services company will be less concerned with export quotas on coal than an extractive industry. And companies will expect different things from international bodies as opposed to national governments. This will also vary from one location to another. Some governments are more liberal than others. Surprisingly, corporations still see themselves as based in one country. Given the concerns about footloose enterprises, it is interesting that corporations still guard some sort of national identity. This will change – for instance, Shell has always had its Dutch and UK components.

Corporations based in Hong Kong face different legislation from those based in Australia, Brazil or the US. There is no global regulator, and companies, although not moving their headquarters, in general, do move the locus of their operations to seek the most advantageous conditions. A government who is less 'corporate friendly' will not lose the headquarters of the corporation except in exceptional circumstances (the end of the UK's lease in Hong Kong saw some companies move their headquarters). Yet, there will be a convergence toward a set of criteria within which a corporation will operate. What these should be are only partially the subject of international discussion. The World Trade Organization (WTO), for instance, practically ignores social questions on its agenda, although recent globalization protests are leading the WTO to a re-think.

What business should expect from government is a large subject, and so what I have done here is simply to list the main concerns of what the private sector could expect from governments in a planetary bargain:

National level

At the national level, private sectors might expect the following:

- a stable environment that ensures open markets;
- a secure legal framework and fully functioning enforcement institutions;
- a non-corrupt, competent, streamlined administrative framework;
- clear investment policy and plans;
- incentives for new (foreign) investment and for domestic investment and savings;
- repatriation of profits and foreign currency;
- a flexible labour code;
- democratic practices;
- no forced labour;
- clearly defined rules of operation;
- a one-stop information bureau for new and existing investors;
- an independent tribunal to adjudicate on disputes;
- fair local banking practices;
- training institutes linked to the needs of the private sector; and
- tax incentives for corporations practising CSR policies.

International level

At the international level, private sectors might expect the following:

- fair and open rules for trading;
- an independent international body to arbitrate disputes; and
- accurate and available information on investment possibilities, impediments to conducting business, and best practices to finance social development.

The fact that dialogue to conclude such a social and planetary bargain has only just begun is illustrated by a meeting held at the UN at the end of

1994 in preparation for the 1995 World Social Summit held in Copenhagen. There, a number of high-ranking UN officials and some senior financial figures sat down to see what common ground could be found between social development professionals and global bankers. These officials included, among others, Juan Somavia, then chairperson of the Social Summit and now director general (DG) of the International Labour Organization (ILO); James Speth, the then administrator of the UNDP; Marshall Carter, chief executive officer (CEO) of State Street Bank in Boston; and former Citicorp banker Walter Wriston. The will was there, but the context was missing, according to Carter, who said: 'When we talked about our fiduciary responsibility – to ensure that stockholders are not exposed to undue risk – you could see the development people reaching for their dictionaries.'[9] Since then, the dialogue has blossomed into a series of global events known as Money Matters in the UNDP, and a Money Matters Institute has been formed. Many other global fora have arisen in recent years to address these issues; the ILO Enterprise Forum held in 1996 and again in 1999 attracted over 1000 businesses and concerned individuals. Following initiatives taken by Marcello Palazzi of the Progressio Foundation in Holland, Habitat organized a meeting where corporations met to discuss their global responsibilities, and both the UNDP and the United Nations Educational, Scientific and Cultural Organization (UNESCO) held similar meetings in 1998.

The UN itself launched, in 1999, its Global Compact initiative that encourages the private sector to sign up to a set of nine principles in the areas of labour standards, human rights and environmental practices. Several hundred corporations have signed up. Whether this has been to associate themselves with the UN's powerful brand name or whether it means positive action on the CSR front has been subject to intense speculation. It is worth noting, however, that the three areas being covered are only a subset of a full-fledged CSR approach as defined in this book. With the possible exception of labour issues, internal stakeholders are not considered in the Global Compact initiative. Nor is there a concern with verifying the claims of corporations that sign up to the Global Compact. Lack of independent verification is likely to lead to the UN being embarrassed, at the very least, should one of its companies be guilty of poor social responsibility even outside of the nine principles. Consequently, although a very useful move toward a planetary bargain, the Global Compact is only a partial response to worldwide global concerns.

What is coming out of all of these dialogues and meetings? As Marcello Palazzi said in an interview when I posed this question to him: 'I proposed to UNESCO that we create an Enterprise Initiative for Cultural and Human Development, a virtual network of business associations and networks that want to do projects together that advance culture and human development.' Little came of that initiative; but, undoubtedly, the intense interest in business partnerships will lead to more and more companies adopting socially responsible policies. Certainly, the number of international meetings around topics such as labour standards, business partnerships and corporate citizenship is noticeably increasing. Cynics will say that this is all talk and no action. To an extent this is so; but talk will eventually lead to concrete action simply because businesses will demand this from their international relationships. As Winston Churchill used to say, albeit in another context, jaw-jaw is better than war-war.

Prisoner's dilemma

The strategy to be adopted by government and the private sector should not be one of confrontation, but – like the strategy required to solve the prisoner's dilemma, a well-known example from game theory – should be one of compromise. The best solution to the prisoner's dilemma was cooperation between the main actors involved. Lack of cooperation led to high penalties. The analogy is that should government or enterprises act alone, albeit seemingly in their own best interest, then this would jeopardize their overall position. The compromise for government and the private sector is to develop a voluntary code of practice or social bargain that both observe. Efforts to create such a code do exist and date from the early 1970s – when the UN developed a commission on TNCs and the OECD developed a set of guidelines for multinational enterprises – and from 1976 – when the ILO's world employment conference on basic needs put forward the notion of 'good citizenship'. In the years since, these codes fell hostage to extreme politicization at the international level and interest varied.[10] More recently, the European Commission (EC), in a White Paper, has urged a voluntary approach to the implementation of CSR.[11] Curiously, the EC actually includes the word 'voluntary' in the actual definition of CSR, which it defines as 'a concept whereby companies integrate social and environmental concerns in their business operations and in their interaction with their stakeholders on a voluntary basis'. This is curious since it rules out an important debate that is currently ongoing about whether CSR should be voluntary or compulsory. My view (see the following section) is that the answer lies somewhere between a totally voluntary approach and complete legislation. The exact pointer is to be arrived at through negotiation.

This is also where my metaphor of the prisoner's dilemma falls down; as with all good metaphors, they only go so far. The compromise reached was not based on negotiation, since the prisoners were kept in isolation, but on a tacit knowledge that this is the only wholly viable outcome for both prisoners.[12] The actors in the CSR debate are often aware of each other's position. For instance, the EU invited responses on its White Paper and received around 250 replies, of which about half of the responses came from employers' organizations, business associations and individual enterprises. Trade unions and civil society organizations accounted for another large portion of the responses.

At the national level, the current debate concerning increased regulation of corporations by the US government as a result of various corporate scandals is being carried out among a whole host of institutions. As Alan Blinder noted: 'While changes in private-sector behaviour will eventually fix many of today's accounting and corporate governance problems, the markets are clamouring for decisive government actions now.'[13] Who in the market and what are the actions are ignored by Blinder, who nevertheless noted in the same article the ambivalent attitude toward government intervention when he wrote: 'When things go well the markets want to be left alone, but when things start to fall apart they want Washington help.'

A planetary bargain and globalization

What is meant by globalization?

What is the link between CSR and globalization? First, what is meant by globalization? Essentially, it means that money (financial capital) can move to wherever its owners wish at the flash of a computer button or the click of a mouse. In practice, it also means that the world has become a smaller place because concomitant with these massive capital flows have come advances in telecommunications and travel. The use of Global System for Mobile Communications (GSM) telephones or the internet can put the investor in Iceland in direct contact with Wall Street. There is hardly a place on Earth where it takes more than a day to travel to from almost any other part. But, of course, it all depends where you start from – as in the old witticism, where a person asking for directions in Dublin received the reply: 'Well, I wouldn't start from here.'

Globalization, meaning access to markets, is fine for those with the physical, human and social capital to access them. Those without these attributes, the Bushmen in the Kalahari or nomads in Somalia, for instance, find it just about impossible. On the other hand, reductions in telecommunication charges will eventually enable farmers in developing countries, for example, to communicate directly with the industrialized world, thereby enhancing trade and improving living conditions. One of the many problems is that telecommunication charges are often in the hands of public monopolies in developing countries, who use these charges as an alternative taxation system. A one-minute telephone call from a small flower grower in Kenya to a buyer in the Netherlands might cost the equivalent of a day's flower harvest. Globalization that enhances internet services and insists on competitive telecommunication charges will help – at the margin, at least – to lower costs and therefore to raise living standards for such producers.

Some readers may reject this flowery example of trade theory in action without institutional constraints. But returning to the nomads in Somalia, or at least their descendants, globalization is helping development in one part of Somalia. In the self-proclaimed independent state of Somaliland, in northern Somalia and a former British protectorate, civil war led to the complete destruction of utilities. Without a public telecommunication monopoly to protect Somaliland, Somalilanders use wireless mobile phone technology linked to satellite transmitters to conduct their business. Costs of international calls are fiercely competitive due to the plethora of mobile phone companies who operate there. Problems exist, of course. Somaliland government ministers have half a dozen phones on their desk since competing networks do not allow talk across different networks – an example of where a strong government could enhance actions taken by the private sector. The government in Somaliland is weak partly through lack of international recognition and partly through historical reasons. A planetary bargain of compromise between public and corporate sectors could, therefore, also be implemented at the local level. Compromise between the fledgling government in Somaliland (to regulate telecommunications) and the telecommunication private sector (to allow cross-talk on their networks) would be to everyone's advantage. Cross-talk would reduce the costs of government in having so many networks; the market would increase as the population would be able to talk across all networks; and the companies would benefit through a larger market.

Will globalization lead to lower wages?

The fear behind increasing globalization is that production will increasingly be allocated to the lowest cost producers, thereby impoverishing the currently richer part of the world. This is known to economists as 'factor price equalization', where the wages of the unskilled in the richer countries fall and those in the poorer countries rise.[14]

But do the wages rise, in practice? In many fast-growing developing nations, unskilled wages have risen (at least until the recent Asian crisis) – Malaysia, Thailand, South Korea, Taiwan, Chile, Tunisia and so on. There, new consumers have been created to replace those supposedly left behind in the richer nations. Their new consumption leads to new exports for the richer nations, who have become more efficient because of the relocation of unskilled jobs to the poorer countries. This is a virtuous circle where all can gain.

However, rapid population growth in other developing world nations and the entry of two monster economies into the global trading system – India and China – mean that the pool of unskilled labour is growing rapidly. Merely relocating production to these countries does not necessarily mean that unskilled wages will rise. Wages normally rise in an open economy to match productivity increases. But even if productivity increases, wages can be kept down in at least two ways. First, employers can simply employ other unskilled workers from the already large labour surplus; second, through seeking lower production costs (economists call this rent-seeking), multinational firms can allow their new investment to float elsewhere, to other low-wage unskilled nations. In these countries, wages should be allowed to rise, along with social benefits, to create the 'virtuous circle'. This can be helped through a voluntary and global bargain between the key actors in the business sector, so that new markets for consumers can be created.

A voluntary bargain can be undermined by rogue companies, and one company can always undercut another. However, if a 'bargain' existed to exclude rent-seeking behaviour to the lowest common denominator, it would be in everyone's interest – workers would see their wages rise, company profits would not be undercut by another firm using bargain-basement labour and new consumers would be created. A 'rogue' company that fell out of this bargain could be treated in a number of ways. If the bargain was voluntary, the rogue company might simply chose to ignore it; but it would then be subject to peer pressure. If the bargain was compulsory, who would enforce it? The voluntary solution is preferable because it means a lower burden in the cobweb of already complicated rules for doing business. The voluntary solution is less democratic, however, because it allows the company to choose what actions to take with only lip service to its constituents. Basic codes of ethics for international business have been introduced at a rapid rate in recent years (see Chapter 4), and companies are increasingly observing them.

Thus, codes of ethics, as well as the wider issues implied in my definition of the planetary bargain, are part of globalization. They will ensure that enterprises will employ beggar-thy-neighbour policies less and less. Will the costs of doing business rise? Yes, they will, as the planetary bargain is gradually accepted. But profits will not necessarily fall as new markets are generated from the newly enriched consumers.

A key component of any agreement is that the main private-sector companies in the world should participate. This, of course, is difficult because it means private global trading concerns agreeing to work toward better conditions for their workers, wherever they may be. But this is the aim of the UN's Global Compact initiative, and steps are already being made in that direction. Furthermore, with an international agreement between the largest trading concerns to do this, then all gain, because the playing field in which all compete remains level. The competition is then based on new products, services, technology and price, but not upon who manages to exploit their workers the most. Such global Keynesianism (but see the following sub-section) will stimulate demand for goods in both rich and poor countries.

One of the key results of such a planetary bargain or social agreement will be to improve social protection for workers around the world. Obviously, the type of social protection devised has to be carefully constructed so as not to over-burden business with meaningless regulation that leads to inefficiency and increased unemployment. However, social protection that increases workers' pecuniary benefits worldwide through pensions, maternity leave, better pay, and so on is in everyone's interest because it will stimulate effective demand, consumption and, consequently, increased growth. It is in the interest of private TNCs that social protection should rise at the same rate everywhere to prevent competitors or rogue countries from benefiting from short-term gains through inflicting misery on their people. It is in the interest of nation states because those who have attempted to improve the lot of workers will not be undercut by the same rogue countries. Germany has often complained that its high level of social protection, gained since 1945, might now have to be dismantled to compete with the sweat shops of the developing world. The goal, however, must be to move everyone to German levels, rather than to move German levels to those of, for instance, Somalia, Rwanda or Bangladesh.

Labour conditions and trade: The social clause

The idea of relating improved labour conditions to trade is not new.[15] At the international level, this has come under the heading of a *social clause*. Discussions to include this in international agreements have also been underway for many decades.[16] The intention is to help to promote fair competition between developing country exporters by ensuring that those who respect minimum labour standards are not penalized for their efforts to promote human development.

Progress in including a social clause in effective international agreements has been painfully slow. This is because some developing countries feel that the industrialized countries' concern about working conditions is due, above all, to their export success and to the growing pressure for protectionism that has arisen from high unemployment. A social clause is seen as a disguised form of protectionism – a Trojan horse – which is tantamount to interference in their internal affairs, while they are being asked for reciprocity in social obligations in return for trade concessions. The private sector sees it as yet more restrictions on its ability to provide the best quality products at the lowest possible prices.

Thus, any negotiation at the international level has to be handled carefully; the benefits and costs for both industrialized and developing countries must be clearly spelled out. This is something that neither the WTO, with its limited staff and research capability, nor the ILO, which finds it politically very difficult to support research and analysis of its labour standards, have accomplished to date. And whether the agreement should be voluntary, because it is in everyone's best interest, or regulatory is worthy of further reflection. On this latter point, it is worth mentioning that since its establishment in 1919, the ILO has not achieved the passage of any of its conventions and recommendations on labour standards into any form of international law. Although many countries have included ILO labour standards within their national laws, there is no international obligation to do so.

Attempts were made to include a linkage between a social clause and trade in the Uruguay Round of the General Agreement on Tariffs and Trade (GATT) that pre-dated the WTO; but the link was rejected and only faltering attempts have been made in the relatively new WTO. Given the importance of this matter, it is somewhat surprising to see that progress on it at the international level has been so slow. There were no provisions within GATT to ensure pursuing an improved social clause, nor are there in its successor, the WTO. The ILO, who is responsible for ensuring the application of labour standards, has been slow (even ignored) in its championing of this at the centre of international discussions.

The ILO has, however, been active in producing labour standards through its conventions and recommendations, and at the last count there were 174 conventions and 80 recommendations.[17] Yet, it appears to be more active in creating new instruments, thereby spreading itself too thinly, rather than conducting research on the impact and value of its labour standards and in identifying a minimum set of labour standards that could be included in a social clause or a social agreement.[18] For instance, in June 1999 the ILO members adopted Convention 182, banning the worst forms of child labour. But, as Gijsbert Van Liemt, one of its former analysts, noted:

> The ILO constitution gives no indication of priorities for the application of international labour standards and the wide range of areas covered makes it impossible – particularly in developing countries with their weak administrative machinery – to expect most or even many of them to be implemented.[19]

The standards generally mentioned, Van Liemt says, are those on freedom of association, the right to organize and bargain collectively, the minimum age for the employment of children, freedom from discrimination in employment, freedom from forced labour, and occupational safety and health. Thus, the emphasis is not so much on the economic aspects as on the legislative. The economic aspects would include social protection, pensions, health insurance, and so on, all of which could stimulate effective demand for new products. But another weakness of ILO policy advice is that it normally raises the cost of labour and hardly ever considers the economic benefits to the institution who has to pay the increased charges implied. This is not a moot point, since few would question the desire to implement many, if not all, of ILO social policy. What is missing is to prioritize social policy in terms of what is essential and what is affordable. The core labour standards approach, which has been picked up by the Global Compact initiative, is a step in the direction of prioritizing, but on political not on economic grounds.

A recent OECD study *International Trade and Core Labour Standards* backed up some of these statements when it noted that 'there remains a continuing gap between the international recognition of core labour standards and their application'.[20,21] Based on published observations of the ILO Committee of Experts on the Application of Conventions and Recommendations, the OECD study finds *no* indication in recent years of substantial progress, overall, in reducing non-compliance with respect to freedom of association and the right to collective bargaining among a broad sample of 69 countries who have ratified the two corresponding ILO fundamental conventions.

The same OECD report noted that the WTO members, in their December 1996 Singapore conference, rejected the use of labour standards because they saw them as protectionist. In classic UN prose, the conference 'recognized' the ILO as the 'competent body to set and deal with core labour standards'. The translation for this is: we don't want to deal with this controversial issue; let the ILO deal with it. Hiding the problem under the carpet in this way is a legitimate cause of concern to critics of the WTO, and at least to some of the active demonstrators known, mistakenly, as anti-globalization protestors.

At the third WTO ministerial meeting in Seattle in December 1999, proposals by the US, Canada and the EU to set up a WTO working group on the relationships between appropriate trade, developmental, social and environmental policy choices in the context of adjusting to globalization were rejected! However, as noted above and by Stephen Golub, there is some light at the end of the tunnel as the ILO (together with the OECD) has moved toward adopting a 'core' set of labour standards.[22] These follow the list applied in much US trade legislation that comprises:

- freedom of association;
- the right to organize and bargain collectively;
- the prohibition of forced or compulsory labour;
- a minimum age for the employment of children; and
- a guarantee of acceptable working conditions (possibly including a maximum number of hours per week, a weekly rest period, limits to work by young persons, a minimum wage, minimum workplace safety and health standards, and the elimination of employment discrimination).

As Golub remarked, this list blends labour 'rights', such as freedom of association, with regulations on working conditions and wages, which are economic in nature. The OECD/ILO's core list is similar to that of the US, except that the fifth standard is limited to the elimination of employment discrimination.

In 1997 the ILO's DG put his weight and that of his organization behind this core set as, indeed, has the new ILO's DG, Juan Somavia, but language has been guarded:[23]

...although it is up to each member state to decide upon the areas and social priorities which should benefit from the fruits of growth and prosperity generated by globalization, there is nevertheless a 'minimum' programme that each should try to achieve.[24]

Indeed, a social clause could go further than just trade, and also be linked to public capital flows, such as official lending and aid, and to strategic relations, such as defence treaties. After all, countries spend billions on their defence industries, largely to prevent the have-nots from obtaining access to that possessed by the haves. Efforts that go into raising living standards through a social clause are likely to have much higher payoffs in terms of peace than is the encouragement of, and therefore the need for, expensive armies.

There have been several other attempts at establishing a social clause at the international level, but these have, so far, resulted in failure. For example, the EC endeavoured to include a social clause with the African, Caribbean and Pacific (ACP) countries that come under its Lomé Convention. But the convention, signed in 1984, made reference only to respecting human rights without a follow-up or control mechanism. Similarly, some international commodity agreements contain a social clause – for example, the 1979 Natural Rubber Agreement stated that its members would endeavour to maintain labour standards designed to improve the levels of living in their respective natural rubber sectors – but there is no monitoring or control or legal provision to ensure observance.

Evidence is already accumulating that a planetary bargain or global compact that goes much further than the UN's so-called Global Compact initiative is required.[25] Companies who have already trail-blazed a green path over the past five years in the UK wanted to see dramatic progress in reporting on emissions, spending and social impacts, generally (according to John Elkington, chairman of SustainAbility, in a report published with the United Nations Environment Programme (UNEP)). Elkington predicted an explosion of activity over the next few years, even without mandatory requirements, as demands for greater transparency force more companies to report beyond their traditional financial boundaries. Already, we see several hundred companies sign up to the UN's Global Compact. However, all of these companies have ignored or skated over the question of a wider ranging global compact than that of the UN and how it could be set into motion. Clearly, more thinking must take place on precisely what kinds of measures should be put into practice by whom and when. Nonetheless, the UN Global Compact initiative has set into motion a number of working groups to handle some of these issues; but, to date, it lacks the necessary financial resources and in-depth analytical work if progress is to be made.

What, then, could a planetary bargain or global compact contain, and to whom should it be directed? There are three main criteria:

1   At the international level, there is a case for vigorously pursuing a minimum priority set of labour standards and social protection that should be included in international agreements within the WTO.
2   Private companies should be encouraged to work toward a set of minimum working conditions that all individuals will respect. This could be accomplished through such bodies as the UN, the ILO, the OECD and the EU, and it is in the private sector's own interest to do this. The leading figures in the major companies in the world should be brought together to thrash out a first agreement.
3   Individual nations should work actively to agree and to respect a minimum code of ethics for their trade with other nations.

Since the first edition of this book, there has been a number of moves to require companies to adhere to a set of global principles, such as the Global Reporting Initiative, UN Global Compact, AccountAbility 1000 (AA1000) and the OECD Corporate Governance Principles. Some companies have indicated their willingness to abide by such principles and even to be subject to sanctions for non-compliance. This is because they would be willing to accept a 'level playing field' to which their main competitors would also adhere. Legislation is difficult since implementation of a code by one country would punish those companies headquartered there to the benefit of companies headquartered elsewhere – for example, the Cayman Islands, the Netherlands Antilles, Panama, etc – where poor levels of corporate governance are legendary. Such a code could not be a once-and-for-all negotiation to produce a global guideline since society changes too fast for this.[26] What is envisaged is a continuing process of dialogue between governments and enterprises.

Who should represent both sides? In fact, such a process has already started within international organizations, as I noted above, at the OECD Corporate Governance fora, the World Bank Business Partnership and Corporate Governance discussions, the UN Global Compact initiative, the UNEP sustainability dimension and Global Reporting Initiative, and ILO annual tri-partite conferences of employers, trade unions and governments.

Who should represent enterprises? This is more problematical. At the ILO, where enterprises have been represented for generations normally by chambers of commerce, rarely do the large corporations show up. The UN Global Compact has had more success, and ILO is represented; but the agenda, to date, has been limited to only a few stakeholders. Nevertheless, enterprises are active in a variety of NGO settings, such as Business for Social Responsibility (BSR), the European Business Network for Social Cohesion (EBNSC), the World Business Council for Sustainable Development (WBCSD) or the International Chamber of Commerce (ICC). Yet, in each case the agenda is different and concepts are vague.

What about other stakeholder groups, such as the trade unions, consumers, non-unionized workers, distributors, retailers, suppliers, shareholders, and so on? To date, no one body has involved all of these groups, as well as governments and enterprises. The nearest organization is the ILO; but its debates are intensely political and the ILO has found it nearly impossible to implement even one specific area of CSR: that of a core set of labour standards.

Should the planetary bargain to promote CSR be voluntary or compulsory?

There is currently much discussion on how the planetary bargain should promote CSR. The scandals in the US have led congress to advance legislation on some aspects of CSR – the corporate governance part. On 24 July 2002, both the house and senate agreed on a broad overhaul of corporate fraud, accounting and securities laws aimed at curbing the abuses that shook Wall Street. They also prohibited Wall Street investment firms from retaliating against research analysts who criticize clients of the firm; barred companies from extending unusual loans to executives; prohibited accounting firms from offering nine types of consulting services to public companies they also audit; and prevented officials from facing judgements related to securities fraud violations from using bankruptcy court to escape liability.

In the UK, legislation is already a little more stringent than in the US and a minister of CSR has been appointed by the government; but, to date, there has been little or no action. The inaction has led to a coalition of NGOs, known as the Child Survival Collaborations and Resources Group (The CORE Group), demanding the UK parliament for legislation concerning CSR. Predictably, according to Janus, the UK's business association, the Confederation of British Industries (CBI), stated: 'We believe that CSR should remain market driven. We do not support a mandatory approach and believe that a one-size fits all policy is just not possible.'[27]

The EU, as noted previously, believes in a voluntary approach to CSR. One of the EU's most active members, France, has devised legislation calling for all large companies to produce social reports on an annual basis by the year 2004. On the other hand, Adrian Henriques has wisely noted that the most common reason given for why new legislation would set CSR back is because of the 'lowest-common denominator argument', and he continues: 'If there were legislation on CSR, then companies would deliver what the law requires, but never more.'[28]

A bargain of a much harsher nature than envisaged here was mooted by Adam Smith in his *Wealth of Nations*. According to one interpretation by Bernard Avishai, writing in the *Harvard Business Review*, Smith's writings set forth a compact by which entrepreneurs were bound.[29] In being so constrained, they owed the government their support only as far as it furthered their companies' commerce. It was unreasonable for government to interfere with supply and demand in any market, including the poor law. But, as Avishai noted, this contract or bargain underestimated how explosive unemployment could be. Consequently, by the end of the 19th century, democratic radicals had pressed successfully for ending child labour, shortening the work day, increasing public schooling and establishing some form of unemployment insurance. Arguably, this new social contract or bargain eventually led to the downfall of communism.

It was the exploitation of labour, the foundation of Karl Marx's theories in *Das Kapital*, that eventually led to the Leninist worker revolution and to the communist state.[30] Marx argued that workers would rise up against capital as they saw their standard of living stagnate, compared with that of the owners of capital. The Soviet Union turned (without permission) into Marx's experimental laboratory. But the success of the market system in allowing workers to become stakeholders in private capital, through the rise and increasing power of the trade union movement, eventually led to market capitalism growing stronger rather than collapsing. Indeed, the strength of the market economies, and the wealth created therein, led to the collapse of Marx's experimental state, the Soviet Union, as it proved hopelessly inefficient at delivering a decent standard of living to its workers.

'Substitution of altruism for self-interest on the part of business enterprises is not called for in resolving environmental problems – indeed, an attempt at such substitution might have mischievous consequences', wrote Jerome Rothenburg in 1974.[31] This seems excessively naive now, after nearly two and a half decades of consciousness-raising and campaigns against polluting industry. However, Rothenburg is correct to say that self-interest is not simply 'to be left intact; it is to be relied upon'. He says that it is the responsibility of the public sector to enact policies that elicit socially responsible behaviour from firms who are following self-interest. The task for governments is to induce firms to act in ways that are socially desirable in the aggregate. This is so not only for governments, but also for the informed public, NGOs, campaigners, associations and the like.

In practice, evidence is already accumulating that businesses are taking it upon themselves to act socially responsibly, and this is much ahead of any legislation either proposed or even dreamed of. Many companies, such as British Petroleum (BP), The Co-operative Bank, Shell, British Telecom (BT) and Asea Brown Boveri (ABB) believe that their existing behaviour exceeds most existing standards and, of course, wish to bring other companies, especially their competitors, up to the same level. They welcome the naming and shaming of rogue companies thereby encouraging limited legislation. On the other hand, Janus observes that few companies have a sophisticated approach to CSR – or even any approach at all![32] He continues: 'Were legislation to be introduced now, most companies would not be able to comply.'

Thus, businesses need prodding to ensure that CSR is on their agenda. As Samuel Brittan of the *Financial Times* remarked: 'It is doubtful whether managers have the knowledge to take into account the second- and third-order effects of their actions on national (or international, for that matter) well-being.'[33] This knowledge problem is 'often overlooked by so-called ethical economists', he says. And while a simple profit-maximization model provides 'subsidiary performance indicators for decentralized managers within a corporation', this does not apply to the much 'vaguer stakeholder objectives'.

How will a planetary bargain come about? Pressure is now being put by many consumers, employees, campaigners and shareholders on enterprises to become socially responsible, which they are actually doing. It would be nice to imagine, as I proposed above, a planetary bargain that arises from all of the major companies in the world sitting around a table and horse trading, eventually producing a final document. Anti-trust provisions will not allow this; but stakeholder pressure will be society's 'invisible hand', guiding, suggesting, protesting, campaigning and regulating the wilder excesses that will create the planetary bargain. It will not occur by itself without vigorous actions or attempts to document and suggest alternative ways of conducting business. The socially responsible 'invisible hand' will have to be guided by the millions of concerned people who care about such things. Given that more and more enterprises see that such a course is in their long-term interest, the ground is fertile for this guidance to take place.

So, a planetary bargain is already on its way. Even as far back as 1976, both the OECD and the ILO produced guidelines for the conduct of international business by TNCs.[34] The ILO report stated that: 'This declaration sets out principles in the fields of employment, training, conditions of work and life and industrial relations which governments, employers' and workers' organizations and multinational enterprises are recommended to observe on a *voluntary* basis.'[35] The Caux Principles (see Chapter 4) provide a philosophical set of principles encompassing business and environmental issues, as did the original Global Sullivan Principles of Corporate Social Responsibility, developed during the 1970s.[36] And the US Council on Economic Priorities (CEP) has developed an overseas labour-auditing process. As its executive director, Alice Tepper Marlin, says: 'CEP has set universal standards for labour conditions, getting companies to say they'll only contract with those who comply...companies almost certainly will begin implementing this'.[37]

The CEP, now known as Social Accountability International (SAI), has called this Social Accountability 8000 (SA8000), and it takes as its core nine ILO conventions (on such topics as forced and bonded labour, freedom of association, home work, and so on, as well as the Universal Declaration of Human Rights and the UN Convention on the Rights of the Child, see also Chapter 7).[38,39]

The ILO's labour standards, the area in which one would imagine such work would have been carried out, have never applied to business because employers' organizations carry one fourth of the vote on the ILO's governing body. Historically, employers' organizations have been against any standards set by the ILO for business, even though ILO standards are not followed up by any legislative body. But times are changing, and businesses, especially in the industrialized countries, are starting to realize that social responsibility pays, and that they have nothing to fear from reasonable standards of conduct.

What, therefore, are the pluses and minuses of CSR regulation?

Pluses of CSR legislation

The benefits of legislation include the following:

- It would help to avoid excessive exploitation of labour, bribery, and corruption.
- Companies would know what is expected of them, thereby promoting a level playing field.
- Many aspects of CSR behaviour are good for business (for example, reputation, human resources, branding, the ease of locating in new communities, etc), and legislation could help to improve profitability, growth and sustainability.
- Some areas, such as downsizing, could help to readdress the balance between companies and their employees.
- Rogue companies would be penalized because of their lower standards.
- The wider community would benefit as companies reach out to address some of the key issues of underdevelopment around the world.

Minuses of CSR legislation

The negative impacts of legislation include the following:

- Additional bureaucracy and, therefore, the costs of observance would rise.
- Costs of operation could rise above those required for continued profitability and sustainability.
- Critics already argue that the CSR of companies is simply to make a profit, and legislation would increase the vocalization of these concerns.

In conclusion, I stand on the minimalist side of the debate on legislation. Clearly, no legislation at all is untenable simply because so much legislation already exists, particularly for corporate governance. Nevertheless, full legislation for CSR, whatever that would mean, is also untenable since business could grind to a halt simply in chasing up all the new CSR laws on the statute book. Thus, the sensible position for a planetary bargain is sufficient legislation to allow for a level playing field. This legislation must apply to all corporations wherever they are located or it simply will not work. How to enforce even minimalist standards in remote locations from the Dutch Antilles to the Maldives, and even in China or India, is a challenge for the legislators.

Is a planetary bargain simply global Keynesianism?

John Maynard Keynes's theories, developed in a series of tracts and books during the 1920s and 1930s, were a response to high levels of unemployment and world recession.[40] A recent popular view of his ideas, and an advocacy of 'why Keynesian economics is best' is covered in a chapter in Will Hutton's book *The State We're In*.[41] Keynes's work was a powerful response to the neo-classical economists, whose theories underlined the importance of market forces in bringing systems into equilibrium. The neo-classicals' focus (as well as that of their many acolytes today) was on the regulatory role of prices. Markets for goods or labour did not clear, they believed, because of distortions in the price system. Remove the distortions, and the markets would clear. For instance, unemployment would occur because the price of labour (wages) relative to the price of capital (interest rate) was too high. If labour reduced its price, then it would be absorbed.

In his challenge to most neo-classical ideas, and to the supposed inevitability of unemployment, Keynes considered that capitalist systems were perfectly viable, were it not for artificial barriers.[42] Keynes was no great egalitarian, and felt that an unequal distribution of wealth was necessary to maintain the level of savings high enough to supply the abundant demand for capital formation. He argued that the volume of employment in equilibrium depended upon, first, the aggregate supply function; second, the propensity to consume; and, third, the volume of investment.[43] This was the essence of his 'general theory of employment'. The neo-classical economists insisted that prices would change to make supply equal demand in product, capital and labour markets. Keynes argued, essentially, that quantities rather than prices would alter to achieve equilibrium, and that real wages were much too rigid to be expected to fall (or rise) quickly enough to restore equilibrium. It was once thought by some Marxist economists, such as Paul Sweezy of the US, that the class-based division inherent in government would not allow the liberal social reform required by Keynesian economics.[44] The convergence between Marxists and Keynesians is strong in neo-Keynesian economics, where vigorous government intervention is suggested to achieve full employment. And both economic schools agreed that capitalism faces the problem of aggregate demand – that is, will the level of aggregate demand generated by any level of output be sufficient to purchase the whole of that output?[45]

Implementation of a Keynesian approach does, indeed, require an activist government to achieve full employment. As Bhatt asked, how can governments assume responsibility for the maintenance of adequate investment growth without enquiring further into the pattern of investment, which is so relevant to the nature and structure of growth and welfare?[46] And decisions relating to the *volume* of investment cannot be isolated from decisions relating to the *pattern* of investment.

Global Keynesianism advocates stimulating demand in all countries so as to absorb excess production and to create full employment. The weakness, its critics argue, is that the stimulation of effective demand leads to inflation when production is constrained. In developing countries, even when there is surplus labour, Keynesianism falls down, say Berry and Sabot.[47] They point out three contributing factors. First, although there is abundant labour – at least of unskilled types in the poorer nations – a general increase in demand will not lead to a general increase in output, because other cooperating factors are needed to work with labour. The traditional one to take is capital – that is, real capital equipment – because 'nothing much can be done with bare hands alone'. Second, demand deficiency tends to ignore longer-run influences on output, such as the negative effects of population growth and the positive effects of technological change and capital accumulation. Third, the specificity of location and the pattern of unemployment, which, in less developed countries (LDCs), may be urban surplus and rural scarcity, contradict the Keynesian models that maintain that the direction, if not the rate, of change in aggregate demand is the same in all sectors.

Yet, investment need not only be in physical capital. In developing countries, investment is required in both social capital (notions of trust, reliable legal frameworks, cultural and ethnic tolerance, pride in one's work and so on) and human capital (education, training, use of technology). This, coupled with effective demand, need not lead to inflation. But great care must be taken not to control inflation solely with monetary measures, such as controlling money supply through raising the real rate of interest, because this can lead to a rising real rate of exchange that destroys any gains from the stimulation of Keynesian demand.

The movement known as *monetarism* attacks the Keynesian model by asserting that, first, governments are poor drivers of the economy and, second, the economy's brake and accelerator have little to do with fiscal policy.[48] Indeed, in a study of the determinants of 1000 years of growth, Angus Maddison puts the rise in living standards down to three main causes:

1   The conquest or colonization of relatively under-populated areas.
2   International exchanges and the movement of capital.
3   Technological and institutional innovation.[49]

Nevertheless, he traces the golden age of growth in industrialized countries between 1950 and 1973 to these latter two points, as well as to the promotion of high levels of demand and employment.[50] The current orthodoxy among economists is that there is a role for both monetary and fiscal stimulus, with attention turning to the question of aggregate supply and how firms can be induced to lift productivity.

How does all of this relate to CSR in a planetary bargain? Raising the living standards of workers and their productivity around the world through socially responsible polices of enterprises will help to stimulate output, growth and effective demand. This, in turn, will allow workers to purchase the goods that the enterprises are offering. Beggar-thy-neighbour policies by rogue companies outside of the planetary bargain may work in the short term, but in the longer term they are self-defeating. Neo-classical economics, which concentrates on the maxim that what is good for profits is good for society, does not necessarily ensure global rises in living standards (see also Chapter 1). Profits can be maximized through using the cheapest source of labour and moving to other sources of labour across national boundaries should problems occur, such as wages starting to rise. With growing numbers of unskilled workers as a result of rapid population growth, socially irresponsible enterprises can always find labour to exploit. Consequently, a neo-classical approach will continue to exist, feeding upon low labour costs. Global Keynesians believe, though, that such an approach is eventually self-defeating (leaving aside the moral argument of whether the exploitation of labour globally is acceptable). This is because it will lead to downsizing in the rich world and to lower effective demand there, while the low wages paid to the masses in the poor world cannot allow them to purchase the goods they make. So, yes, the basis of a planetary bargain is based upon the notion of a form of global Keynesianism. But differing from old-fashioned Keynesian thought, it is also based on the notion that wages cannot outstrip productivity increases, that governments have a regulatory role but are poor at choosing where enterprise should flourish, and that private capital flows should be encouraged.[51]

Let us take an example.[52] The Maldives is a chain of a thousand islands mid-way between the Indian and African continents. It is enriching itself through tourism, which takes advantage of its pristine waters. A fact that is little known, though, is the use of one of its islands for producing clothes for the European market by Sri Lankan entrepreneurs. Because the quota for Sri Lanka for textile exports to the EU has been met, the Maldives, with its own quota, provided a blind eye is turned to abhorrent labour practices, is an attractive place for textile production. Four hundred Sri Lankan women are confined to what some would call a paradise island. Surrounded by a clear blue sea, bordered by waving palm fronds and white coral sand beaches, the island is only about 2 kilometres long by 1 kilometre wide. The main industry is concentrated in two large buildings, one of which is a dormitory and the other an assembly plant. The women work ten hours a day, with one day off per week, in theory. Because they cannot leave the island for two years, and the island is a five-hour boat ride from the capital city Male, there is nothing to do except work for meagre earnings on a piecework basis every day of the week and year. The women's earnings range from about US$100–$200 a year, which, because all their needs are looked after, can be saved. The flight home is paid for every two years. They assemble jeans, jackets and so on for well-known brand labels. But they cannot possibly afford any of the products that they assemble. Unless their manufacturing enterprise enters the world of social responsibility, these women will be confined to a poor livelihood and will never be able to buy the clothes they make. The neo-classicists would be happy with this situation since the women would not be in the Maldives if they could earn higher wages elsewhere. A planetary bargain, on the other hand, would examine the responsibility of the company involved and would likely lead to improved working conditions, thereby stimulating both production, through improved human capital formation and the effective demand of these Sri Lankan women. This would translate into more flights home and, eventually in a small way, more production for Boeing or Airbus.

Chapter 3

The Seven Azimuths: Who Are the Stakeholders?

Introduction

The word 'stakeholder' conjures up images of early gold rushers bashing bits of wood into the ground to establish their claim. It is an ugly word but one, nevertheless, that has passed into common usage among the growing community concerned with corporate social responsibility (CSR). There is no general agreement on who or what are the stakeholders of a firm, and stakeholder theory offers 'a maddening variety of signals on how questions of stakeholder identification might be answered.'[1] Anne Svendsen has come up with a useful and practical, if uncritical, look at the application of stakeholder strategy to corporations.[2] She traces, conceptually, the evolution of corporate stakeholder theory from what was once a defensive style, where managers paid lip-service to its stakeholders en route to making a profit, to a lukewarm interest, especially in customers as essential to make a profit in today's collaborative and 'systems' approach – where interactions with stakeholders provide a win–win situation.

Whatever theory eventually emerges, practice has shown that in terms of social responsibility there are at least seven azimuths, communities or stakeholders that the business spectrum is involved with – namely:[3]

1   owners/investors (shareholders or stockholders);
2   management;
3   employees;
4   customers;
5   the natural environment;
6   the wider community (including government); and
7   contractors/suppliers.

What is the social responsibility of the company to each group and what, in turn, are the responsibilities of each group to the company? These are the questions that are explored in this chapter.

Owners and investors

As will be noted in Chapter 4, it is not, generally, owners and investors acting as shareholders or stockholders that companies generally address, either in terms of ethics or in terms of their responsibilities to them, other than that of making a profit. Increasingly, shareholders are asking questions about business practices. For instance, in 1995, developing-world debt campaigners in the UK started buying single shares in Lloyds Bank so as to be able to attend the company's annual meetings.[4] At the bank's meeting that November, both male and female protestors removed their clothes to reveal anti-debt slogans on their bodies. This was meat and drink for the UK's tabloid press, who gave unprecedented coverage to the issue of debt forgiveness. Five months later, a more measured approach by church-based anti-smoking campaigners in the US won such significant support from pension-fund shareholders that they almost forced the board of RJR Nabisco at its annual general meeting (AGM) to split the food and tobacco multinational into separate parts.[5]

The rising importance of ethical investment funds is also a testament to the changing role of shareholders. As noted in Chapter 1, the US-based Social Investment Forum claims that more than US$1 trillion were under management in the US during 1997, compared with US$639 billion during 1985 (see Chapter 5) – although my own research found, in July 1997, that there were only US$4.5 billion invested in socially responsible mutual funds.[6] Definitions seem remarkably 'fluid' in this area! The Banque de Scandinavie in Switzerland completed a survey of enterprises to judge their level of social responsibility before setting up a number of socially responsible investment funds. In the UK, there is a growing number of investment funds that together have over US$2.4 billion invested in socially responsible companies.[7] Undoubtedly, this trend will continue into the future; however, it remains to be seen how much of it was to do with the bull market up to the end of 2000, and the picture of socially responsible investment is likely to change in the bear market of 2002/2003. However, change is difficult to predict since the bear market that started in the US was exacerbated by corporate scandals. This should be good news for socially responsible investment funds. Nevertheless, socially responsible investment funds have not, to date, gone into the details necessary to uncover financial irregularities of the sort seen in Enron, WorldCom and Andersen. Such investigations would, anyway, be too expensive to carry out, which eventually will lead to a shake-out in the fledgling social investment industry.

Managers

It is the managers – especially the chief executive officer (CEO) – and the board of directors – especially the chairman – who drive any company and are the key force behind whether it is socially responsible or not. Few have been trained in the notion of social responsibility, although business schools are increasingly including ethics in their curricula. In the US, the majority (58 per cent) of executives of Fortune 1000 companies surveyed in 1997 strongly agreed that corporations have a responsibility to address social issues, such as work/family, diversity, equal rights and the environment, while only 14 per cent strongly agreed that corporate leaders were doing a good job addressing those issues.[8]

Furthermore, according to the *Financial Times*, 'ethics and entrepreneurship' are the two hot topics on the executive education agenda.[9] The Harvard Business School requires students to complete a not-for-profit section before graduation. That ethics and questions of CSR are considered to belong only in 'not-for-profit' courses illustrates the hold that Milton Friedman still has on that organization, even with the Keynesian John Kenneth Galbraith just over the park! One of the top business schools in Europe, the International Institute for Management and Development (IMD) in Lausanne, Switzerland, will also put greater emphasis on the need for its one-year MBA students to be aware of the social responsibility of companies. This is something that the course convenor, Professor Meehan, believes will become 'much more important over the next decade'.[10] Yet another leading business school in Europe, INSEAD (Institut Européen d'Administration des Affaires), based in Fontainebleau, France, is promoting the issue of CSR under the guise of 'business in society', and INSEAD believes that CSR will be an essential tool in the future. More importantly, INSEAD believes that CSR is not simply an add-on to business school's agenda but should be an embedded part of corporate strategy.[11] Thus, the power that managers have in driving a company has not gone unnoticed and is the reason for the increase in ethics codes (see Chapter 4) that seek to optimize their behaviour in socially responsible ways.

An important topic under discussion in the boardrooms and business schools of the US is how much is good governance worth? Investment funds, such as the Teachers Insurance and Annuity Association – College Retirement Equities Fund (TIAA-CREF) and the Californian Public Employees Retirement System (CalPERS), seek to impose boardroom guidelines on large US corporations.[12] Unsurprisingly, those companies that were well governed, according to CalPERS, obtained an additional 1.5 per cent to 2 per cent on average in annual returns to shareholders.

This debate came further to light when Heinz CEO Anthony Reilly flew in 500 guests to a racecourse in Dublin during the summer of 1997 at the company's expense, in the midst of laying off 2500 employees. He himself received US$182.9 million in remuneration over a six-year period, which ranked him as one of the world's best-paid CEOs. Yet, he won the dubious distinction of being among the five CEOs cited by *Business Week* as giving its shareholders the least for their money. And in *Business Week*'s first ranking of corporate boards in November 1996, Heinz was the third worst in the US (behind Archer Daniels Midland Co and Champion International Corporation). Governance experts believe that boards should have no more than two or three inside directors, with key audit, nominating and compensation committees being composed entirely of outsiders.[13] Heinz had, in 1997, nine outside directors, all of whom are considered as 'insiders'. Good corporate governance is just one aspect of CSR, albeit an important one, as was discussed in Chapter 1. Heinz's muddying of the waters between insiders and outsiders is an example of poor governance and, consequently, poor social responsibility. Furthermore, since the first edition of this book, the well-documented scandals of Enron, WorldCom and Andersen have come to light.[14]

However, CEOs – with a few exceptions – don't have much time, a problem made worse by the fact that they tend to last in their positions, on average, about four years. At a CSR conference, a former CEO said with some humour: 'The first year is getting to know the job, the fourth year is spent working out how to save your job, and so there are only two years in which a CEO can take on a cynical board and fight for CSR.'[15] He advised CSR professionals to be more commercial – if they are lucky, they will initially have, at most, five minutes in which to convince a CEO of the merits of a CSR policy.

So, what should an advocate of CSR say to a CEO?[16] There are, perhaps, four main points:

1   What is CSR all about (see Chapter 1)?

2   What are the key advantages of being socially responsible? The main advantages are:
    ■   Reputation is improved among staff and customers.
    ■   Productivity is improved through increased innovation and efficiency.
    ■   Shareholder value is increased as social investment funds target the company.
    ■   The customer base is widened, with no risk of losing existing ones.
    ■   Motivation and commitment of staff is improved. Recruitment of young bright people is enhanced.
    ■   The personal satisfaction of management is increased.

3   What are the main steps that need to be taken? These steps will, of course, build upon many activities already underway, but probably in different departments, divisions and countries. Therefore, what does business need, at minimum, to do? This is likely to proceed in stages; but immediate actions would include:
    ■   win board support for its introduction of a CSR policy;
    ■   lead from the front;
    ■   appoint a CSR manager, but keep responsibility shared;
    ■   understand available CSR measures;

- decide upon the key stakeholders;
- take stock of measures already underway;
- decide on whether to produce a social report;
- report adherence to standards; be open;
- contribute to CSR dialogue (for example, on Social Accountability 8000 (SA8000)); join institutes such as AccountAbility, the Global Reporting Initiative (GRI) and Social Accountability International (SAI).

4 What are the costs likely to be? These are:
- increased costs of focus group sessions with stakeholders;
- CSR manager and budget;
- training of staff on CSR;
- production, publication and distribution of social report;
- website section devoted to CSR.

Employees

During eras of downsizing, employees have a hard time. Yet, most companies are aware that good-quality staff is crucial for business success. This is translated into human resource policies that emphasize career development, flexible work practices, training both on and off the job, profit-sharing, incentive schemes, a voice in management, and so on. The economics of any business makes it sensible to retain employees in whom many years of investment have been made. This human capital is every bit as important as physical capital, and it is surprising that business leaders have sometimes ignored this in the past. They have done this to their peril, as Collins and Porras showed, and their message is gradually being taken up.[17]

For example, The Co-operative Bank in the UK, which considers itself an ethical business, found from a survey of its customers that customers were 'sick of the increasing profit focus among most British companies'.[18,19] The bank asked all its million-plus customers for their views on the Co-op's partnership approach, which had attempted to balance the needs of customers, staff and five other stakeholder groups. Analysis of almost 100,000 initial responses challenged the conventional wisdom of 'shareholder value', which makes maximizing profit the main objective of commercial business. The bank's chief executive, Terry Thomas, remarked that:[20]

> ...aggressive treatment of staff by managers and megaphone diplomacy with trade unions sends out a negative message to consumers. It says this company is more concerned with profits and keeping its shareholders happy than its staff and customers, who actually create the profit potential in the first place.

This view came over most strongly when customers were asked to rank the bank's seven stakeholder groups in importance. Shareholders came bottom of the list, with staff at the top as the group to whom the bank should pay most attention. But the gap between top and bottom was very small, with 90 per cent saying that shareholders were important, which emphasizes the difficulty facing a company in balancing the needs of different interest groups.

Recognizing the importance of developing human resources in UK companies, the then Conservative government introduced a training standard and award, known as Investors in People, or Investors for short, in 1990.[21] This was the government's response to the massive Training in Britain survey, which at the end of the 1980s had raised fundamental concerns about the quality and quantity of training in the country.[22] Unlike other government programmes that focus largely on unemployed people, the Investors award is concerned solely with the training offered by employers to their staff. The scheme has four principles: *commitment*, in which an Investor in People makes a commitment from the top to train all employees to achieve its business objectives; *planning*, where regular reviews of the needs and plans for training and development of all employees are made; *action*, which is taken to train and develop individuals on recruitment and throughout their employment; and *evaluation* of the investment in training and development in order to assess achievement and improve future effectiveness.

But did Investors make a difference? A study by Hillage and Moralee of the Institute of Employment Studies (IES) found, in a multiple regression analysis that examined the relationship between Investors' recognition and profitability, while controlling for other variables, that being a recognized Investor in People was positively related to profitability per employee.[23] It was not a statistically significant result, however, which is not surprising given that going for an Investors award without doing anything else would not be enough on its own to make a difference to profits. Nevertheless, about 40 per cent of the employers interviewed in the IES study said that Investors had made a direct contribution to improved business performance.[24]

Another study by the Profit Impact of Market Strategy Group (PIMS) in the UK confirmed the results of the IES work.[25] PIMS gathered data on 3000 strategic business units, half of which were in Europe. These units were divided into those considered good or poor in managing their human resources (HR); behaviour was then examined in two different types of market environment – one complex and turbulent and the other stable. The criteria used to divide companies into good and bad HR included feeling of belonging; equitable compensation; absence of conflict; sense of accomplishment; participation in decisions; sharing of information; and willingness to challenge. The comparison of the financial results of the two groups showed that those rated highly received a return on investment 16.7 per cent higher than those rated poorly. This was for those operating in complex and turbulent environments. When the business environment was more stable, the difference of 3.5 per cent was much less significant. Of course, causality cannot necessarily be established. It might be that good financial results simply allow more progressive HR policies.

Marcello Palazzi and George Starcher also cite another study, this time conducted in the US, of 700 publicly held corporations. The firms using best HR practices had a return on capital of 11 per cent, more than twice as high as the remaining firms that were not considered to have best-practice HR policy for their employees.

Trade unions usually cause company managers and shareholders to roll their eyes and furrow their brows. They have reduced in importance over the last decade and a half, particularly in the US and UK. This reduction of importance probably started in the 1980s, partly because of President Reagan's anti-union moves, which included his famous firing of all air traffic controllers whose union came out on strike, and in part because of Prime Minister Thatcher's vigorous objections to union activity, which culminated in the running fight with the National Union of Mineworkers that her government eventually won.

At the turn of the century, trade unions are again making their presence felt. Starting in the US with the 1997 capitulation of employers to the United Parcel Service (UPS) courier company and the current UK Labour government being challenged by its trade unions, who believe that rising UK prosperity has passed many workers by, this potentially heralds a new era for trade unions. As argued previously, the fight of trade unions for better living conditions and workers' pay prevented the collapse of capitalism that Karl Marx had predicted. This, in turn, showed the communist countries that market capitalism also cared for its workers while making great strides in efficiency. A socially responsible enterprise and a socially responsible trade union will have mutual respect; they will therefore be better able to forge partnerships in less than acrimonious surroundings. This must be the future of trade unions and their acceptance by CSR corporations.

One of the major issues confronting trade unions is the degree of ownership, partnership and profit-sharing enjoyed by employees in their company. This has spawned an immense literature – one too vast to cover adequately here. Suffice it to say that when employees have an interest in their firm, results are normally much better than in those companies where workers feel alienated from management.

Female employees are gradually getting their fair share of benefits on the principle of equal work for equal pay. However, there is no doubt that much more remains to be done by enterprises in recognizing women's role in the workplace. To help promote these values, the campaign Opportunity 2000 was launched in October 1991 in the UK by Business in the Community – a group founded in 1982 with the aim of making community involvement a natural part of successful business practice; of increasing the quality and extent of business activity in the community; and of improving the quality and quantity of women's work at all levels, based on ability, in both private- and public-sector organizations. This is not solely a social issue, important as it maybe; rather, the belief behind the campaign is that organizations who fail to utilize fully the nation's female resource are putting a brake on performance and compromising their competitiveness. The campaign started with 61 enterprise members and by 1996 had over 300 members in both the public and private sectors.

Customers

The statement that 'the customer is king (or queen)' has never been truer than today. The UK prime minister before Tony Blair, John Major, drew up a Citizen's Charter that would have been unheard of just a decade earlier. Major's target was the poor and sloppy service given to customers (for him, the electorate) by the public services. At the same time, the former nations of the Warsaw Pact countries have had to turn their thinking on its head, from 'count and supply' to 'listen to customers and then create, cost and supply'. The two new notions of cost and customer sovereignty had to be dealt with almost instantaneously.

The rapid onset of globalization has made it easier, in principle, for unscrupulous businesses to circumvent tiresome environmental or health-and-safety rules by relocating production overseas, says Rob Harrison of the *New Internationalist*.[26] Interestingly, in this era of globalization, many companies still retain their national identity and observe national rules. This can be noted by the number of large companies who are quoted on the stock exchange of their original country – British Telecom (BT) of the UK, Nestlé and Novartis of Switzerland, General Motors (GM) of the US, and so on. What many managers fear, however, is becoming the target of a powerful single-issue campaign group. Rather than waiting for it to happen, managers are taking pre-emptive action. This may take the form of environmental product labelling, or engaging with such ideas as codes of ethics and social audits.

Harrison notes that there are at least ten ways in which consumers can run an effective campaign, should they wish. These are as follows:

1   *Consumer boycotts*: one of the most successful boycotts in recent years was when German politicians called for a boycott of Shell over the dumping of the *Brent Spar* oil platform, and Shell was forced to capitulate when it saw its German sales fall by 70 per cent in a two-week period.
2   *Direct action*: this includes plugging effluent pipes or occupying offices.
3   *Shareholder action*: an example of this is the Lloyds campaign by developing world debt sympathizers, mentioned above.
4   *Letter writing*: today's modern political activists are likely to be writing as many letters to companies as to politicians.

5 *Ethical competition*: for example, during the early 1990s, Greenpeace commissioned an East German factory to manufacture a completely chlorofluorocarbon (CFC)-free refrigerator, and within six months mainstream refrigerator manufacturers in Germany were marketing identical products.

6 *Labelling*: here, campaigners play some role in monitoring companies' adherence to a set of ethical standards.

7 *Specialist campaigns*: these are set up specifically to oppose unethical businesses, such as Corporate Watch in the UK, and specialize in direct action.

8 *Specialist consumer guides*: these guides are published in most industrialized countries and tend to give symbols (sometimes incomprehensible) to companies to indicate such things as quality of products, employee treatment, social record and so on.

9 *Ethical screening*: for example, this is done by investment funds around the world to encourage investment in ethically sound companies.

10 *Anti-consumerist or limits-to-growth agitation*: this opposes business as usual because of concerns, often well thought out, about the sustainability of Western consumerism; it then goes on to advocate – and, in some cases, live – lifestyles that are less materialistic and less reliant on non-renewable resources.[27]

Companies are riding the trend to greater social responsibility, and have seen that this is to their advantage. For instance, Alison Thomas, head of research at PriceWaterhouseCoopers in London, found in a study of the banking sector that customer satisfaction translates into higher stock price returns.[28] However, she also found that there was little appreciation of 'intangible assets', such as customer satisfaction, to the extent that improved investment decisions would be made by shareholders if such information were more easily available and digestible.

Moreover, Mark Suzman has found that schemes such as cause-related marketing (CRM), where companies associate themselves with one or more charities or projects, and thereby link directly with particular values, are of increasing importance.[29] According to a survey by Business in the Community (BitC) in the UK, nearly 70 per cent of marketing directors believe that CRM will increase in importance over the next two or three years. And Suzman, again, believes that confusion and misallocation of resources in developing new initiatives can be minimized with proper planning. Amoco, the US oil company, has developed a simple, 12-step process for planning a programme of socially responsible initiatives that, it believes, should help weed out inappropriate programmes. These steps are:

1 Identify business goals. What is the purpose of the programme? What do you want to accomplish?

2 Identify problem areas or areas of opportunity.

3 Identify key audience(s):consumers; regulators; employees?

4 Assess the internal/external environment. What are the issues in the community or company? What are the barriers?
5 Evaluate the costs and benefits associated with the issue or proposal.
6 Define visions. What do you want to be in the future?
7 Identify and brainstorm programmes and activities to help reach this vision.
8 After you have brainstormed ideas, evaluate what resources you will need in terms of people, money and technology. What do you have and what do you need? Is the project feasible?
9 Identify the costs and benefits of the proposals.
10 Implement the activity or programme.
11 Market the activity/programme to key activists.
12 Evaluate the project against costs/benefits.[30]

Natural environment

The strongest social movement to insist on responsibility from business has been the environmental lobby. It has both 'Brown' and 'Green' parts, the former dealing with issues such as smokestack pollution and nuclear waste, the latter with biodiversity: the protection of ecosystems and landscapes, and plants and animals.

Concerns about possible environmental limits to human development extend as far back as one is willing to look. Plato, in *Critias*, lamented that agricultural activities had transformed the land of Attica into the 'bones of a wasted body...the richer and softer parts of the soil having fallen away, and the mere skeleton left.' However, the origin of the modern debate on sustainable development probably dates from at least two centuries ago, when Malthus characterized human well-being in terms of the ratio of environmental resources to human population.[31] Malthus's assessment was bleak, for he saw in food production a land-limited resource that could not possibly be increased quickly enough to keep pace with a growing human population. This was quickly refuted by those who argued that the socio-economic system would automatically correct itself through the price mechanism, adjusting wages and so on. Such was Adam Smith's vision, competing with that of Malthus, and positing that an 'invisible hand' would guide markets to respond to resource shortages. The debate has remained within the same limits ever since and is characterized by Burton and Kates:

> In its extreme form, one pole is determinist in its view of nature, Malthusian in its concern with the adequacy of resources, and conservationist in its prescription for policy. The opposite pole is possibilist in its attitude toward nature, optimistic in its view of technological advance and the

sufficiency of resources and generally concerned with technical and managerial problems of development.[32]

It is no secret that those who are in the sustainable development school of thought tend to gather around the first or conservationist pole; while those of the human development school, of which this author is one, tend to hover nearer to the second or possibilist pole, with a liberal eye on the first.

Both poles have been articulately and extensively defended in the literature. The conservationist school had a major impulse from the publication, in 1962, of Rachael Carson's *Silent Spring*, which brought home to many people that there was a limit to the biosphere's power to tolerate unthinking human activity.[33] Ten years later, the United Nations (UN) conference in Stockholm on the human environment declared the need to defend and improve the human environment for present and future generations, and to establish goals for peace and worldwide economic and social development. Malthusian doomsters were greatly encouraged by the publication of Donella and Denis Meadows et al's book on *The Limits to Growth*, which concluded, using a 'systems dynamics' model of the world, that the combination of rising populations and resource limitations would lead to increased pollution and a catastrophic fall in the quality of life by the middle of the next century.[34] This view was soundly refuted in *Thinking About the Future* by the Sussex University team of H Cole et al, of which this author was a member, and which was essentially based upon 'possibilist' arguments.[35] Although the notion of sustainability was used both in the Stockholm conference and in *The Limits to Growth*, it was the World Commission on Environment and Development (WCED), headed by the Norwegian prime minister of that time, Gro Harlem Brundtland, and the publication of its book *Our Common Future* (known as the Brundtland Report), that has stimulated the recent impetus to concerns about sustainable development.[36]

In June 1992, the UN Conference on Environment and Development (UNCED), better known as the Rio or Earth Summit, gave a further impetus to sustainable development with the endorsement of Agenda 21, which extends to 600 pages. One of the major voices for business present was the World Business Council for Sustainable Development (WBCSD), a coalition of more than 120 businesses who share a commitment to the environment and a commitment to economic growth and sustainable development, with members in more than 36 countries across 20 major industrial sectors.[37]

Since the resounding political mandate at Rio to implement sustainable development, some confusion has set in as to what it is all about. Clearly, the Brundtland Report and the UN Earth Summit had tried to reconcile the two poles of thought in a compromise position. This led one commentator, Sara Parkin, in *Green Futures* to state that such an aim was self-defeating because it called for sustainable development to be fuelled by increased economic growth, and it was precisely this type of development strategy, currently pursued in both rich and poor countries, that was proving to be unsustainable.[38] Herman Daly and John Cobb also noted this compromise, and mused that one of the reasons for the unanimity of support for the Brundtland Report and its concept of sustainable development was precisely because it had been left rather vague.[39] Development was not distinguished from growth, nor was there any distinction between strong and weak sustainability.

Sustainable development means improving the quality of human life while living within the carrying capacity of supporting ecosystems. Therein lies the problem. Until a collapse occurs, we often do not know when we are living within the limits of the Earth's carrying capacity, nor has anyone proposed how else we can know. The conclusion of the ecologists is to be on the side of extreme caution in the use of *any* natural resource in case this suddenly disappears, but this approach is not acceptable to those who are living in absolute and relative poverty, or to profit-maximizers in the rich countries. Yet, the alternative view – that what is required is simply to 'get the prices right' – is also risky. There, it is proposed, perfect markets will give price signals to determine that a resource is running out, which will then provide an impetus to substitution possibilities – a view held by the neo-classical school of economists. More recently, it has been argued that prices should reflect full social marginal opportunity costs, and should be clearly linked to human development concerns. However, this is frequently ignored, in practice, and has meant that many large-scale projects have avoided environmental concerns. Clearly, there has to be a middle way, and the challenge is to develop indicators that will allow us to determine when we are approaching the limits. Otherwise, the normal human response is to experience catastrophe before we act.

One of the main reasons why economics and business have been slow to internalize environmental externalities (Goodland and Daly) is that economics deals with scarcities, and until relatively recently many environmental goods were not scarce.[40] Scarcity value is the trigger for economics to address any concern. Environmental goods, such as clean air, clean water, intact ozone shield and intact biodiversity, have become scarce at different times, but mostly relatively recently. The second main reason is that many environmental goods and services are unpriced and therefore cannot be traded. The predominant paradigm of neo-classical market economics works better with traded than with non-traded commodities.

Not all is negative in the relation between business and the environmental lobby, as a cursory reading of any major newspaper suggests, in general. An example of a positive relation is that of GM, who purchases US$70 billion's worth a year of materials from its suppliers.[41] GM is working with thousands of its suppliers across the world to achieve significant cost savings by increasing energy efficiency and reducing pollution. This process, known as 'greening the supply chain', is being carried out in partnership with governments, NGOs and university groups, as well as with suppliers. GM is also one of around 120 corporations who belong to Climate Wise, a government initiative in the US aimed at implementing energy-efficient and pollution-prevention projects that lower operating costs while reducing emissions linked to global climate change.

Belonging, of course, is not the same as acting – GM was not included in the '100 Best Corporate Citizens', ranked by *Business Ethics* in their study of 1000 corporations in the US.[42] In the follow-up to the Earth Summit held in New York during the summer of 1997, the US advocated reducing global warming while admitting that it was the main culprit in that area. No new initiatives were taken by the US, however, and it remains the world's largest energy consumer. The alleged involvement of Exxon in lobbying the young Bush administration to withdraw from the Kyoto Environment Treaty is troubling; this was accompanied by howls of protest from environmentalists and even from some European governments. Anita Roddick, CEO of The Body Shop, is leading a campaign to boycott Exxon (also known as Esso) petrol stations. With energy prices taxed relatively lowly compared with Europe, there are few economic incentives (albeit growing in number) to encourage the consumer and producer towards energy-efficient cars.

Despite the difficulties, environmental reporting, followed by action, is likely to increase substantially.[43] Initiatives such as the Californian environmental propositions for auto emissions reduction; the International Chamber of Commerce (ICC) Charter; the UK Employer's Environment Business Forum (part of the Confederation of British Industries (CBI)); the British Standards Institute (BSI) Environmental Management Standard in the UK; the UK Sigma Project, designed to develop sustainable development guidelines; and the European Union's (EU's) eco-audit scheme will all encourage this.

Indeed, corporate sustainability is increasingly being taken up by corporations, leading one to wonder what is the relation between CSR and corporate sustainability? As noted above, the term sustainability first came to widespread acceptance in the Brundtland Report in 1987, and at that time the concept and study of sustainable development had hardly left the domain of environmentalists and ecologists.

More recently, the term 'sustainability' has grown to encompass social and economic components, as well as its historical work on the environment. Thus, the sustainability school has split, rather confusingly, into two. The first split is the conservationist school described above (which I denote by sustainability*); the second split has moved out into the social and economic field (which I denote by sustainability**). Corporate sustainability means more than corporations having an environmental policy. This new formulation of 'sustainability' led the UN World Summit on Sustainable Development, held in Johannesburg in August 2002, to wander outside of the environmental school to include social and economic components as well – also known as 'triple bottom-line' issues.

PriceWaterhouseCoopers define corporate sustainability as aligning an organization's products and services with stakeholder expectations, thereby adding economic, environmental and social value. The GRI that grew out of environmental work by the Coalition for Environmentally Responsible Economies (CERES) and the United Nations Environment Programme (UNEP) produced, in June 2000, the GRI Sustainability Reporting Guidelines which cover economic and social performance, as well as the more 'traditional' environmental ones. The world of business is embracing the notion of sustainability, and many businesses are now producing 'sustainability reports' – for instance, the fast-growing European services company Hays publishes its Strategy for Sustainability on its website.[44] But to Hays, sustainability still means sustainability*.

Nevertheless, the Dow Jones Sustainability rankings (using a wider definition of sustainability – namely sustainability**; see also Chapter 7) put Asea Brown Boveri (ABB) as number one in the Dow Jones in 2000 on its 'sustainability' index and noted that there is mounting evidence that the financial performance of good performing sustainable companies is superior to that of companies who are ranked lower. A report by Business in the Environment (BIE) cited a *Financial Times*/PriceWaterhouseCoopers' survey of 750 CEOs who were asked their views on the most important business challenges for companies in 2000. Of those challenges that were listed, increasing pressure for social responsibility was ranked second only to recruitment of skilled staff. In a MORI survey (the UK-based Market and Opinion Research International company), in 1998, 86 per cent of adults considered the environment to be a very or extremely important part of corporate responsibility.

However, the jury is still out on whether having sustainability or responsibility values improves a company's bottom line? But long-term corporate stayers – corporations that have lasted for many decades – do have sound social values, as Collins and Porras impressively showed in their book *Built To Last*.[45] So, should CSR now read corporate sustainability** (CSu)? There is strong semantic attraction for that since it is clear that the notion of sustainability has an attractive ring about it to hard-pressed CEOs trying to keep, and raise, shareholder value, while maintaining an eye on a plethora of social concerns. Responsibility appears, on face value, to do with the 'nice' things that a company should do, rather than simply stay in business and work on shareholder value. In fact, CSR and the new CSu are two sides of the same coin. CSR defines the social responsibilities of a corporation that, if implemented, will lead to the corporation being sustained (Collins and Porras). CSu has moved away from purely environmental issues to encompass both social and economic concerns. Zadek agrees with me when he warned that 'It is simply inaccurate and misleading to talk about "sustainable business". The "sustainable" in sustainable development is just not the same as the "sustaining" of a particular business, irrespective of its social and environmental perfomance.'[46]

The confusion regarding what is meant by 'sustainability' leads me to prefer the term CSR, with its more lofty goals, since it talks not only about issues that will sustain a corporation but also about issues for which a corporation is responsible. Whether there are additional concerns in the CSR toolbox that will, ultimately, provide for longer-term sustainability than those in the CSu toolbox is a point worthy of further discussion.

The wider community

Business has always operated closely with government.[47] However, only in recent years has business started to think about its wider role in society and, in particular, its role in communities, whether local, regional, national or international. Iain Vallance, one time chairman of BT, stated at the time that:

> Our business depends very considerably on the health of the community. If that health is adversely affected by deprivation, crime, vandalism, racial tension, inner-city decay, homelessness or pollution, so, too, is our business health. Our opportunities are reduced, our problems increase, our costs rise. So, rather than moaning about these problems, it makes good business sense for BT to work with others and get involved with addressing them.[48]

Furthermore, Dominic Cadbury, chairman of Cadbury-Schweppes, remarked that:

> Companies across the UK are increasingly recognizing the importance of business engagement with the community. Companies have a wealth of expertise and skills. They also have powerful products and brands. Together, through partnerships with the wider community, they can create and deliver real benefits.[49]

Grand Metropolitan, a huge branded food and drink business, became well known for its community activities before being merged into Diageo.[50] Its chairman at the time, George Bull, remarked:

> Corporate responsibility is not a fringe activity. All of us at Grand Met believe business success cannot be defined solely in terms of earnings, growth and the balance sheet. A truly successful company is sensitive to the concerns of all those on whom it depends: investors, employees, customers, trading partners and the countries and communities in which it does

business. What happens to society matters to us, because it happens to us.[51]

A business relates to the community in at least four ways – charity; social investment, such as supporting initiatives in the areas of education and social problems; partnerships with local organizations through such activities as lending equipment or human resources for specific time periods; and, lastly, through its fundamental mission of providing the goods and services that society needs in a responsible and ethical manner.[52]

Some businesses have always cared about the communities where they locate their plants. In the UK, Port Sunlight near Liverpool is a town set up by the soap magnate Lord Leverhulme of Lever Brothers (now Procter & Gamble) in the late 19th century, as Bourneville was set up by chocolate firm Cadbury's and after which some of its products are named. And Detroit lives or dies as the health of GM fluctuates. But for business to be actively involved in community issues where they don't operate geographically is relatively new – The Body Shop's concern with the Ogoni people in Nigeria was one well-known recent example of this.

The trend to more involvement in communities is increasing, and this is welcome. But where does it stop? How much involvement in community work that is marginal to a company's business should be done so that the company can be considered a socially responsible enterprise? There is no easy answer. Certainly, the society in the neighbourhood of a company should be a concern, whether individuals work for the company or not. Further than that, activities in remoter communities will be dominated by CRM concerns where costs and benefits can be measured, albeit with difficulty. To some, this might seem to be cynical; but a business must also focus upon its own survival, or there will be no community involvement at all!

Suppliers

Should enterprises apply the same rules that they apply to themselves to their suppliers, subcontractors and trading partners? The short answer is yes.[53] However, this is idealistic and, clearly, will not happen over night. The reason is that, in practice, it would mean that most of the export production in the developing world, Central and Eastern Europe and the informal sectors of the industrialized countries would simply disappear. The producers in those countries cannot afford the high standards achieved by a large enterprise in its industrialized country of origin. However, it is increasingly recognized that for suppliers in the same country as the parent enterprise, similar conditions should apply, so that, for instance, both have the same or similar codes of ethical practice.

In other countries, and this must be part of the planetary bargain, it is in the interests of enterprises to ensure that their suppliers start to obey the rules of the parent company – this means adequate pay, clean and safe working conditions, no exploitation, promotion of women's rights, adequate pensions, and so on. Levi Strauss is a leader in this area by having published rules of conduct expected of suppliers throughout the world and monitoring them to ensure compliance (see Chapter 5).

Yet, what is a company to do about trading with China, for instance? Despite a labour law banning the practice, I saw job adverts – during a visit to China in 1997 to assist the labour ministry to create an information system on labour – that specify whether a position is for males or females, a practice banned in most Western countries. Furthermore, unless a rural worker has an offer of a job in an urban area, where most of the new jobs are being created, he or she is not allowed to relocate. Moreover, the enterprise that employs a rural worker must pay a tax of at least the first month's salary to the local authority. This is designed to prevent a flood of largely unskilled rural workers migrating to the cities; but it smacks of coercion and discrimination solely on the basis of where one lives. Again, this is practically unheard of in Western countries. In the short term, this practice will keep the unemployment levels down in urban areas; but in the longer term, China is creating a major income inequality problem for itself that is likely to end up in internal conflict.

China is not the worst offender, according to the 2000 Corruption Perception Index devised for Transparency International.[54] China is 63rd in the list; below it, in descending order, are such countries as Egypt, India, the Philippines, Venezuela, Ecuador, Russia, Vietnam, Azerbaijan and the Ukraine. Nigeria is last of the 90 countries considered. The top country is Finland (followed by Denmark, New Zealand, Sweden and Canada). Second-placed Denmark, in the year 2000 rankings (through its ministry of social affairs), has been one of the most active in promoting social responsibility through social partnerships, both within Denmark as well as elsewhere.

So what to do? No one seriously believes that companies should stop trading with *all* rogue nations, which, in the end, may include half the world. The answer is not clear cut. Public bilateral and multilateral aid agencies have been grappling with these problems for decades, yet their funds are drying up. The World Bank, at its annual meeting in Hong Kong in 1997, put anti-corruption at the top of its agenda, with its teeth (along with the International Monetary Fund, or IMF) biting into rogue nation Kenya for the first time anywhere. Yet, anti-globalization protesters are succeeding in influencing these institutions – for example, the reduction to two days of the World Bank Annual meetings from the usual ten days or so in Washington, DC, in September 2001.

Now it is the turn of the private sector to grapple with these issues. As the many examples in this book show, it is no use turning a blind eye to the problem because it will rise up at some point and hit you in the face.

On the positive side, many enterprises (Shell, Levi Strauss, Nike, Gap, The Body Shop and Diageo, to name just a few) have realized and have started different types of programmes of assistance around the world in ways that were unknown even a decade or so ago. This, undoubtedly, is the way ahead, with enterprises working with their suppliers and trading partners wherever they are across the world to improve their lot.

Chapter 4

Codes of Ethics

Introduction

Today, the term 'corporate code of ethics' has tended to replace the original phrase 'code of conduct', which is still widespread but is more usually restricted to discussions of the conduct of public officials. A corporate code of ethics is, typically, a set of principles that state the moral obligations of the company in its relations with a wide audience of subjects or stakeholders. These codes have grown in prominence in the US and, more recently, in the UK after a series of scandals. Companies with headquarters in other countries are less well known in their application of codes of ethics, though this probably has more to do with specific cultural values than with being any less concerned with ethics than their counterparts in either the US or the UK. Nevertheless, in South Africa, for instance, the King Committee on Corporate Governance has included a set of recommendations on what should be in a code of ethics for enterprises.[1] In countries such as Canada, Denmark, Norway, the Netherlands, India and Brazil, groups are actively involved in developing ethical guidelines for companies. However, in this fast developing field, this chapter focuses primarily upon US and UK experiences in this area.

There has been a measurable increase in both company awareness of ethical issues and public disquiet about standards of business behaviour. According to Nigel Harris, professional codes have increased nearly tenfold in the last 30 years.[2] Many companies now have codes of ethics for both themselves and their suppliers.

A landmark in the US for the development of ethics programmes was the US Sentencing Commission's 1991 Sentencing Guidelines for Organizations. The guidelines fixed a legal standard to assess whether a company has an 'effective compliance programme' that would then allow a reduction by up to 60 per cent of fines for corporate misbehaviour. This was a major incentive for companies to build ethics programmes. The UK is also a good example of the development of social and ethics initiatives related to the business world that seem to crop up on a daily basis – a 'social investment' forum exists; many universities teach corporate social responsibility (CSR) programmes; the government has inspired an Ethical

Trading Initiative; Business in the Community (BitC) promotes codes of ethics for its members; and the New Economics Foundation (NEF) and its offshoot, the institution AccountAbility, are successfully promoting social auditing.[3,4]

Nash (1992), in a comparative study, showed that in the US corporate ethics activity was, in comparison to five years previously, more widespread, more sophisticated and moving deeper into the organization than in Europe.[5] Many European firms, on the other hand, were still not attracted to ethics statements and codes. In Europe, codes and ethics programmes appeared to be less frequent, more recent and more frequently dominated by large companies than in the US.[6]

Initiatives in Europe have mainly come from the trade unions, employers' associations and the European Union (EU). France has been prominent in these activities, and in 1995 (during its presidency of the EU) presented a proposed social charter to promote basic social rights in multilateral trade relations. Nevertheless, France is still a highly centralized state, with many public corporations or quasi-private ones that operate within rules developed at the central level (Crédit Lyonnais, for instance, has been bailed out by the state at huge cost for every living French person). This is illustrated by the fact that in the European Business Ethics Network (EBEN), no prominent French academicians are members. However, since the first edition of this book, initiatives are gathering pace and a new institution was set up in 2001 by French trade unions and a number of companies to promote socially responsible investment and CSR activities: the Observatoire sur la Responsabilité Sociétale des Entreprises (ORSE). The French government has also published a draft law for quoted companies in France to publish social and environmental reports. It is anticipated that the first results of the law will appear in company reporting in 2003.

Privatization, too, has galloped along in the UK, but has been much slower in the other large European nations – France, Germany, Spain and Italy. In the smaller European nations – the Scandinavian countries, Portugal, the Netherlands, Belgium and Austria, for instance – privatization is underway but is still far behind the levels seen in the US and UK.

According to Jean-Paul Sajhau, in work on codes of ethics in the textile, clothing and footwear industry for the International Labour Organization (ILO), ethical codes and codes of practice that cover principles of operation to regulate the internal operation of an enterprise, and its relations with its trade partners (in particular, its subcontractors), constitute the most tangible expression of the growing sense of social responsibility of the business world.[7] Certainly, the derivation of a code of ethics (and its application and independent verification) constitutes one of the main planks of social responsibility; as illustrated in Chapter 9, this is one of the most important indicators that can be used.

Sajhau cites a 1996 study by Peter Prowse Associates on the annual reports of the 100 main companies quoted on the stock exchanges in

Europe, which notes that enterprises that had applied codes of ethics performed better than average on the stock exchange. He adds, of course, that the conclusion cannot necessarily be drawn that there is a direct link of cause and effect between these two factors. It is generally the most productive enterprises in a given sector that have the human and financial resources that enable them to develop an ethical approach.

There are at least three types of application that enterprises use to apply a code of ethics. The first is passive application, in which the enterprise merely publishes the code in a prominent place but does not always distribute it to staff or contractors. Second comes active application, in which the code is monitored by visits from inspectors or personnel. The third is active application by external monitors – that is, independent bodies such as non-governmental organizations (NGOs), who may be consumer associations, specialized consultancy enterprises or reputable external auditors. The last convey the most probity; but, to date, only a few organizations have subjected themselves to their analysis.

Codes of ethics in the US

In the US, the number and percentage of companies with codes of ethics are higher than in the UK. Weaver (1993) reported two surveys that took place in 1992.[8] In the first, 83 per cent of the companies surveyed had codes in the US and only 50 per cent in Europe. The second survey, of the Fortune 1000 companies, reported that 93 per cent had codes.

One of the most famous cases is that of the clothing retailer Gap, who was among the first enterprises in the US to draw up a code of ethics.[9] Gap bought in clothes from the Mandarin International Apparel Factory, situated in the San Marcos free-trade zone of El Salvador. It came to international prominence when a number of workers in Mandarin, an independent supplier to Gap, were dismissed for trying to set up a trade union in response to poor working conditions – more than 12 hours of work a day, overcrowded and overheated premises, coercive measures and very low wages of the order of US$0.56 per hour. The US National Labour Committee (NLC) sounded an alarm, and although Gap was not the only enterprise working with Mandarin, the NLC focused pressure on the company. Because Gap was well known for living up to its public image, it became a target of the NLC campaign. Arguably, a company with a poorer image would have been less of a target, but then would not reap the benefits of a positive consumer reaction.

In the event, Gap at first cancelled its contract in El Salvador; but on reflection that this would not help improve conditions there, it signed an agreement with NLC that it would renew its contract only if working conditions improved and the leaders of the trade union movement were reinstated. It also promised to give specific assistance in improving working conditions in Mandarin, and to have its code of ethics monitored independently – until then, monitoring had been carried out by employees of Gap. An independent group was formed to do this monitoring at the beginning of 1996, in conjunction with two established bodies, the Interfaith Centre on Corporate Responsibility and Business for Social Responsibility (BSR). They established the main goals as being to:

- detect violation of the Gap's code of ethics and applicable local law;
- promote practices leading to compliance with Gap's code of ethics and applicable local law;
- encourage training programmes for workers on the basis of their knowledge about their own rights;
- deter abuses against workers;
- provide a safe, fair and credible mechanism for dispute resolution;
- foster a productive, humane working environment; and
- promote utilization of existing processes within the plant to resolve problems as rapidly as possible.

Gap's monitoring system at that factory continues to this day. However, while Gap received good publicity for this move, it failed to implement all the reforms. According to Global Exchange (an NGO pressure group set up to monitor the application of companies' codes of ethics in the US), it put minimal resources into the monitoring system and reneged on its pledge to extend such monitoring to other factories in the region.[10]

With these resolutions and the establishment of the independent monitoring group, Gap, according to Sajhau, has gone further than other US enterprises who have developed codes of ethics but have not authorized an independent monitoring of their application. This agreement could provide a model for socially responsible enterprises, at least for their dealings with third parties. It also illustrates that the application of socially responsible principles is not pie in the sky, and that one major company (and there are many; see the discussions in Chapter 5) is putting social responsibility for both itself and its contractors on a par with profit maximization.

That Gap will enhance both its public image and, consequently, its eventual profitability is something to be expected, according to the arguments put forward in this book; only time will tell.

Table 4.1 gives an overall appreciation of ten large and well-known US enterprises in the retail sector and the sorts of items they include in their codes of ethics. The scores attributed are approximate because they are based upon a secondary source. If an item was not mentioned, then it was given the number 0 in the table; if the item was mentioned, it was given the number 1. Of course, the results say nothing about the intensity of application, or whether the company respects the items in all countries and for all subcontractors with which it works.

Table 4.1 *Synoptic table of codes of ethics content in ten major US firms*

Issue – items on:	Levi Strauss	Sara Lee	Phillips-van Heusen	Gap	Reebok	Nike	Wal-Mart	Sears-Roe-buck	JC Penney	Wool-worths
Child labour?	1	1	0	1	1	1	1	1	1	1
Prison labour?	1	1	1	1	1	1	1	1	1	1
Discrimination?	1	1	1	1	1	1	1	0	1	0
Coercion of workers?	1	1	1	1	1	1	1	0	1	1
Limited and reasonable working hours?	1	0	1	1	1	1	1	1	0	0
Salary minimums?	1	1	1	1	1	1	1	1	0	0
Social benefits paid?	1	1	1	1	1	1	0	1	0	0
Safety and health at workplace?	1	1	1	1	1	1	1	1	0	0
Subcontractor conditions?	1	1	1	1	1	1	1	1	1	1
Pro-natural environment?	1	1	1	1	0	1	1	0	0	0
Human rights in country?	1	1	1	1	1	1	1	0	0	0
Communication of code to staff?	1	1	0	1	1	1	1	1	1	1
Monitoring independent?	1	0	0	1	0	0	0	0	0	0
Mean score	1.00	0.85	0.77	1.00	0.85	0.92	0.85	0.62	0.46	0.38
Rank	1	4	7	1	4	3	4	8	9	10

Source: adapted from reports in Jean-Paul Sajhau (1997) 'Business Ethics in the Textile, Clothing and Footwear (TCF) Industries: Codes of conduct', Working Paper, Industrial Activities Branch, Sectoral Activities Programme, SAP 2.60/WP.110, International Labour Organization, Geneva

The pattern of codes of ethics remains more or less the same – they are against child labour; do not countenance prison or forced labour; have non-discrimination rules for reasons of sex, age and race; and have rules on wages, social benefits and working hours that normally respect but go no farther than 'what is normally accepted in accordance with local standards'.[11] Many multinational companies actually pay wages and offer conditions above local standards; but this is not stipulated in the codes of ethics examined. Statements noting compliance with pro-environmental aspects and concern with human rights in the countries where they work are weaker (although six out of ten and seven out of ten of the companies, respectively, are concerned). More problematical is the monitoring of the codes of ethics. The enterprises normally distribute their codes of ethics to staff, but only Levi Strauss and Gap use independent evaluators to check on compliance. These latter two companies both have excellent codes of ethics, ranking first, equally, in Table 4.1, and are followed closely by Nike, Reebok and Sara Lee. Woolworths, J C Penney and Sears-Roebuck fare less well, and have the three lowest scores of the ten companies considered. Whether or not having a code of ethics has affected this, Levi Strauss, Sara Lee and Wal-Mart stores (ranked 1, 4 and 4 respectively) are included in *America's 100 Most Admired Companies*, with our first-placed Levi Strauss ranking 16 there (but see Chapter 5).[12]

Marjorie Kelly, in her reflections of 15 years of CSR, noted that despite many companies in the US espousing CSR, she felt that 'ethics in business are worse than ever'.[13] Nevertheless, I feel that she is exaggerating this since there is no doubt that CSR is part of the agenda of large corporations as never before. I agree with her observation that much, if not all, CSR work that has been going on fails to uncover much corporate wrongdoing and financial mismanagement. She is obviously affected by the Enron scandal and observes that 'Enron issued a triple bottom-line report, gave speeches at ethics conferences, and in 2000 won six environmental awards.' Clearly, until CSR becomes part of the corporate system and culture, it will remain, more or less as now, an add-on to a corporation rather than embedded in its system. But only five years ago, when I wrote the first edition of this book, most companies I spoke with thought I was off the wall when I talked about CSR. Today, most companies I speak with know about the concept and are more concerned with what to do to implement CSR and how CSR affects their bottom line.[14]

The Caux Principles: The international standard?

There is, currently, no accepted international standard for codes of ethics. One of the first to grow in prominence were the Global Sullivan Principles, set up by the late Reverend Leon H Sullivan during the early 1970s.[15] The focus was more on supporting economic, social and political justice than codes of ethics per se. Neither Social Accountability 8000 (SA8000),

AccountAbility 1000 (AA1000), or the Global Reporting Initiative (GRI) Principles (see Chapter 7) are, currently, as wide reaching as the Caux Principles described next.

The Caux Roundtable is an international group that consists of business leaders from Europe and Japan, as well as the US, and is committed to energizing the role of business and industry as a 'vital' force for innovative global change.[16] It was founded in 1986 by Frederik Philips, former president of the Dutch multinational Philips Electronics, and Olivier Giscard d'Estaing, brother of the former French president and vice-chairman of the business school INSEAD, in response to concern about growing trade tension among industrial countries.[17] The first meeting of 30 senior businessmen in Caux, Switzerland, has turned into a regular six-monthly event around the world. It has focused upon the importance of global corporate responsibility in reducing social and economic threats to world peace and stability.

The members of the roundtable are expected to adhere to the Caux Principles, which were devised in 1994 and 130,000 copies of which were distributed to business leaders. These principles are rooted in two basic ethical ideals: *kyosei* and human dignity. The Japanese concept of *kyosei* means living and working together for the common good, whereas human dignity is defined as the sacredness or value of each person as an end, not simply as a means to the fulfilment of other individuals' purposes or even majority prescription. Swallowing this might seem heavy for some tastes. The appeal to a philosophical rather than an economic and social notion, as advocated in this book, as the basis for a code of ethics for businesses may well drive away more conservative company managers.

Nevertheless, the Caux Principles provide a baseline from which an international consensus is emerging. The principles have three main parts.[18] The first is an introduction or preamble to the Caux philosophy. The second part contains seven general principles:

1   The responsibilities of business beyond shareholders to stakeholders.
2   The economic and social thrust of business toward innovation, justice and world community.
3   Business behaviour beyond the letter of law toward a spirit of trust.
4   Respect for rules.
5   Support for multilateral trade.
6   Respect for the environment where it recommends businesses should embrace the Coalition for Environmentally Responsible Economies (CERES) environmental principles (see 'Applying the Caux Principles' later in this chapter).
7   Avoidance of illicit operations.

A third part outlines how a company should behave towards its six types of stakeholders – customers, employees, owners/investors, suppliers, competitors and communities.

The Caux Principles

Preamble

- The mobility of employment, capital, produce and technology is making business increasingly global in its transactions and its effects.
- Laws and market forces are necessary but insufficient guides for conduct.
- Responsibility for the politics and actions of business, and respect for the dignity and interests of its stakeholders are fundamental.
- Shared values, including a commitment to shared prosperity, are as important for a global community as for communities of smaller scale.
- We affirm the necessity for moral values in business decision-making; without them, stable business relationships and a sustainable world community are impossible.

General principles

- The responsibility of business is beyond shareholders and toward stakeholders.
- The economic and social impact of businesses in foreign countries is toward innovation, justice and world community.
- Business behaviour goes beyond the letter of law toward a spirit of trust.
- Respect international and domestic rules and recognize that some behaviour, although legal, may still have adverse consequences.
- Provide support for the multilateral trade systems of the General Agreement on Tariffs and Trade (GATT) and the World Trade Organization (WTO).
- Respect the environment and, where possible, improve it, promote sustainable development and prevent the waste of natural resources.
- Avoid illicit operations, such as bribery, money laundering and other corrupt practices. Do not trade in arms or other materials used for terrorist activities, drug trafficking or other organized crime.

Stakeholder principles

Customers should be treated with dignity, irrespective of whether they purchase products and services directly or indirectly.

Employees' interests should be taken seriously and business has a responsibility to:

- provide jobs and compensation that improve workers' living conditions;
- be honest;

- listen;
- engage in good faith negotiations;
- avoid discriminatory practices;
- guarantee equal treatment and opportunity in areas such as gender, age, race and religion;
- develop skills;
- be sensitive to unemployment problems; and
- promote disabled employment.

Owners'/investors' trust should be honoured. There should be a fair and competitive return on investment and disclosure of relevant information. Owners' assets should be protected; requests, suggestions, complaints and formal resolutions should be respected.

Suppliers should be treated fairly and should be free from coercion and unnecessary litigation. Long-term stability with suppliers should be fostered; they should be integrated within the planning process; they should be paid on time; and suppliers should be sought whose employment practices respect human dignity.

Competitors should have fair competition. Open markets should be fostered, and competitive behaviour that is socially and environmentally beneficial should be promoted. Stakeholders should:

- refrain from either seeking or participating in questionable payments or favours to secure competitive advantages;
- respect both tangible and intellectual property rights; and
- refuse to acquire commercial information by dishonest or unethical means, such as industrial espionage.

Communities: we believe as global corporate citizens that we can contribute to such forces of reform and human rights as are at work in the communities to whom we are open. Human rights and democratic institutions should be respected, and they should be promoted where possible. Stakeholders should:

- collaborate with those forces in the community dedicated to raising standards of health, education, workplace safety and economic well-being;
- promote and stimulate sustainable development and play a leading role in preserving and enhancing the physical environment and conserving the Earth's resources;
- support peace, security diversity and social integration;
- respect the integrity of local cultures; and
- be good corporate citizens through charitable donations, educational and cultural contributions and employee participation in community and civic affairs.

Applying the Caux Principles

Writing in *Business Ethics*, Robert MacGregor, president of the Minnesota Centre for Corporate Responsibility (MCCR), reflects on how what was originally a naive idea – a world standard of ethical business behaviour, accepted by competitors and applied across cultures around the globe – now works.[19] The MCCR originally developed the set of global business principles that were subsequently revised by Japanese and European groups and then adopted by the Caux Roundtable. According to MacGregor, they have now become the 'most widely circulated in the world'. As such, they provide some of the key elements for a planetary bargain.

There has been some advance in this area. MacGregor says that the principles have been translated into seven languages, presented at conferences in dozens of towns and distributed to major business schools, while some firms in Malaysia and Australia have registered the principles as part of their charters and a number of consulting firms in the US and Europe use them for their ethics training.

To date, more companies have adhered to the CERES environmental principles than to the Caux Principles per se. Although when CERES was created in 1989, only 13 of the Fortune 500 companies issued any public environment report, today – according to Bob Massie, its executive director – such firms number in the hundreds, and nine of the Fortune 500 companies had, at that time, endorsed the CERES principles.[20]

Nevertheless, the Caux Principles cover the essential parts that can be found in most business codes of practice these days. The codes hint, but do not elucidate, that beggar-thy-neighbour polices in international trade, where production goes to the lowest common denominator, should be avoided. Consequently, to promote a planetary bargain, a wider set of principles are required that cover international business better than the present ones do.

Codes of ethics in the UK

In the UK, more and more companies are adopting codes of ethics. Simon Webley of the London Institute of Business Ethics sent a short questionnaire to the chief executives of the largest companies operating in the UK.[21] The questions were similar to those asked in a 1987 survey, which queried whether the company had a statement of philosophy or a code of practice or ethics as guidance for employees. Of the 300 companies surveyed in the UK in 1988, 100 gave usable responses, which showed that 55 (55 per cent) had a code or other statement of business ethics. In 1992, Webley surveyed 400 of the largest companies, and from 159 usable responses found 113 (71 per cent) with codes or other statements – a rise of 26 per cent in four years. When Webley asked whether they had a written code, in 1987 18 per cent of the sample claimed this, while by 1992 this had increased to 28 per cent. Of the 62 firms stating that they had no code or other written statement in the 1991 survey, 18 (29 per cent) indicated that – while they took the matter seriously – they did not consider a code to be beneficial, or else they incorporated ethical matters within staff handbooks and similar documents. Another study surveyed 1481 UK companies in 1990 and, on a response rate of 25 per cent, reported that 50.5 per cent had codes of ethics, 22.8 per cent had a policy statement on ethics and 42.6 per cent had guidelines for the proper conduct of business.[22]

Burton and Myanmar

The response of Burton, a UK clothes retailer, to adverse criticism in the press about the production of some of its textiles in Myanmar (formerly Burma) is interesting, and is different from the approach taken by Gap in the US. The criticism led Burton to instruct its suppliers to place no further contracts for sourcing in Myanmar and to terminate all existing contracts.[23] The Burma Action Group had mounted a letter-writing campaign against Burton's investment; it noted that Burton's action showed that UK consumers are increasingly ethical consumers, and this had sent a very strong signal to the military in Myanmar that they faced increasing world isolation.

When Gap had a similar problem in El Salvador, it first wanted to withdraw its production, but then reviewed its position and brought pressure on its suppliers to improve working conditions in El Salvador. Myanmar, of course, is currently a pariah country, while El Salvador has been struck off this list – a list that is not official in any way and presumably depends upon how friendly the country is to the West.[24] The fact that Myanmar is a military dictatorship cannot be the main reason, because the West continues to work with other repressive regimes – for instance, Nigeria or Algeria.

The result of Burton's withdrawal from Myanmar, presumably, will be that the military junta and its cronies will not be able to exploit child labour and poor working conditions. But what does this mean for these children and their fellow workers, who will now not even have their meagre wages to help eke out a living? With few alternatives available in Myanmar, this will most likely entail increased impoverishment, which translates into malnutrition for the children, no hope of ever going to school, starvation for the families of the workers and a continuing sullen acceptance of their lot, with even reduced energy to challenge the military junta. The dilemma, therefore, is should Burton have continued in Myanmar – implicitly supporting a repressive regime – while providing employment for a few, or withdraw and accept public praise?

The conditions in Myanmar may well have led Gap to have acted as Burton did, because experiences are never the same from one country to another. However, a more complex, and perhaps thoughtful, strategy would have seen Burton assisting its workers in Myanmar, trying hard to reduce exploitation and opening a dialogue with the military junta on working conditions. At the same time, it could have mounted a public campaign to explain what it was up to. This is probably what Gap would have done.

Such decisions are not easy, as the experience of Levi Strauss, one of the US's most admired companies, illustrated. It retreated from Myanmar in 1992 because it was 'not possible to do business in Myanmar without directly supporting the military government and its pervasive violations of human rights'. Perversely, this admirable sentiment may well have increased the power of the military government because its action further weakened the people of Myanmar themselves.

Premier Oil, an oil-exploration company based in London, has had its operations criticized for exploring and pumping oil in virgin land in Poole Harbour in the UK, as well as for similar activities in Myanmar. Premier has continued both operations in the face of criticism and has countered attacks by working closely with the corporate citizenship unit at Warwick University. Premier appointed a corporate citizenship manager and reports annually through its corporate citizenship report. It has explained its activities in Myanmar, where it has tried to engage the authorities to respect human rights, and has developed several community participation projects. Without an in-depth independent review of its activities, I cannot judge how successful its activities have been. However, I believe that simply leaving a corrupt or nasty country just leaves the crooks behind. What George Soros is doing in another corrupt country, Kazakhstan, is preferable: he has tried to get the foreign oil-exploration and production companies together to bring pressure on the government.[25] This is part of a planetary bargain – get the good guys together and out the crooks!

Cadbury, Greenbury, Hampel, Turnbull

In response to a number of financial scandals in the UK, ranging from Guinness to Maxwell to Polly Peck, public clamour urged the then Conservative government to do something. A number of reports ensued, the first of which was by Lord Cadbury, who was appointed to draw up a code of best practice to suggest specific procedures. His Committee on the Financial Aspects of Corporate Governance made its report in December 1992, offering guidelines to large companies on how they should conduct their affairs. Although these procedures are not mandatory, the London Stock Exchange (LSE) now requires every listed and Unlisted Securities Market (USM) company to include a statement in its annual report confirming that it is complying with the Cadbury Code, or giving details of, and reasons for, any areas of non-compliance. The statement must include the following four elements:

1   An acknowledgement by the directors that they are responsible for the company's system of internal financial control.
2   An explanation that such a system can provide only reasonable and not absolute assurance against material misstatement of loss.
3   A description of the key procedures that the directors have established and that are designed to provide effective internal financial control.
4   Confirmation that the directors (or a board committee) have reviewed the effectiveness of the system of internal financial control.[26]

The Cadbury Code was, essentially, one for financial control and for the responsibilities of directors and the operation of boards – only a part of which could be in a fully fledged ethical code. In a survey of its members, the Confederation of British Industries (CBI: the most important UK employers' association) found that 81 per cent of respondents said that the Cadbury Code had caused them to review the structure and operation of their boards, while 71 per cent believed that their institutional shareholders were concerned about ensuring compliance with the code, but 90 per cent believed that the code had no positive effect on their financial performance.[27]

Following further scandals about the excessive remuneration of company directors, in July 1995 the Greenbury Study Group on Directors' Remuneration issued its code of best practice for listed companies. It recommended that company boards publish a statement regarding their compliance with the best-practice provisions on remuneration committees. These would consist solely of non-executives. Again, compliance is not compulsory and the experience to date has been, according to the CBI survey, that 47 per cent of respondents considered that the Cadbury and Greenbury codes would alter the character of UK boards, while 46 per cent believed that the effect on their company would be adverse and only 16 per cent believed it would be beneficial.

Adherence to the Cadbury and Greenbury codes does not imply that a company is necessarily an ethical organization:

> It may still produce shoddy or dangerous goods, pollute the environment, impose adverse condition on its workforce or tell lies in advertising. However, the following of a code such as that found in the Cadbury report is more likely than not to lead to a corporate governance regime with greater openness of information, less likelihood of domination by one or few people and fewer excesses in the remuneration packages of senior executives. (Alan Kitson and Robert Campbell.)[28]

In June 1998, the LSE issued its principles of good governance and code of best practice that have become known as the *Hampel Report*. This time, it applies to all listed UK companies as of January 1999. Although only a limited number of code provisions are new, and are not derived from either

Greenbury or Cadbury, it brings in a strong control framework to be administered by the LSE. As well as rules concerning directors' and non-executive directors' roles, the code insists that each board should review annually the effectiveness of all controls, including operational, financial and compliance controls and business risk management. The purpose is both to protect and increase shareholder value. However, the code shies away from introducing an explicit code of ethics and has made almost no distinction between the governance standards expected of larger and smaller companies. Thus, the code falls short of an earlier announcement in July 1997 by Clare Short, secretary of state for international development of the need for an ethical trading initiative (see the following section).[29]

The three reports of Cadbury, Greenbury and Hampel were compressed by the LSE into what is now known as the Combined Code. The latest link in the UK corporate governance chain was the September 1999 publication, named after its chairman, the *Turnbull Report*.[30] This report aimed to provide some guidance to companies on how to interpret the Combined Code. The sections most relevant to CSR covered the following:

- Are the significant internal and external operational, financial, compliance and other risks identified and assessed on an ongoing basis?
- Does the company communicate to its employees what is expected of them and the scope of their freedom to act?
- Are there established channels of communication for individuals to report suspected breaches of laws or regulations?
- Are there specific arrangements for management monitoring and reporting to the board on risk and control matters of particular importance?[31]

The Association of Chartered Certified Accountants (ACCA) report on Turnbull noted that compliance may well require boards to adhere to previously 'marginal accreditation' mechanisms, such as SA8000 and AA1000 (see Chapter 7).

Along with these increasing moves in the UK to improve corporate governance came two further initiatives. The first was the 1999 launch of the UK government's 'Company Law Review' consultation paper, in which a key element concerned the responsibilities of company directors to external stakeholders. Its revision, in March 2000, stressed the value of reputation and set out new reporting proposals covering aspects of social and environmental performance. Secondly, there was a change in UK law in July 2000 that requires pension fund trustees to include in their statement of investment policies a comment on the extent to which they take social and environmental issues into account in determining their investment policy.

All of these initiatives have shaken the UK company establishments and have driven pension funds to consider ethical issues. However, as

British Telecom's (BT's) CSR guru, Chris Tuppen, noted: 'Social and environmental reports do not in themselves meet the requirements of Turnbull, but they can be useful contributors to the identification of risk and the establishment of appropriate internal control mechanisms.'[32]

Ethical Trading Initiative (ETI)

This initiative is based on the principle of incorporating internationally agreed standards within codes of labour practice. These latter are the ILO's core conventions (forced and bonded labour; freedom of association; right to organize and collective bargaining; equal remuneration for male and female workers for work of equal value; no discrimination in employment and occupation; minimum-age provisions), and the initiative also notes as 'especially relevant' other ILO standards (workers' representation; occupational safety and health; vocational rehabilitation and employment of disabled persons; home work).[33]

When announcing this initiative, a number of partners were identified from the business sector (such as the Co-operative Wholesale Society, Sainsbury's, Safeway, Littlewoods and C&A), from trade unions (such as the Trades Union Congress – TUC; the International Confederation of Free Trade Unions – ICFTU; the International Textile, Garment and Leather Workers' Federation – ITGLWF; and the International Union of Food Workers – IUF) and from NGOs (such as Christian Aid, Oxfam, the World Development Movement, the New Economics Foundation and the Fair Trade Foundation). Since then, the ETI has published its first annual report for 1999 and 2000, and its business membership list has risen to 16.[34] One of the conditions of ETI membership is for members to provide an annual progress report relating to their supply-chain monitoring and to describe their activities under a number of headings:

- Company profile and code of conduct.
- Management responsibility for ethical trade.
- Communication about ethical trade policies.
- Overview of compliance monitoring.
- Areas of significant non-compliance.
- Corrective actions.
- Suppliers disengaged (if any).
- Priorities and targets for the year ahead.

Fourteen companies had been members of ETI long enough to make a report for 1999, and of these 11 apparently showed the degree of progress expected by the ETI board while 3 appeared to be at an earlier than expected stage.

Clearly, the ETI is one step toward a 'planetary bargain'; but it has not made this achievement without controversy. The UK government's moves toward ethical trading were brought sharply into focus when Foreign Secretary Robin Cook played down efforts to promote ethical trading initiatives among defence contractors and supplies to 'favoured' nations such as Zimbabwe and Indonesia. One of its business founders, C&A, has since pulled out of the UK (for commercial not for ethical trade reasons) and some, such as Safeway, were not included in the 'good' companies when the FTSE4good screening indicator was announced in July 2001 (see Chapter 7 for a further discussion on FTSE4good). Yet another controversy that is looming is whether ILO labour standards introduce 'rigidities' into labour markets, thereby making them uncompetitive. The ILO has avoided such analysis of its oft-promoted labour conventions and standards. The ETI has not considered this aspect either, and I wonder whether the 16 companies who adhere to the ETI have considered such competition aspects?

Contents of contemporary corporate codes of ethics

There is no generally accepted formula for the ethical code of a company. Most codes, however, stem from a basic philosophy on how business is to be conducted. The ethical code of the once widely admired The Body Shop – the UK supplier of 'ethical cosmetics' – is based upon a declaration:[35]

1   *The Body Shop goals and values are as important as our products and our profits.*
2   *Our policies and our products are geared to meet the needs of real people, both inside and outside the company.*
3   *Honesty, integrity and caring form the foundations of the company and should flow through everything we do.*
4   *We care about each other as individuals; we will continue to endeavour to bring meaning and pleasure to the workplace.*
5   *We care about our customers and will continue to bring humanity into the marketplace.*
6   *We care about humanizing the business community; we will continue to show that success and profits can go hand-in-hand with ideals and values.*[36]

In work for the Institute of Business Ethics, Simon Webley studied 96 codes and other statements of companies.[37] He found that one of the outstanding features was the almost universal agreement that the corporation has moral obligations to other individuals or groups than its legal owners – that is, its shareholders. Most codes (for instance, that of Caterpillar Inc) went to considerable lengths to set out these duties, although they concentrated more on obligations to employees than on responsibilities to other stakeholders. Surprisingly, few of the companies stated that they exist to maximize profits and long-term results, and they frequently mention that the investment returns they produce should be 'fair', 'acceptable' and 'satisfactory'.

One code in every five of those Webley analysed came from a subsidiary of a foreign corporation – most often a US one. Typically, such codes were longer, more extensive and more detailed than UK ones. In the codes of these companies, there was less reticence in the wording than in those of the UK-based companies. For instance, some went as far as to state an annual target for their earnings growth, while at the same time emphasizing the duties they owed to all stakeholders.

The majority of codes divided their statements of obligations to stakeholders into five main headings: employees, shareholders, suppliers, the community and the customer. Webley summarized the contents of the codes for each stakeholder as follows:

1 **Company obligations to employees:** companies viewed their obligations to employees in different ways. Some saw them as company assets, while others claimed that they best met their obligations to their employees by being competitive, dynamic and innovative. Most stated that they were committed to an equal opportunity policy, and nearly all acknowledged that their obligations to their employees included keeping them informed while also listening to them. Some references were made to the company's obligation for remuneration and the development of their employees.

2 **Company obligations to shareholders:** companies in Webley's survey made few comments on their obligations to shareholders or other providers of money. They were mentioned only in the context of general statements about duties to stakeholders.

3 **Company obligations to customers:** nearly all the companies mentioned their obligations to customers in their codes. The companies who made no mention of them tended to be those who did not list their responsibilities to any stakeholder, and approached ethical conduct in a different way. Webley believes this is because they would probably say that such responsibilities are obvious. Many companies stated clearly that they depended totally upon winning customers, and it was commonly stated that the customer must come first. 'Value', 'quality' and 'service' were words that regularly occurred in the statements. 'Fair price' and 'safety' were also words that cropped up commonly. Where service to customers was stressed, it was often amplified with phrases such as 'courteous', 'first class', 'best possible' and 'high standard'. This indicated that the company staff were expected to provide such service, and that customers who did not receive it had grounds for complaint. There were few references to ethical matters as such, though some mentioned integrity

in dealings with customers and others the 'reliability' or 'dependability' of their products.

4 **Company responsibilities to suppliers:** only a small proportion of companies specifically stated that they had obligations to their suppliers. The majority of codes, even if they did not make any direct mention of 'responsibilities' or 'obligations' in this area, dealt in some detail with one aspect of the subject – namely, the relationship of their individual employees with suppliers. This normally took the form of a company rule on receiving gifts, money, excessive entertainment, and so on. The clear reason was to make sure that the buyer's judgement was not distorted by personal inducements. Late settlement of accounts by large customers was one of the most consistent complaints of small companies, and has been the subject of campaigns by the CBI and other bodies. However, only two suppliers dealt explicitly with the subject and stated explicitly that suppliers should be paid on time. On the specific issue of the giving and receiving of gifts or other tokens of thanks, companies in the survey were quite clear that only minor items could be given or received, and that anything doubtful should be reported. The overriding objective was transparency in dealings with suppliers and any other person or organization with whom the company had a relationship. Few companies had a stated policy about sourcing in other countries – for instance, those in the developing world – nor did they have a policy toward 'rogue' countries. These aspects appear to be much more advanced in US companies than in UK companies.

5 **Company responsibilities to the community:** there were numerous views, ranging from general statements about the role of companies in society 'to operate efficiently and profitably', to specific aspects such as company donations to charity. Three major themes arose under this heading. First, by providing goods and services that are required in an effective manner, the company serves the community well. Second, by encouraging and operating in a competitive setting regulated by law, the community is better off than under other systems. Third, employees should be encouraged to play a full part in their community. North American firms, in particular, gave considerable play to the avoidance of anti-competitive practices by their employees, probably because of the rigorous anti-trust legislation there. Few UK firms mentioned employee involvement in the community; but most North-American-based organizations did.

6 **Other stakeholders:** companies also set out their position in other ethical areas, such as product policy, animal experiments, taxation and currency transactions, and the environment. Of these, environmental concerns were the most important. This ranged from statements by chairpersons at annual meetings to the issuing of a specific publication. This concern was also on the increase, as demonstrated by attempts to

introduce environmental auditing to monitor company practice in areas such as factory emissions, noise, materials usage and waste disposal.

Implementation of codes

In the same study, Webley found that many companies had broadly drawn codes. It was only when specific and questionable situations arose that guidelines had to be definitely applied. Indeed, in the use of codes, it appeared that very few companies provided a mechanism for an employee to report an infringement. Moreover, not all boards of directors agreed that written codes of behaviour were required to set or raise standards. Some were well satisfied with their performance and said that they did not require a written code. Others felt that detailed ethical policies should be left to their operating companies, or preferred to incorporate such matters in the staff handbook, or even just as part of the terms and conditions of employment.

In another detailed study of 125 UK companies in 1992, Manley suggested the following factors as crucial to the successful implementation of a code of ethics or similar policy document:[38]

- management involvement and overseeing;
- constant consciousness of written and codified values and standards in recruiting and hiring;
- an emphasis on code values and standards in educating and training employees;
- recognition and tangible rewards for conduct that exemplifies desired values and standards;
- ombudsmen or other designated persons assigned to field employees' questions and reporting;
- thorough consideration of high-risk jobs and areas in terms of violating code values and standards;
- periodic certification and auditing to ensure compliance with code values and standards;
- well-defined and fair enforcement procedures, including sanctions.

Later, Kitson and Campbell added to these the requirements that a code must be:[39]

- the result of an extensive period of research, consultation and discussion by, on behalf of and between all affected parties;
- owned by all who are affected by it and not merely imposed by executive fiat;
- backed by a programme of staff development and training that is ongoing and that opens the code up to amendment in the light of experience.

Who is to monitor the application of the code? In 1973 in the UK, the Fair Trading Act of 1973 gave authorization to the Office of Fair Trading (OFT) 'to encourage relevant associations to prepare, and to disseminate to their members, codes of practice for guidance in safeguarding and promoting the interests of consumers'. The OFT monitors these codes. In 1993, it changed its policy to emphasize independent monitoring: 'When considering whether to support a code, we now seek an element of independence in both redress and disciplinary procedures, beyond the requirements stated in the guidelines.' This was in response to the increasingly numerous requests for assistance that the OFT was receiving, because the enforcement of codes had been a major problem in the past.[40]

A European initiative to assist companies in developing and applying codes of ethics, known as the Quality of Social and Ethical Responsibility of Corporations (Q-RES) Project, aims to provide a framework for managing CSR and codes of ethics.[41] It was developed by Simone de Colle of the accounting firm KPMG and Professor Sacconi at the Cattaneo University of Castellanza, Italy. The Q-RES model embraces six building elements for CSR management:

1   Corporate values and mission.
2   Corporate code of ethics.
3   Ethics training and communication.
4   Ethics infrastructures (organizational systems and internal control).
5   Social and ethical accountability processes.
6   External verification (third-party verification).

The Q-RES project follows the social contract theory rooted in the original work of the American philosopher John Rawls.[42] According to Rawls, a social contract purports to be an *ideal* contract that includes the following points:

- Force, fraud and manipulation must be put aside.
- Everyone must follow the ideal procedure of putting themselves in the position of every other stakeholder, taking the position of each in turn.
- Everyone will find out the terms of agreement that she/he is ready to accept and conform to.
- Game theory tells us that there is at least one agreement that everyone will accept given that she/he knows that it must also be acceptable by any other stakeholder.

The social contract defines the terms of agreement that are acceptable from the point of view of an impartial spectator when considering the problem from every stakeholder's point of view. The fair corporate action, decision or strategy is therefore the result of a mutually advantageous agreement among free and rational individuals.

Given this approach, it follows that ethics training has a crucial role within any organization, as it relies on the ability of single individuals to apply the ideal of the social contract to their day-to-day decisions and actions.

Sajhau insists that the codes of ethics must be applied in a way that leaves no doubt in the minds of observers outside of the enterprise.[43] Obviously, monitoring the application of the code by insiders, even those who have been specially trained for the purpose, or whose integrity is unquestionable, will not be as easily accepted as by an independent group of monitors. Even then, this can be questionable if the outside monitors have links to the company, such as future contracts. For instance, Nike asked Goodworks International and its co-chairman, Andrew Young (see also Chapter 5), President Carter's one-time ambassador to the United Nations (UN), to evaluate its operations in the developing world. Nike prides itself on its social responsibility and feared no adverse criticism. It was rewarded by a positive report by Young.[44] Shortly thereafter, one of Nike's suppliers in Vietnam was found to have 'one factory official convicted of physically abusing workers, another fled the country during a police investigation of sexual-abuse charges and a third under indictment for abusing workers'.[45] Young had not visited this particular location; this shows how the pitfalls of a single case can badly damage a previously impeccable reputation.

Chapter 5

Corporate Social Responsibility in Practice

Introduction

This chapter draws on a number of specific experiences and case studies of socially responsible enterprises to illustrate the application of some of the ideas already expressed in this book, and to illustrate the growing importance being attached to these ideas. It covers The Body Shop's values report; although now a little long in the tooth, it is still worth discussing because it was innovative in being one of the first to carry out such a widespread review of its activities using the new tools of social auditing. It has also attracted considerable coverage, both positive and negative. The chapter then highlights what the Levi Strauss company has done in the area of supplier sourcing, where it is one of the world leaders but not without controversy. This is followed by a report of Nike's activities in the area of social responsibility. Since the first version book of this book was published in 1998, many companies have written social reports. This chapter looks at some of the most well known (for example, British Telecom (BT), Van City, The Co-operative Bank, British Airways (BA) and Camelot) and draws out some of their unique characteristics.

Chapter 3 noted that as corporate social responsibility (CSR) takes the higher ground, many in the environmental movement have also turned their attention to the concept and practice of CSR. This chapter describes how one medium-sized company in the UK, B&Q, went from concerns about the environmental impact of its products to the wider issues of social responsibility in its help for a community supplying it with timber in Papua New Guinea. Next, a specific example involving two concerns in the health area is presented, where one concern acted socially responsibly and the other did not. The former made less profits to begin with, but eventually won out as the other's lesser social responsibility led it to find a slope more slippery than it had anticipated when the legal forces moved in.

To date, there are still few large companies who have taken social responsibility to heart in the same way as The Body Shop and Levi Strauss, though the number is growing every day. There is a certain scepticism by large companies about social responsibility – that this is just a marketing

Box 5.1 The Soho Pizzeria

Matthew Bennett is an extraordinary man to find in the centre of notorious Soho in the heart of London. Soho is known for its sex and sleaze and not for social responsibility. Yet, Matthew is chairman of Soho's community environment fund to reduce homelessness in central London, and was behind the conservation scheme for Piccadilly Circus, which preserved the front of many old buildings. Less known was Matthew's successful campaign to make rooms in these buildings available to the homeless. His social responsibility extends to his business, too. In his recent venture, the Soho Pizzeria, Matthew has an unusual menu item that says: 'African Neptune: tuna, anchovies, olives, capers, onion, tomato, fresh garlic – 30 pence from every Neptune sold will be donated to third world charities'. In his busy restaurant, even this small sum raises over £1000 a year. Matthew says: 'There is no reason why small-scale enterprises cannot be as socially responsible as larger ones.' He is one entrepreneur showing the way.

ploy for companies, or even that the companies are just platforms for the social conscience of their owners. To illustrate that this is not the trend, I cover the subject of where some large sums of money are going: the ethical investment field. This has grown enormously over the past decade, and is perhaps one of the most influential determining factors of company activities. If a company does not behave socially responsibly, then it risks seeing its rating slide and investors withdrawing their money. To date, this affects perhaps only 5 per cent of publicly quoted companies. Many large companies still do not take the ethical fund business too seriously; but this is beginning to change as the new index supported by the London Stock Exchange (LSE) – the FTSE4good – illustrates. This index is discussed here and some of its limitations pointed out.

Finally, this chapter includes some thoughts about CSR, using original data provided by the UK Market and Opinion Research International (MORI) survey company. The survey results provided the striking conclusion that the people surveyed in the UK (a representative sample) were more concerned about social responsibility than they thought enterprises themselves were. It suggests that enterprises need to move quickly to capture this new consumer mood.

The companies discussed here are medium or large; I say little in the book about small companies with, for example, less than US$10 million turnover per year, or those employing less than 50 people. This would fill another book; but to illustrate that social responsibility is not just the concerns of larger companies, I include a short piece on social entrepreneur Matthew Bennett and his Soho Pizzeria (see Box 5.1).

The Body Shop's social report

Whenever the phrase 'social responsibility' crops up, it is quickly followed by references to The Body Shop. The Body Shop, Traidcraft, a developing world import and trading company in the UK, and Ben & Jerry's ice cream in the US were among the first to produce elaborate, and sometimes bewildering, moral statements and analyses about their business. The Body Shop is as near as any one company has come, to date, to being a socially responsible enterprise; but it has not escaped controversy, as argued by Jon Entine (see the end of this section). It is also considered one of the leading exponents of social auditing, and has worked closely with the New Economics Foundation (NEF) in the UK to set up precise guidelines for social auditing.

I have followed The Body Shop's progress with interest. Having been a researcher at the University of Sussex in Brighton, I visited, as a customer, Anita Roddick's shop many times during the early 1970s, located in a decrepit part of Brighton. Being a snooty-nosed researcher at the Institute of Development Studies, little did I realize that my research should, indeed, have started there and not in faraway places. But it is never too late, and some 20 years later I was invited to address The Body Shop franchisers on my research on indicators that purport to measure socially responsible enterprises. I learned more than I imparted from a very active and alert group, who had come from all over the world. From campaign director Gavin Grant's talk at the same workshop, I also learned about The Body Shop's attempts to save the life of Ken Saro-Wiwa of the Ogoni tribe in Nigeria. This was my first introduction to cause-related marketing (CRM).

The Body Shop describes itself as a large multi-local business – not a one-woman show but a global operation with franchises running their own businesses and thousands of people working towards common goals. It says:

> *We want it to be obvious for anyone to see why we do what we do – and how we do it. This applies to every level of our business, from the manufacture and marketing of skin and hair care products to our activities as a socially responsible company.*[1]

The Body Shop's first social statement appeared in early 1996, following the company's threefold 'mission' statement that it, first, believes that business has a moral responsibility to tell the truth; second, is a high-profile advocate of social and environmental causes, so that (because sometimes this upsets people) if a company wants the licence to campaign on public issues it must demonstrate its own commitment to reflection and self-improvement on issues such as environmental protection, animal protection and human rights; and, third, has – if it is to continue to mix business with politics, and cosmetics with campaigns – to take its supporters and stakeholders (including customers, employees and suppliers) along with it.

It is curious to see a company so specifically committed to social causes, and it is hard to imagine other companies, in the future, following the same route. Yet, the thesis of this book is that this is inevitable. In the first edition of this book I said: 'This does not mean, of course, that companies such as Shell will campaign against themselves; rather, they must ultimately be convinced that acting socially and responsibly is not only good for business, but essential if the planet is to survive peacefully into the future.' Since that time, *The Shell Report* has been listed as one of the most prominent social reports published (see 'Avant-garde social reports' later in this chapter). I also wrote: 'Obviously, not all companies will have the passion of The Body Shop, but it may not be too long to see Ms Roddick's dream come true.' It has come quicker than I thought! Anita Roddick wrote:

> *I would love it if every shareholder of every company wrote a letter every time they received a company's annual report and accounts. I would like them to say something like: OK that's fine, very good. But where are the details of your environmental audit? Where are the details of your accounting to the community? Where is your social audit?*[2]

The Body Shop's four-volume social statement document dealt with all aspects of the company's environmental impacts, animal testing and protection policy, ethical basis and social positions.[3] It surveyed shareholders, of which 371 returned questionnaires covering a total of 28 aspects of the company's relations with its institutional and individual investors. Of all shareholders responding (and the share price has long been a 'roller coaster ride'), 90 per cent agreed that 'The Body Shop takes active steps to make its business more environmentally responsible' and 78 per cent were satisfied with the information they received on the company's financial performance.[4] However, 29 per cent disagreed that 'the company enjoys the trust of the financial community,' and one third were dubious whether The Body Shop had a clear long-term business strategy.[5]

I only cover, briefly, three of the 'audits' because my main concern is with social issues, not environmental, animal protection or even ethical issues in any great detail. These are all amply discussed in other publications. The company's environmental audit covers its principal sites of operation in the UK – eventually, the company plans to cover its international operations. It follows the protocols and framework set out in the European Commission's (EC's) regulation for a voluntary Eco-Management and Audit Scheme (EMAS), which was approved by the European Council of Environment Ministers in March 1993. The Body Shop's own environmental statement follows what it considers to be the most important of its operations – namely, energy efficiency (transport, electricity, gas); waste (waste water, solid waste); product stewardship; training and finance; together with a verifier's statement (performed by an independent group known as Environmental Resources Management – ERM). Interestingly, the audit also included a 'non-verified' section on environmental targets, international markets, UK retail sales, its soap works supplier and a report from the NEF on its contribution to the UK's carbon dioxide (CO_2) emissions. The ERM verified that all three of The Body Shop's manufacturing sites in the UK 'broadly' met the requirements of the EMAS regulation.

The company's animal protection statement draws its inspiration from the company's aim to eliminate the use of animals from the testing of cosmetics and toiletries worldwide. The Body Shop rejects animal testing, and its report includes an independently verified assessment of its procedures and purchasing criteria and how they relate to the international standard ISO9002. This standard is aimed at assessing how a company's suppliers conform to specific requirements. The independent verifiers, SGS Yarsley ICS, certified The Body Shop's compliance. This did not stop a huge row in the press over whether The Body Shop did or did not use animals for testing; as is often the case, the incident illustrated that when mud is thrown it tends to stick, whatever the merits of the case.

The Body Shop's ethical statement is, essentially, a summary of what it does in its three audits for the environment, animal protection and social matters. Of interest is that The Body Shop set up an ethical audit department to provide support for the company's ethical stance in three areas: policy, auditing and training. The audit department is not usually responsible for day-to-day management of ethical issues, but reported at the time directly to the chief executive officer (CEO), Anita Roddick. She created a 'values-and-vision' group, as well as the more normal corporate structure (marketing, sales, finance, legal departments and so on), in which the ethical audit unit is lodged, as well as a public affairs unit, a CEO support team and a team concerned with fair trade. The ethical audit unit has six areas of professional expertise – animal protection; environmental protection; social issues; health and safety at work; information management; and training. The unit is organized along stakeholder lines, with each of the main professional groupings taking special responsibility for the needs of particular stakeholders. This, it is believed, streamlines communications, and avoids head office departments and stakeholders being confused by differing values-related audit demands.

The largest volume by far was the one dealing with The Body Shop's social situation (the social statement). Anita and Gordon Roddick write, in the foreword to the statement:

> *We went into the social audit with a sense of damned if we do, damned if we don't...we are already finding that it is helping us to run our business better...different parts of the business recognize the improvement points necessary to*

maintain the support of their stakeholders. We now have a list of strategic targets and priorities for action for each stakeholder group.[6]

The methodology they use draws on their own research, as well as the experiences of the Sbn Bank in Denmark, Traidcraft in the UK, the NEF, the Council on Economic Priorities (CEP) in the US and Ben & Jerry's in the US. Questionnaires were delivered to stakeholder groups and quantitative indicators of social performance of relevance to each group were devised. The purpose of the social audit was not to focus on specific criticisms or issues, but to deal, broadly, with only one accounting period. It did not investigate individual allegations of wrongdoing or inefficiency. The social statement focused on ten key stakeholder groups: employees; international franchisees; local franchisees in the UK and US; customers; suppliers; partners in Trade Not Aid relationships; shareholders; local community in one town in UK; UK-based non-governmental organizations (NGOs); and organizations applying for funding from The Body Shop Foundation. Each of the stakeholders had a dedicated part of the social statement that covered one year – 1994–1995 – to coincide with the financial statement of accounts. The report itself has sections for each stakeholder, as well as one on health and safety at work. What is commendable in each section is a section that deals with the next steps that the company should take. The fact that this was taken seriously was indicated by the hiring of Kirk Hanson by The Body Shop, the professor of business ethics and social responsibility at Stanford University Graduate School of Business, to review the social statements. He was very thorough and, in the main, very complimentary.[7] Nevertheless, he was concerned that The Body Shop tended to exhibit a pattern of exaggeration and to intimidate critics. The reactions of the Roddicks to the Hanson report was: 'one of the difficult lessons we have learned [is that others'] perception and our view of reality are often poles apart'.[8]

What came out of the social statement? Table 5.1 reproduces a chart from the report that provides a good summary of the main lessons learned. In fact, it is difficult to see what The Body Shop could have derived from the chart because the variance of the scores is low and bunched around the grade of 4 – that is, most of the stakeholders agree or strongly agree that The Body Shop is doing a good job. The highest score is 4.9, where its international franchisees strongly agree that the company does not test or commission tests on animals (the NGOs, with a score of 4, are less sure), while the lowest score is 3.4, where the NGOs, again, only just agree that the company trades fairly with producers in the developing world.

The Body Shop itself concluded various things from the study. It came up with 95 specific 'next steps' allocated for its stakeholder groups as a result of its review. These ranged from 'publish and communicate a career-development policy statement for its employees', to 'develop a strong new product and promotional calendar that recognizes the unique aspects of

Table 5.1 Stakeholder perceptions of The Body Shop's social performance (average scores)

Statement about The Body Shop	Staff	International franchisees	UK franchises	US franchises	Customers	Suppliers	Share-holders	NGOs	Foundation applicants
n	1799	23	56	42	1000	109	372	43	32
Cares about its staff, customers and other people affected by the company	3.8	4.2	3.9	3.8	3.6	4.0	3.9	3.9	3.9
Campaigns effectively on human rights, environmental protection and animal welfare	4.3	4.6	4.4	3.8	3.8	4.3	4.0	4.0	4.0
Takes active steps to make its business more environmentally responsible	4.3	4.8	4.6	4.0	3.9	4.3	4.2	4.1	4.3
Trades fairly with producers in the developing world	4.0	4.2	4.0	4.1	3.8	3.7	3.8	3.4	3.8
Assists its business and trading partners to improve on their performance on social, environmental and animal welfare issues	3.9	4.0	4.0	3.6	not asked	3.6	3.8	3.4	3.7
Does not test or commission tests on animals	4.6	4.9	4.8	4.6	4.5	4.4	4.2	4	4.1
Provides reliable and honest information to stakeholders on social, environmental and animal welfare issues	4.1	4.2	4.2	4.1	3.8	4.1	3.9	3.5	3.6

Note: the scale used was 1–5. 1=strongly disagree; 2 = disagree; 3 = neither agree nor disagree; 4 = agree; 5 = strongly agree.
Source: The Body Shop (1995) Social Statement 95, The Body Shop, Littlehampton, UK, p131

The Body Shop in the US market', to 'a special initiative on educating customers on the naturals issue', to 'create partnerships without playing God'. The independent auditors from the NEF were complimentary, but thought that a more detailed analysis of the stakeholder survey results would have been useful.

Not everyone is complimentary about The Body Shop's efforts. In September 1994, accusations of using animals to test products; products filled with petrochemicals; a history of penurious charitable contributions; troubled employees and disgruntled franchisee relationships; and the fact that the name, store and package design, and product line were copied from another cosmetics company surfaced in a Jon Entine article for *Business Ethics*.[9] This set off a firestorm of press coverage, which was one of the reasons that The Body Shop opened its books to the social auditors. The Body Shop's biggest challenge, according to Entine, is not its competition but itself.[10] Its faltering financial situation coincides with a reversal in its image as a leading socially responsible company. It has experienced embarrassing problems with franchises, product quality and vendor relationships, as well as challenges to its integrity.

This aside, one of the key questions not addressed by The Body Shop is whether all of their very noble efforts are, in fact, good for business. Could the firm have reduced some of its campaigning and community contributions, and thereby have increased profits to the benefit of its shareholders? Certainly, other companies who may be interested or eventually required to produce a social audit may well ask, perhaps unkindly, whether The Body Shop is not a business mainly, or even partly, organized to provide a platform for its founders to promote social causes on a world stage. Even if, as it seems, the social causes are admirable, the answer might well be an unkind yes! This would weaken the case, stated above by Anita Roddick, for each shareholder to ask their company: 'Where is your social audit?' if it implies that each company must not only issue a social statement but also list social campaigns that may only be tangential to their business. But I leave the last words on this to Anita Roddick, who said:

> *Very few chief executives publicly challenge the role of business itself to try to connect their activities to wider social objectives except in a strict economic sense. Some of our best companies still retreat into shareholder value justifications for excellent community outreach programmes when they should simply celebrate and say: 'This is what business should be about.'*[11]

Then in 2001, the London *Evening Standard* reported that:

> *Anita Roddick has branded the cosmetics chain a 'dysfunctional coffin', claiming it had lost its soul since*

floating on the stock market. 'I wanted every shop to challenge the World Trade Organization, to ask every member of parliament, and they won't do that', Roddick told the Edinburgh International Book Festival. She also questioned The Body Shop's future as a publicly quoted company, saying the underlying drive of the financial system towards yielding greater profits was killing its spirit.[12]

Levi Strauss sourcing guidelines[13]

Levi Strauss was once *the* world leader in providing strict guidelines to its worldwide contractors. Even the arch critic of socially responsible business, Jon Entine, admitted that 'of the high-profile retailers, Levi Strauss has distinguished itself for at least devoting considerable resources to identifying which shops supply its suppliers, and bringing direct pressure to establish minimum wage standards and working conditions'.[14] With intense pressure to keep costs down, many contractors, especially in developing countries, compromise on health and safety standards. Levi Strauss devised its guidelines (see Box 5.2) to regulate health, safety and environmental standards that have now been implemented by 700 contractors in 50 countries. In addition, the company established country selection criteria (see Box 5.3) to decide whether it should sever its relationships with contractors in countries where human rights abuses are pervasive and where employers are at risk because of social or political problems. It was also concerned, quite naturally, with whether putting these values into practice and adhering to its own code of ethics had an impact on its bottom line.

The company was founded in 1850 by Levi Strauss, a Bavarian immigrant of Jewish descent. In the latter part of the Californian gold rush, Levi Strauss made durable clothing, first out of heavy canvas and later out of denim. Today, the company is the world's largest manufacturer of branded clothing, producing jeans, shirts and jackets for men, women and children.

The company went public in 1975, but the Levi Strauss family realized that shareholders were primarily concerned with financial results and gave little importance to the company's value system at the time. Consequently, the family bought back the company through a leveraged buyout in 1985. When CEO Jacobi travelled to Asia and Latin America in 1993, he noticed major discrepancies between the way in which workers were treated there and in the US. For instance, in Mexico workers were exposed to bare wiring with no insulation whatsoever. In Costa Rica, female workers were dismissed if they became pregnant – Jacobi was told that this was basic economics, because the subcontractor was forced to do so to stay competitive to win major orders from companies such as Levi Strauss.

Box 5.2 Levi Strauss business partner terms of engagement

Our concerns include the practices of individual business partners, as well as the political and social issues in those countries where we might consider sourcing.

Environmental requirements: We will only do business with partners who share our commitment to the environment.

Ethical standards: We will seek to identify and utilize business partners who aspire as individuals and in the conduct of their business to a set of ethical standards not incompatible with our own.

Health and safety: We will only utilize business partners who provide workers with a safe and healthy work environment. Business partners who provide residential facilities for their workers must provide safe and healthy facilities.

Legal requirements: We expect our business partners to be law-abiding as individuals and to comply with legal requirements relevant to the conduct of their business.

Employment practices: We will only do business with partners whose workers are in all cases present voluntarily, not put at risk of physical harm, fairly compensated, allowed the right of free association and not exploited in any way. In addition, the following specific guidelines will be followed.

Wages and benefits: We will only do business with partners who provide wages and benefits that comply with any applicable law or match the prevailing local manufacturing or finishing industry practices. We will also favour business partners who share our commitment to contribute to the betterment of community conditions.

Working hours: While permitting flexibility in scheduling, we will identify prevailing local work hours and seek business partners who do not exceed them except for appropriately compensated overtime.

Child labour: Use of child labour is not permissible. 'Child' is defined as less than 14 years of age or younger than the compulsory age to be in school. We will not utilize partners who use child labour in any of their facilities. We support the development of legitimate workplace apprenticeship programmes for the educational benefit of younger people.

Prison labour/forced labour: We will not knowingly utilize prison or forced labour in contracting or subcontracting relationships in the manufacture of our products. We will not knowingly utilize or purchase materials from a business partner utilizing prison or forced labour.

Discrimination: While we recognize and respect cultural differences, we believe that workers should be employed on the basis of their ability to do the job, rather than on the basis of personal characteristics or beliefs. We will favour business partners who share this value.

Disciplinary practices: We will not utilize business partners who use corporal punishment or other forms of mental or physical coercion.

Box 5.3 Levi Strauss guidelines for country selection

The following country selection criteria address issues which we believe are beyond the ability of the individual business partner to control.

Brand image: We will not initiate or renew contractual relationships in countries where sourcing would have an adverse effect on our global brand image.

Health and safety: We will not initiate or renew contractual relationships in locations where there is evidence that company employees or representatives would be exposed to unreasonable risk.

Human rights: We should not initiate or renew contractual relationships in countries where there are pervasive violations of basic human rights.

Legal requirements: We will not initiate or renew contractual relationships in countries where the legal environment creates unreasonable risk to our trademarks or to other important commercial interests, or seriously impedes our ability to implement these guidelines.

Political or social stability: We will not initiate or renew contractual relationships in countries where political or social turmoil unreasonably threatens our commercial interests.

However, Levi Strauss thought that it could not maintain two different standards for workers, one in the US and another in developing countries. To deal with this, the company had already formed, in 1991, a Global Sourcing Working Group to develop its sourcing strategy. This essentially stated that contractors must respect safety and health standards, as well as environmental standards. Child labour and prison labour are not allowed.

The sourcing guidelines were implemented first in Asia, where the majority of the company's subcontractors were located. Auditors designed a two-day training programme for Levi Strauss employees in 13 countries, and this was followed up with a centralized database of all sites and audits. The auditors receive training and attend a yearly conference. The sourcing staff receive an internal newsletter that encourages them to bring problems within contractor plants to the attention of the company.

Since instituting this policy, the company has severed ties with 5 per cent of its contractors. For instance, a contractor in Saipan was dropped because he had violated the law, and contractors in Uruguay and the Honduras were eliminated for sewing another company's brand and designs without authorization. A Filipino contractor was dropped because of poor working conditions and personnel practices and, even in the US, a contractor in Alabama was sacked for using prison labour, but agreed to phase out the practice in six months and was reinstated. Regarding child labour, the company at first thought to end the contractual arrangements but found out that this would lead to hunger in families and that the children would resort to begging and prostitution. The company decided to pay the children to go to school until their 14th birthday, and then give them the opportunity to come back to work at the factory.

Regarding its country selection guidelines, Levi Strauss struggled with the dilemma of how to assess human rights. The company based its guidelines on the Universal Declaration of Human Rights, but developed its own definition of 'pervasive' or widespread human rights violations through looking at such things as what part of the population suffers from abuses, was the country a pariah nation internationally, what was the overall trend, and what was the policy of the country. This led Levi Strauss, for example, to judge that China was worse than Guatemala and to abandon the former country until its human rights record improved.

Levi Strauss was one of the first to adopt global sourcing guidelines in 1991, and since then other companies have followed suit – Reebok, Nike and Timberland have developed sourcing guidelines. US retail stores Sears, J C Penney and Wal-Mart have decided only to sell products that are manufactured under some form of 'fair' conditions. Its sourcing and country selection procedure show, to invert former UK Prime Minister Ted Heath's saying more than 20 years ago (applied to board-room battles at Lonhro), the 'acceptable face of capitalism'![15]

However, a common problem with large companies at one time or another is the question of 'downsizing'. Levi Strauss has been no exception. In November 1997, it announced the firing of one third of its 18,800 factory workers in the US and the shutting of 11 of its 37 factories. Earlier that year, the company announced that 1000 white-collar jobs would go, saving US$80 million. However, it gave the workers eight months' notice and spent US$31,000 on each worker to help them find new jobs. Then CEO Robert Haas treated seamstresses in the same way that other firms treated senior executives. That, according to *The Economist*, would count as weakness in the 'chain-saw school of management'; but Haas reckoned that there would be benefits in the attitude of employees left behind.[16] The difference between Robert Haas and his rivals, continues *The Economist*, remains his refusal to concede that treating his employees well is an avoidable cost: 'In an age where human capital is becoming increasingly important, it is hard to believe that this particularly quiet American has it wrong.'

Thus, once seen as a beacon, events during the late 1990s illustrated how hard it is to retain high levels of social responsibility when markets turn against your product. Suffering from a devastating plunge in sales, the company retrenched with massive layoffs and joined its competitors in moving the bulk of its production overseas to low-wage contractors. It continues to struggle under the burden of a huge bank debt that Robert Haas took on in 1996 to finance the concentration of the private company's ownership among selected family members. Nevertheless, according to Karl Schoenberger, an author of a recent book on Levi Strauss, by the middle of 1999 indications were that Levi Strauss did not intend to turn its back on its values.[17] It toned down its commitment in a more tersely worded document that deleted the old headline 'responsible commercial success' and changed its mission statement from 'We will conduct our business ethically and demonstrate leadership in satisfying our responsibilities to our communities and to society' to a single line: 'to achieve and sustain commercial success as a global marketer of branded apparel'. But the core values remain. Whether these will see them through past and present difficult times remains to be seen. What is clear, once again, is that CSR is important, but that a company cannot ignore market conditions.

Nike's independent audit

Independent audits of progressive companies who believe that they are socially responsible do not always go well. One of the most celebrated cases in recent times, as noted at the end of Chapter 4, was the commissioning of Andrew Young to carry out an independent assessment of Nike's code of conduct and to evaluate the company's effectiveness in applying that code to factories where Nike apparel and footwear products were manufactured. The initial main finding by Young, after visiting Nike factories in the spring of 1997 in Hong Kong, China, Vietnam and Indonesia, over a period of ten days, was: 'It is my sincere belief that Nike is doing a good job in the application of its code of conduct. But Nike can and should do better.'[18]

Nike is essentially a holding company who does not do any manufacturing directly itself. It has, so far, produced the bulk of its footwear products in Asia, originally in Japan, Taiwan and South Korea and, more recently, in China, Indonesia and Vietnam. Young took particular care not to be duped by Nike and to be shown only 'good' Nike factories. He visited four factories in China, four in Vietnam and four in Indonesia, which represented the 'work sites' of 40 per cent of the total Nike contract employees in Vietnam, 25 per cent in Indonesia and 45 per cent in China. Factories were chosen that were considered the 'best' and 'worst' based on the audit reports that had been reviewed in the US. An average of three to four hours was spent in each factory, and talks were held with individual employees at each factory, randomly selected by Young. Young also had talks with both local and international NGOs, usually without Nike personnel present. Such ex-post evaluation is commonly used by international organizations such as the United Nations (UN) or governments for their major foreign aid programmes, and the author has been a UN evaluation team leader on numerous occasions. The methods used by Young are common when time and money are at a premium, which is the case with most ex-post evaluations. However, it is inevitable that the detailed knowledge required for a full evaluation cannot possibly be obtained in only a rapid visit. Furthermore, hostile commentators can always find one case that will shed doubt on the honesty of the commission's report, and even on the integrity of the evaluators themselves. Such was the case with Young's report, particularly because Nike executives were so pleased that they immediately took out full-page ads in *The New York Times*, the *Washington Post*, *USA Today* and other papers. The ads quote Young as saying: 'It is my sincere belief that Nike is doing a good job...but Nike can and should do better,' and the company's response: 'Nike agrees. Good isn't good enough in anything we do.'[19]

Young organized his report to cover eight topics:

1   Factory conditions.
2   Abuse of workers and violations of human rights.
3   Plant management–worker relations.
4   Workers' rights.
5   Third-party reporting and monitoring.
6   Living conditions at factories.
7   Processes and systems.
8   Education and training.

Under each heading, he came up with a number of findings and, finally, produced six major recommendations. These were that Nike should:

1   Continue its efforts to support and implement the provisions of the Apparel Industry Partnership.
2   Take more aggressive steps to explain and enforce the code of conduct.
3   Take proactive steps to promote the development of 'workers' representatives' in the factories who can effectively represent the workers' individual and cumulative interests.
4   Insist that the factories that manufacture its products create and enforce a better grievance system, which allows a worker to report a complaint without the fear of retribution and abuse.
5   Expand its dialogue and relationship with the human-rights community and the labour groups within the countries where they produce goods and with their international counterparts.
6   Consider some type of 'external monitoring' on an ongoing basis as a way of demonstrating its commitment to the code of conduct and to ensure its effective application.

Bob Herbert of *The New York Times* led the critique of Andrew Young's report. Young had said that he found no evidence of child or prison labour; but, Herbert wrote, he did not seem to realize that those were not the problems that critics of Nike's operations in China, Vietnam and Indonesia had been complaining about. The issues in those countries were wretchedly low wages, enforced overtime, harsh and sometimes brutal discipline and corporal punishment. In Ho Chi Minh City, for example, Nike workers are paid the equivalent of US$1.50 a day, which is not enough to cover the cost of food, shelter and transportation to and from work.

However, Young's report did not address the issue of wages. 'It is not reasonable', the report says, 'to argue that any one particular US company should be forced to pay US wages abroad while its direct competitors do not'. Nike's critics, including Herbert, argued that the company's full-time overseas workers should be paid at least a subsistence wage for the areas in which they live. It is worth mentioning that a US$1.50 a day is more than a subsistence wage in Ho Chi Minh City.

The setting of wages is a fundamental issue but a difficult one. There is no universal agreement on what level wages should be set at, or whether there should be a minimum wage, or – where there is one – what it should be. These are issues that have been studied over a considerable period of time by labour economists; Young, or even Herbert, could not be expected to resolve them during the time spent on them. This is not to dismiss the idea that a 'living wage' is not important – it is simply difficult to come to an agreement on what it should be. The World Bank's rule of thumb is that anyone living on less than US$1 a day is living in absolute poverty. Yet, US$1 a day will get you nowhere in Portugal, for example, but a long way if you are a subsistence farmer in sub-Saharan Africa or a slum dweller in Madagascar. Local price levels are important and, indeed, are the reason that companies such as Nike locate their production in cheap labour countries. Normally, multinational companies such as Nike pay higher wages than local companies; but as Young said in response to his critics:

> The salary issue may be considered by many as primary structural abuse. I do not feel qualified to determine a living wage in China, Vietnam, or Indonesia; but I saw the presence of workers, with whom I talked, both in and out of the factory grounds, who spoke of saving and sending money home to help parents. Western clothing, bicycles, motor scooters and the roadside merchants present at the factories, even where food was provided, did not give the impression of starvation wages. In Indonesia, where there were TV sets and antenna visible in quite a few of the crowded rooms, one could get a clear sense of economic mobility.[20]

According to Herbert, however, Young dodged the issue of corporal punishment as well. He acknowledged that there had been problems, but said he found no evidence of 'widespread or systematic abuse'. Other investigators, including Thuyen Nguyen, an American businessman who founded a group called Vietnam Labour Watch, have confirmed numerous reports of Nike workers undergoing serious and sometimes harrowing abuse. Nguyen also noted that Nike had been operating in Vietnam for less than two years, and already one factory official had been convicted of physically abusing workers, another had fled the country during a police investigation of sexual-abuse charges and a third was under indictment for abusing workers. Young retorted: 'Occasional abuses? Yes! Widespread systematic human rights violations? No!'[21]

Young asked Nike to report back on its response to his recommendations, and it has done so. But what is important about this case study is Nike's willingness to be examined by an independent evaluator and to profit by, or suffer from, the consequences accordingly. A less socially responsible company, of which there are many, would not accede to an independent evaluation, or allow the report to be published and be easily available on the internet; nor would it let itself be examined for possible abuses. Nike must be applauded for its honest attempt in this field, even if the spin put on its pronouncements has been somewhat exaggerated.[22]

B&Q moves from environment to social responsibility

Environmental concerns are not the main thrust of this book, but a socially responsible enterprise is assumed to have environmentally friendly policies. For this reason, I have included here the discussion of an impressive company, B&Q, who have published, to date, three reviews of its environmental policy. Its latest, with the picturesque name of *How Green Is My Patio?*, was published by the company in 1998.[23] The company itself is the UK's biggest home improvement and garden centre retailer. It has 321 stores employing 33,000 people, with a 13.5% share of the repair, maintenance and improvement market. In 2002/2003 B&Q and Screwfix Direct had a combined turnover of US$6 billion with profits of US$580 million.[24]

The foundation of B&Q's policy was the acceptance by its board, in 1990, that each of the 40,000 products sold has an impact on the environment. For instance, its use of timber can contribute to the destruction of the world's natural forests; its paint solvent when drying will evaporate into the atmosphere and may contribute, albeit in a small way, to global warming; and peat used for potting compost has led to concerns about its extraction from areas recognized as important for conservation. The company also believed that the working conditions of its suppliers had to improve because this would 'become one of the most significant ethical environmental issues facing retailers in the future'.

The company found that applying the environmental standard BS7750 to its suppliers was heavy on its suppliers, who did not have the resources to implement the standard, and that the standard itself was rather bureaucratic. Consequently, in 1995 B&Q developed its own standards and came up with an innovative method to rank its suppliers on a number of environmental grounds. The assessment process, known as QUEST for Suppliers (QUality, Ethics and SafeTy) is based on an average score derived from ratings awarded on a scale of 1 to 5 for each of ten QUEST principles (see Box 5.4). It subsequently launched QUEST for Stores and, in 1998, started to introduce QUEST for all other B&Q departments.

As can be seen, the interpretation of each principle is largely subjective, making it much harder for individual suppliers to comply or even know what is expected of them in any detail. Suppliers were given a preliminary classification and a year in which to challenge that classification or to improve.

In the event, paint suppliers consistently came top of the classification, reflecting the industry's early response to their high-profile impacts, such as the effects of volatile organic compounds. Timber suppliers were more problematical, and B&Q stated its timber policy as: 'B&Q will only buy timber whose harvesting has not caused the destruction of, or severe damage to, a natural forest anywhere in the world. Indigenous people and forest inhabitants must not be harmed and, ideally, should benefit from the forest management.' This was a target originally set by WWF, and B&Q was the first retailer to adopt it.

Like Levi Strauss, B&Q also use a country rating system when no details have been supplied about forest management; but the location of the source leads B&Q to suspect that the sources will be typical for the country concerned. B&Q does not rely on what it calls the 'glossy brochure' approach because it realizes that self-certification alone is not good enough.

The rating, also subjective, like QUEST, is built up by asking approximately 20 forestry experts from around the world to rate the countries from which B&Q sources timber according to the potential certifiability of a typical source within that country. The rating has six components on a (rather curious) scale, from a top score of 25 per cent (certification very likely) to a bottom one of –10 per cent (certification unlikely) for the following:

■ quality of national forestry legislation;
■ implementation of legislation;
■ support for certification;
■ support for the Forest Stewardship Council (FSC);
■ degree of support from NGOs; and
■ access to information.

B&Q does not stop at certification; it makes an attempt to help the people themselves. For example, in 1992, B&Q sponsored the Baining people of East New Britain in Papua New Guinea (PNG) for three main purposes: first, to benefit local people by giving employment, income and self-reliance; second, to provide incentives to maintain viable forests, thereby preserving biodiversity and local culture; and, third, to produce timber to B&Q's specifications. The Baining people have traditionally had very few sources of income, apart from the fact that the indigenous peoples of PNG are legal owners of the land they inhabit. Thus, their forest is their major

Box 5.4 B&Q's QUEST for Suppliers

QUEST Principle 1 – Advice and support to B&Q: This is the degree to which a supplier supports and advises B&Q on how to improve the quality and environmental objectives of B&Q.

QUEST Principle 2 – Cooperation with B&Q Quality and Environmental Department: In the past, up to 25 per cent of the department's time was spent chasing suppliers for replies to questionnaires and letters. The rating goes down or up depending upon the level of cooperation.

QUEST Principle 3 – Product safety and integrity: This reflects the measures taken to ensure that the product is safe and fit for the purpose for which it is sold.

QUEST Principle 4 – Quality management systems: The supplier has to ensure that quality is consistent by implementing systems that are appropriate for the product.

QUEST Principle 5 – Quality performance: This grades the performance of a supplier and the product in store with the customer. Qualitative and quantitative measurements are compiled for each supplier and used in the analyses. These include reject reports at central warehouse, product refund data, trading standards enquiries and store manager anecdotes.

QUEST Principle 6 – Environmental policy and awareness: A supplier's understanding of the environmental issues associated with its products and its commitment to resolving them are graded by assessing its published environmental policy.

QUEST Principle 7 – Environmental action and achievements: To ensure that a supplier's environmental achievements consist not solely of writing a good policy, a supplier's achievements are awarded a separate grade for action.

QUEST Principle 8 – International supply chains: B&Q believes that the issue of poor working conditions in factories in developing countries will become a significant issue for retailers. A supplier's understanding and commitment to this issue is awarded a separate grade.

QUEST Principle 9 – Packaging and environmental claims: The supplier's ability to meet all of the possible future legal requirements to minimize the amount of packaging used and design for recycling is jointly assessed with the accuracy and benefits or problems caused by any environmental claims on a product.

QUEST Principle 10 – Timber: This involves the supplier's ability to meet B&Q's present and future requirements of its timber policy and targets.

Source: B&Q (1998) *How Green is My Patio? B&Q's Third Environmental Review*, B&Q, Eastleigh, UK

asset, and over the last few decades they have sold the rights of vast areas to foreign-owned export logging companies or for conversion to plantations. While the windfall income is attractive, it is quickly gone, along with the forest and any future opportunities. B&Q provided a grant to stop the clans from having to sell off their land and to help them manage their forest appropriately. Total funding to date has been around US$250,000. B&Q has also helped the local communities to bring their timber production up to the standards of their certification levels.

Thus, B&Q started with environmental concerns, like many other companies, but also found that it could not then ignore social issues, as the Baining people's example illustrates. This is the route taken by many companies, and that will be taken by even more as they see that environmental enterprise concerns are just one issue, albeit a very important one, in the whole area of CSR.

Avant-garde social reports

Since the first edition of this book, many companies have gained prominence in social reporting and have won prizes to this effect. The United Nations Environment Programme (UNEP), for instance, has started to rank company *environmental* reports based upon 50 sustainability indicators and gives annual awards.[25] Of the 100 companies for which reports were available, The Body Shop, BA, Bristol-Myers Squibb and British Petroleum (BP) were highly regarded.

This section briefly examines some of these companies, but from a *social reporting* perspective – namely, The Co-operative Bank, Camelot, Van City of Canada, Shell, BT and BA.

The Co-operative Bank: *Partnership Report 2001*[26]

This report is the fifth in a series of annual reports on social responsibility and sustainability. The Co-operative Bank in the UK is one of the world leaders in the presentation of social reports and was cited as such by UNEP. Its *Partnership Report 2000* was also the winner of the year 2000 Institute for Social and Ethical Accountability (ISEA) award for the best social report. The report takes the stakeholder approach and develops a number of innovative indicators for each stakeholder group – similar in nature to the ones suggested here. The report insists (and this is worth insisting upon) that any indicator must follow a SMART approach: it should be specific, measurable, achievable, realistic and timely. Of particular interest in the Co-op's work is the attempt to assess the costs and benefits of its ethical and environmental interventions. It admits that its methodology is in an early stage (and does not present it in the report), but assesses the benefits less costs to be about 15–18 per cent of pre-tax profits.

Camelot: Social reports[27]

Camelot runs the UK lottery and has published two social reports, to date, in 1999 and 2000. Both reports have similar formats and follow a straightforward 'stakeholder model' of reporting, with each stakeholder having a separate section – the public, employees, community, retailers, suppliers, pressure groups, the environment and shareholders. The most controversial aspect of Camelot, and one addressed in the report, is that its product is not only an alternative form of taxation but is a regressive one. Poorer players tend to spend more money on lotteries than richer ones. Camelot addresses this, commissioning work from the Personal Finance Research Centre of the University of Bristol in the UK, and shows that as the average weekly household lottery expenditure rises, in absolute terms, the higher the household's income decile. It does not reveal the proportion of expenditure by decile that would show this declining as one moves up the decile distribution – or, in other words, it does not show that £1 for a poor person is more valuable than for a richer person.[28] Nor does it explain how poor an investment a lottery ticket is compared to the stock market, for example. But then, why would it?

An innovation in Camelot's report is the use of ISEA's Quality Scoring Framework (QSF), developed for AccountAbility 1000 (AA1000) (see Chapter 7). The QSF is based upon eight strangely named principles: inclusivity, comparability, completeness, evolutionary, embeddedness, communication, external verification, and continuous improvement. These are further broken down into a set of 56 criteria; an assessment of the organization's social accounting process is then rated on a scale of 0 (not satisfied) to 4 (satisfied to a high extent). The scores are added up and averaged for each principle and then compared with a benchmark scale of five stages: basic, foundation, intermediate, advanced and sustainability. Camelot scores high enough to be in the 'advanced' stage. The procedure was followed in 1999 but not in 2000. It is a rough-and-ready manner to see how a company compares to others; but the principles are a little far-fetched to believe that a high mark on each will lead to glory in the fifth stage – business sustainability! The fact that Camelot at first lost its bid against a consortium led by Richard Branson of Virgin fame, and then was declared the winner for a further period in 2000 after a well-publicized high court case, indicates that the ISEA's scale requires more attention.

Van City of Canada

Van City, a small financial service company based in Vancouver, produced its first externally audited social report in 1997 and is highly regarded as one of the first to use a stakeholder approach under the influence of the UK-based NEF.[29] Its stakeholders are its members, staff, associated credit unions, community, environment, suppliers and business alliances. Its audit report (signed by Simon Zadek of NEF) is refreshing; it notes that the report provides a reasonable basis for understanding the social impact of Van City, but observes critically that not all stakeholders were included.

Shell

Royal Dutch/Shell Group of Companies has, at the time of writing, produced six annual reports on its social, economic and environmental activities.[30] At first sight, *The Shell Report 2002* and *The Shell Report 2001* appear to devote only 12 out of 50 pages to social issues in a section headed 'Social performance', albeit up from only 6 pages in *The Shell Report 2000*. However, the confusion of separating out environmental and economic from the over-riding concept of CSR leads the report to sprinkle social responses throughout its pages. The space devoted in the report to the discordant views of its various stakeholders is unique. For instance, 'Exploit or explore? The arrogance is almost unimaginable. I will continue to boycott Shell' is juxtaposed with statements such as: 'I shall feel further reassured when I next fill up the tank – that I am supporting a company that is not only socially responsible and accountable but is also concerned for the world my children will inherit.'

The report's 'Tell Shell' report card, which readers and stakeholders are invited to fill in either through a pre-paid form or via the internet, is innovative, as is the space devoted to a key performance indicator framework of economic, social, environmental and governance, and values indicators. As readers of this book will know, I am of the school that strongly believes in measurement – not of the school that says that if you can't measure it, then it does not exist. Most things can be measured, but some things are just more difficult to measure than others.

British Telecom (BT)

Unusually (but what can be expected from a telecommunications company?), British Telecom (BT) chose to launch, in 2001, its social, economic and environmental report solely through its website.[31] This is fine if you can read on screen or, lamentably, as did the author, have a fast printer. The idea is to use the internet to update the reports and to use 'interconnectivity' to link with pages within the website, and to other parts of BT's web presence, as well as to some external sites. But, as the chairman of BT, Christopher Bland, stated in his Introduction: 'the Better World site...is not like a book that has a start and an end and a logical story running through it.' Too bad, I say! Nevertheless, what is in it reflects chief author Chris Tuppen's wide experience in the area of CSR and covers many essential-to-read items, such as a value statement; a choice of indicator; stakeholder engagement; an environmental impact assessment; and an interesting attempt to link CSR to economic values in a section called 'Economics and the big picture'. There, BT sees CSR as 'embracing the activities a company can take towards a wider goal of sustainability', which is based on BT's definition of sustainable development as a concept that 'has increasingly come to represent a new kind of world – a world in which economic growth delivers a more just and inclusive society, at the same time as protecting our natural heritage'. In other words, BT bases its concept of sustainable development on the environment, as so many others do, but then raises the stakes through linking sustainable development, implicitly, to a fairer society where the fruits of economic growth are shared equitably. One may well ask what all that has to do with a telecommunications company – and one that has seemingly over-reached itself through massive investments in licences to operate broadband telecommunications. Perhaps, like Levi Strauss, BT will water down the rhetoric as its share price continues to dive and as take-over threats loom. That would be a shame.

Nevertheless, in an innovative approach to examining the bottom line of its activities, BT has produced a report that analyses the effects of its 'social responsibility' activities on its business activities.[32,33] Its approach has been to establish a relationship between various factors and satisfaction levels among its 19 million residential customers. BT identified four drivers of customer satisfaction – the most important being direct contact with the company when reporting faults, making complaints and so on. This is obviously no surprise; but what was surprising was the finding that reputation and image are 'a major determinant of customer satisfaction', and 'over a quarter of the overall figure for image and reputation was attributable to CSR-related activities'.

BT's research suggested that, taken together, its customers perceive a 1 per cent change in issues such as trust, employee care and social responsibility as of much greater importance than a 1 per cent change in call and rental charges. The figures express the relationship as a ratio. So, for example, if BT's overall image and reputation rose by 1 per cent, its customer satisfaction rating would rise by 0.42 per cent. BT's Chris Tuppen also stressed the subjective nature of much of the data. 'Customer satisfaction is, after all, a perception measure. A detailed statistical analysis of the underlying information does allow one to identify the main components; but even here things are not straightforward', he says. 'Trust, for example, includes technical issues, such as knowing the phone will work when you pick it up. We're really looking at trends in customer satisfaction levels to identify the strongest contributors to image and reputation.'[34] The contributions of trust, environmental responsibility, social responsibility and 'cares about customer needs' were all 'pretty high'. The analysis was based on tens of thousands of customer interviews over 80 months, with questions on issues including cost of service, employee care, social responsibility and the way in which the company dealt with complaints. 'Once we had established the degree to which people were satisfied, we then asked subsidiary questions to build a picture of what elements lie within customer satisfaction. We have spent a lot of effort disentangling masses of data to understand the cause and effect linkages in mathematical terms.' The BT method did not attempt to quantify shareholder benefit directly. Instead, it addressed the position of the company in the marketplace. As BT Retail's monopoly weakens, customer satisfaction levels become correspondingly more important: each of BT Retail's 8 million most valuable customers delivers an annual average of £70 (US$100) earnings before interest and taxes (EBIT). If, as the BT studies strongly suggests, CSR activities play a role via image and reputation in maintaining or building BT's market share in a competitive market, then CSR will defend or build shareholder value. This will happen, says *Ethical Performance*, 'regardless of whether the contribution of CSR can be precisely quantified or not, assuming the company manages its CSR expenditure efficiently'.[35] In other business sectors, the CSR contribution to customer satisfaction might be greater or smaller. But this just showed, again according to Tuppen, that the 'business case for CSR will never be found whole. It needs assembling piece by piece.'

British Airways (BA)

British Airway's (BA's) first combined report contains sections on social, environmental and economic factors, as is the case with many reports. One of the reasons of splitting up the economic and environment aspects from the social (the model presented in Chapter 8 sees environment and economic as part of stakeholders' interests when exploring a corporation's CSR) is that many environment groups have moved into the social and economic sphere for the first time. We now hear of 'triple bottom line (TBL)' reporting that arose from John Elkington's book *Cannibals with Forks* and applied through his UK consultancy firm SustainAbility.[36] His influence also extended to the Global Reporting Initiative (GRI), of which he was a founder member, that has built on its environmental work with social and economic reporting aspects.[37] BA's slim 48-page report takes, as might be expected, the environmental impact seriously but is much more limited on social and economic aspects. A stakeholder focus is missing, and BA focuses upon its employees, consumers, business conduct and community programmes under what it calls its citizenship approach.

In John Elkington's review of the BA report, cited in the document, he uses a metaphor of a five-speed gearbox. The gears are recognition of key impacts; focus on internalization of CSR (Elkington also includes corporate citizenship and sustainable development in his 'gearbox'); managing an expanding array of interfaces with stakeholders; joined-up thinking; and linking improvements in TBL performance with customer appeal and the value of the company's brand. He finds that BA has not yet entered fourth gear, where it can find virtuous circles rather than manage vicious ones. Auditors and statements in the report are kind to BA but do not address some key CSR issues critically such as, for instance, BA's move to capture high-income passengers with better service and smaller planes. No room for backpackers and smaller planes means more movements in the air and increasing congestion at airports leading, eventually, to higher prices for BA's less well-off consumers.

A socially responsible private hospital wins out

Being successful in business in terms of conventional measures can be costly, if social responsibility is ignored. The world's biggest for-profit healthcare and hospital company, Columbia/HCA Healthcare of the US, announced in mid 1997 a net profit of US$891 million on revenues of US$10.5 billion.[38] Based in Nashville, Tennessee, it owns 342 hospitals as well as hundreds of outpatient surgery and care facilities. It has prospered by cutting fat from a notoriously inefficient business, partly through take-overs that enabled it to boost its supply-buying power and partly through reducing the layers of bureaucracy. The for-profit mentality has also helped to change the way US healthcare is run, through the setting up of integrated healthcare systems that handle everything from heart surgery to home care. The long-term plan of the company is to introduce disease management that standardizes hospital care in the same way that fast food chains prepare their products.

However, some of Columbia's business practices attracted investigation by federal authorities; approximately 500 federal agents raided dozens of its facilities in July 1997. According to an article in *The Economist*, some of the company's for-profit activities may have been more unethical than illegal, however.[39] For instance, Columbia had partnerships with doctors at hospitals that allowed the doctors to take a stake in their hospital and a share in its profits. This encouraged doctors to refer patients only to specialists at Columbia-owned hospitals, a practice that might not necessarily be in the patient's best interest. Other doctors allegedly referred patients only to affiliated home-care providers, whether or not they offered appropriate or convenient care for the patients concerned. The company, apparently, billed Medicare – the US government-sponsored health service – for blood tests on patients that doctors had not requested; inflated the illnesses of some Medicare patients so that they appeared to have more serious illnesses than they really had, thereby adding to Columbia's fees; paid expenses to specialists who were able to increase the flow of profitable patients; discouraged treatment of uninsured patients at some of its hospitals; and overcharged extensively. Columbia has some other skeletons in its closet, as well. One of its buyouts in the 1980s, Humana, a pioneer of for-profit healthcare, spent much of the 1980s besieged by investigators and lawsuits. Rivalling the US defence industry in excessive charges, it once charged US$7 for one tablet of Tylenol, an otherwise inexpensive aspirin-like drug found in most US supermarkets.

There is now a merger mooted between Columbia and another for-profit health company, Tenet Healthcare, which has a more socially responsible image. (It was not always that way, however; in 1994, National Medical Enterprises – as Tenet was then known then – paid US$380 million to settle charges that it had practically imprisoned healthy patients in its psychiatric hospitals until their insurance ran out.) A merger between Columbia and Tenet may be the main way for Columbia to improve its image. Of course, if it simply changes its name again, and makes no attempt to improve its social responsibility, it will more than likely run into trouble again. Nevertheless, it will continue to make healthy profits in the interim. After its problems with federal investigators, Tenet followed the socially responsible route, with annual healthcare ethics courses for employees, a toll-free number for whistle-blowers and a mission statement that emphasizes integrity and honesty as prime principles. Tenet's profit margins are slimmer than Columbia's; but, as *The Economist* acerbically comments in one of its famous last-liners: 'As Columbia and the rest of the healthcare sector are discovering, being wealthy is not always healthy. Or wise.'[40] Short-term gains achieved through dubious practices may well be in the interest of shareholders who are there for the upswings. But long-term stability is sacrificed, and even the survival of the company itself. If Columbia had imposed a code of ethics earlier, it would have been in better shape today.

Ethical funds

Investing in socially and/or environmentally responsible enterprises has grown spectacularly in recent years.[41] The idea is that people can choose whether to avoid investing in enterprises that produce tobacco or armaments, or those with poor pollution or industrial relation records, or even those that invest in repressive regimes. The change reflects both the increase in wealth in the industrialized world, albeit skewed more to the richer than the poorer, and the change in social conscience. As Lewis et al mention, with such a shift in attitudes:

> ...the possibility that the world may become a better place through individual market choice without the need for government intervention is opened up. There are also strong implications for economic theory, which has traditionally assumed that financial behaviour is primarily motivated by individual interest.[42]

There are numerous funds for investors to chose from. Ethical funds invest only in enterprises that meet certain ethical or environmental criteria. However, there is no agreed definition of 'ethical', and each fund's approach varies. For instance, Ethical Funds, Canada's largest family of

'Green' mutual funds, doesn't invest in companies who sell tobacco products or in utility and mining firms who use nuclear power. Today, there are more than 40 mutual funds (unit trusts) in the US and another 12 in Canada that use some form of positive or negative screens. Together, they hold upward of US$13 billion, with another US$3 billion invested in targeted social investments, such as community development banks. However, this is little compared with the more than US$1 trillion (Entine says US$8 trillion, which is probably exaggerated, compared with the US-based Social Investment Forum figure of US$1 trillion cited earlier) under management in North America; yet, it has a high media profile, and various types of social screen are gradually being adopted by many multibillion-dollar pension funds.[43] A MORI poll of 1000 British adults in 2001 showed that 46 per cent of respondents consider social responsibility to be 'very important' when deciding whether to buy a product or service from a particular company. This is 18 per cent more than a similar MORI survey in 1998.[44]

Socially responsible banking first received national attention in the US during the mid 1970s, when the South Shore Bank turned a poor, decaying section of Chicago into a respectable area with pleasant housing and thriving shops. South Shore did this through investing in its own neighbourhoods with money from its own depositors and from socially concerned savers throughout the country.[45]

A 1995 survey by the Social Investment Forum indicated the relative importance of the issues that have come to dominate the investment screens.[46] These are for negative screens, where companies are excluded – tobacco (86 per cent), alcohol (73 per cent) and weapons/military production (64 per cent) – and for positive screens – human rights (42 per cent), environmental issues (38 per cent), animal rights (24 per cent) and employee relations (22 per cent).

In the UK, the amount of money invested in ethical funds more than doubled between 1994 and 1997, according to the Ethical Investment Research Service (Eiris).[47] Eiris also found that funds managed by ethical unit and investment trusts (mutual funds) rose 35 per cent to £1.47 billion (US$2.4 billion) from 1996 to 1997. This is still small, in comparison with the £150 billion of total funds under management in unit and investment trusts in the UK. Nevertheless, ethical funds have increased by 34 per cent a year on average between 1989 and 1997, which is twice the 17 per cent increase of the industry as a whole. According to Eiris, ethical investors tend to be female and most strongly object to three types of organization: those that manufacture weapons, support oppressive regimes or despoil the environment.

Yet, ethical investing is not without its criticisms. These are fourfold. First, it is primarily the smaller enterprises that are selected, and these tend to be more *volatile* than the larger ones. The reason is that many of the biggest companies are no-go areas for ethical funds, because the bigger the company, the more likely it is that some part of its operations will fall foul of their criteria. Because of this reasoning, the oldest and biggest ethical unit trust, the Friends Provident Stewardship fund in the UK, can invest only in 15 or so of the 100 biggest UK companies, and in about 40 per cent of the wider All-Share index of stocks. Some ethical funds are even more restricted. The Jupiter Ecology Fund has a choice of just 440 companies globally, including 15 per cent of the All-Share line-up.[48] This concentration has also meant that ethical funds have missed out on much of the 1996–1997 rise in the UK stock market, which has been concentrated in a few big banks, and chemical and oil businesses that did particularly well – sectors that can be anathema to ethical funds.

Second, *small incidents* rock the boat for ethical firms much more than those that are known to be more opportunistic. For example, one of the largest ethical funds in the US, the Parnassus Fund, reported in the five years up to 1996 a stellar return of 21.5 per cent, leading the normally caustic commentator Jon Entine to say that this was 'vindication of sorts for a segment of the investment industry that has long believed that ethics and profits need not be mutually exclusive'.[49] But in May 1997, after Entine had written his piece, the fund was accused by the Securities and Exchange Commission (SEC) of 'improper acts' for which the SEC was seeking civil damages. One of the accusations was that Parnassus had improperly made a loan to Margaux of US$100,000, which was outside Parnassus's investment policy.[50] Although Parnassus claimed that the SEC was making a 'highly technical argument that was wrong', it illustrates the new boundaries that are introduced in ethical investing that can then be used against the ethical investor.

Third, the *definition* of what should be in a social screen is sometime unclear. Some say that the field is becoming diluted by the larger fund management groups who are entering the area because they see rich pickings in the trend toward ethical investing.[51] Furthermore, some start-up social funds are not really socially orientated, which leads consumers to question the integrity of 'social funds', generally. Jon Entine remarked that it is clear that it can no longer be assumed that there is unanimity about what constitutes social responsibility: 'A religious fundamentalist in Iowa does not share many social values with a gay activist in New York.' He also cites Shuttleworth of Ethical Funds, who doesn't invest in companies that make packaging for the tobacco industry unless tobacco-related production represents less than 20 per cent of business. Why 20 per cent? 'Well, that's just the cut-off we set,' says Shuttleworth. Other curiosities are not hard to find. For instance, Entine continues, in Canada resource companies make up more than 40 per cent of the Toronto Stock Exchange, and social investors frequently filter out 'messy' industries such as timber, paper products, mining, oil production and so on. Yet, many of the firms in these industries have become leaders in revamping their environmental programmes while offering well-paid jobs in a difficult economy.

Fourth, the collection of *information* on what is a socially responsible enterprise is difficult. As I found myself, for the supposedly information-rich UK (see Chapter 9), the social information about enterprises is difficult to locate and then to rationalize. And many indicators are simply not in the public domain. Jon Entine, again, notes that company research is superficial, even at resource-rich Merrill Lynch and other top firms. Social research firms have even skimpier resources, and for the most part they must rely on non-independently provided company information as their main source. They must also rely on first-level screens; for example, ethical funds say that they won't invest in tobacco, nuclear power or defence industries, but they may not screen banks who may hold huge investments in the very same industries.

Joan Bavaria, president of the Franklin Research and Development social investment enterprise, noted that the business world can no longer be conveniently divided into 'bad' multinationals and 'good guys':

> We are entering a new era in the world of socially responsible managing and investing. It is not a black world or a white world with neat and crisp lines of demarcation. It is the real world of complex systems and internal contradictions.[52]

These comments are particularly pertinent to the widely cited FTSE4good fund that was launched by the *Financial Times* (FT), together with the LSE in mid 2001.[53] But, as I said at the time in a correspondence with the FT, the FTSE4good indicator is not an indicator of CSR, as some of its adherents had suggested, but a screening device (see Chapter 7).[54] Simply eliminating companies whose products you do not agree with is half-baked social responsibility. A better approach would be to grade the 'baddies' (tobacco, nuclear weapons, etc) on a CSR scale, then reduce the portfolio investment in the 'baddies' but not eliminate it altogether. This is because what is bad today may be good tomorrow and vice versa – for instance, tomorrow airlines may be ousted, owing to the, as yet, unrevealed radiation risk of flying and Nestlé, once out, may be in again.

Eliminating a company gives no space, or incentive, for that company to improve its socially responsible rating over time. As socially responsible investment (SRI) funds become ever more important, then investment for 'baddy' activity could dry up. Although most of us would not object to this in the case of landmine or nuclear weapon manufacturers, some (including me) would be very upset if that meant the disappearance of Beaujolais!

This point was illustrated by Gareth Davis, chief executive of Imperial Tobacco, when he noted in reply to my letter that 'as a big UK manufacturer of a legal but controversial product, Imperial Tobacco aspires to apply recognized criteria for good corporate governance, employee relations, health, safety and the environment and wider community relations'.[55] Cynics may smile; but given that people smoke, is it not better to enter a dialogue with the 'baddies' to improve their CSR than to ignore them completely? Some may say that ignoring such companies completely would hasten their disappearance. But what is an unacceptable product today may become acceptable in the future (and vice versa, of course). Therefore, as Gareth Davies stated: 'We believe investors would be better served by a set of indices that represent a fair and objective assessment of identifiable business practices, rather than measures based on inclusion criteria that are completely inflexible and a subjective opinion of a company's products.'[56]

How could such an index be created?

CRITICS (Corporate Responsibility Index through Internet Consultation of Stakeholders), on my company's website, is a questionnaire that I developed to produce data for such a rating.[57,58] An index is then created that is based upon 20 questions about a *company's* CSR activities. The question on products is phrased as follows: 'Do you attempt to ensure that your product is used in a socially responsible manner?' This is then weighted as one of 20 items in the final index. This is not, as Gareth Davies hoped for, a 'fair and objective assessment'; indeed, it is very unlikely that complete objectivity can be achieved in measuring CSR. But the CRITICS approach does allow a company to improve its CSR rating over time and, if included as a criteria for portfolio investing, would provide a more adequate indicator than FTSE4good.

Nevertheless, mainstream financial analysts remain cautious about the idea of social investment. They do not see the relevance of information provided by social or environmental reports in their daily analysis of companies and are unlikely to use the information provided. They believe that it is harder to make money with social investment, given their potentially reduced diversification and active risk exposure, and are very sceptical of social investment indicators such as the Kinder, Lydenberg & Domini (KLD), FTSE4good, Dow Jones Sustainability Index (DJSI) and Jantsi Social Investment Index (JSI), to name some of the well known ones. The scepticism towards the indices is also being shown by dedicated SRI houses. What these indices do, however, is raise awareness of SRI. The fact that mainstream index producers are getting involved in this area further demonstrates that SRI may not be a fashion statement.

Certainly it is early days for social investment funds, as back-tracking of the various indices shows. For instance, the Canadian JSI, from its inception on 1 January 2000 through 31 August 2001, lost 12.47 per cent, while the Canadian Standard & Poor's (S&P)/Toronto Stock Exchange (TSE) 60 and the TSE 300 lost 12.11 per cent and 10.69 per cent, respectively, over the same period. A similar result was estimated for the FTSE4good and DJSI over the same period. Hardly brilliant! An investment in fixed interest bonds over the same period would have avoided any loss. This goes to show that social or any other type of investing doesn't mean putting your head in the sand when you see the investment storm clouds gathering!

Clearly, investment analysts wish to see the 'business case' for social investment and are not carried by the 'moral case'. So, why are mainstream analysts not seeing the business case, where does the problem lie and what can be done about it? Let's look at these questions briefly one by one.

Why the slow uptake of CSR issues by mainstream financial analysts?

- Investors are still mainly interested in making profits or driving value.
- CSR is imperfectly understood and its impact on profits or value creation is not easily measured.
- Some believe that CSR implies a political tinge of social democracy or even socialism/Green party sympathy.
- There is a legacy of belief that CSR issues are the government's responsibility.
- Company reporting is opaque.
- There is a perception that major social responsibility issues are beyond company control.

What does business need to do?

- Understand available measures.
- Report adherence to standards; be open.
- Contribute to CSR dialogue (for example, on Social Accountability 8000 (SA8000)); join institutes such as AccountAbility, the GRI and Social Accountability International (SAI).
- Follow best practice.

What do analysts need to do?

- Understand and popularize available standards.
- Contribute to the debate on business performance and CSR.
- Tell business the results of their analysis.
- Openly state their ideological beliefs on CSR.

As I have shown in the regular 'Monthly Feature' published on my company MHC International's website, the business case for CSR investing is still under consideration. My own 'j-curve' model theorizes gains.[59]

Investment analysts should not, however, ignore *fashion*. They certainly did not in the dot.com boom when many wiser heads were seeing shades of the South Sea Bubble and were rewarded when the Nasdaq declined by half in a few months in 2000. When fundamentals come together with fashion, then the time, in my view, is to jump into CSR investment. A precedent for investing was established by one of the UK's most famous economists and successful investors John Maynard Keynes, who was the brainchild for the Bretton Woods institutions: the International Monetary Fund (IMF), the World Bank and the more recent World Trade Organization (WTO). Alongside developing his general theory of employment during the 1930s in response to the crash of 1929, Keynes was an inveterate investor. Not getting up until midday, he used his 'bedtime' to work with his investment brokers. He was no slave to economic theory and no virgin to price earnings (PE) ratios, shareholder values and the like. Keynes ascribed his success to trying to understand human behaviour – seeing where they were investing and following suit. Now, over 50 years after his death, would Keynes be looking at CSR investment? He would certainly have some ideas on how to handle the current recession and would be quick to spot the next 'fashion'.

The events of 11 September 2001 have spurred interest in social development. None of us in that field welcome the fact that vile acts have given impetus to concerns about social development. Nevertheless, the acceleration of interest in social development, both through the nation state and through corporations, is likely to herald a boom in social investment.

MORI study of consumers about corporate social responsibility

MORI has focused on the issue of CSR and community involvement through multi-client studies in the UK dating back to 1990. In August 1996 it conducted a survey among a nationally representative sample of 1948 people aged 15 or more.[60] MORI's overall conclusions were strikingly in support of increased social responsibility by UK companies; yet, it thought that companies had still not grasped this – four people out of five saw CSR and community involvement of companies as important, while two-thirds thought that companies did not pay enough attention to these responsibilities. Indeed, 71 per cent said that when deciding whether or not to buy a product or service, it was important to them that the company shows a high degree of social responsibility. However, the majority also felt that while enterprises should give help, they should also benefit from this help. This was emphasized by the respondents noting that profitability and financial stability, as well as the quality of the products and services, were the two most important things to know about a company in order to judge its reputation – and this was a trend that had become steadily more important between 1990 and 1996.

The public also expects companies to get involved in the community and not just to donate money. Nevertheless, to date, environmental issues have been the highest concern of the public, with social concerns only recently having become more important. What these social concerns should be is still not clear to the public, who expects companies to be active, even if it cannot name particular programmes. This expectation of involvement also differs considerably by company, industry sector and awareness of current activities.

MORI suggested a list of the kinds of social responsibilities that companies should have. The respondents were asked about the two responsibilities of companies – commercial responsibilities (that is, running their business successfully) and social responsibilities (that is, their role in society and community), and what kinds of social responsibilities, if any, they thought the companies had. These responsibilities were, in order of importance in the 1996 survey, to:

- look after employees' welfare; provide good pay and conditions; ensure the safety of the workforce; (24 per cent)
- protect the local environment (21 per cent);
- become more involved in the local community and/or sponsor local events (12 per cent);
- provide good service to consumers (8 per cent);
- reduce pollution; stop pollution (7 per cent);
- provide good pensions and healthcare schemes for employees (5 per cent);
- be honest and reliable (3 per cent);
- sponsor charities (3 per cent);
- produce and ensure safe/good-quality products (2 per cent); and
- charge fair prices for products (1 per cent).

Over the period of 1990 to 1996, the rankings of these ten items had changed little – environmental issues had waned slightly, while providing a good service to customers had increased a little. In another set of activities that MORI showed to respondents, taking steps to prevent and/or reduce environmental damage was considered the most important of the list shown, while help in job creation came only just behind.

The respondents agreed, overwhelmingly (86 per cent), that a company who supports society and the community is probably a good company to work for. When asked why companies support society and the community, only 1 in 20 takes the cynical view that companies are helping communities only to cover up any anti-social activities. But the public is not naive, and a high proportion accept the 'bargain' – namely, that companies expect to benefit from their programmes while also giving real help to the community.

As a guide to companies' behaviour, MORI asked a rather complicated set of questions and cross-tabulated them. 'How important do you think it is that large companies do certain specified activities?' was cross-tabulated with 'Which [activities] do most companies do at the moment?' Issues that the public thought were very important, but where they thought companies were not doing much, involved encouraging their own employees to be environmentally conscious, crime prevention, support for hospitals, and special services for the elderly and disabled. Surprisingly, in this time of 'downsizing', the public thought that help in job creation was important and that companies also agreed with them on this.

Regarding ethical investment, opinion was divided as to whether companies should aim to get the best return for their shareholders or should invest selectively according to ethical criteria. Four out of ten believed that companies should avoid investing in certain companies or countries.

Questions were not asked by MORI about suppliers, especially those in the developing world. A question was, however, asked about 'Which type of charity would you most like large companies to support?' Most important were medical research, child welfare and housing/homelessness. Far down the list (in 12th position) came overseas/developing world aid. This suggests to large companies with overseas interests that out of sight is still very much out of mind. Yet, only one incident can shock the public, as we have seen many times. The dilemma for a company with overseas interests is difficult. A company such as BP, for instance, is highly respected for its social and business-in-the-community activities. Yet, its payments to former soldiers from the UK's elite counter-terrorist unit, the Special Air Service (SAS), to provide covert training to Colombians to guard its pipelines in Colombia have harmed its public image because it is suspected of dealing with private armies, paying off drug dealers and so on.[61] Although it may have done this in the most socially responsible way, given that its job is to find and produce oil products, its image has been hurt by one incident. A large company, with the best will in the word, can't police every activity it undertakes, even if it wants too.

Chapter 6

Corporate Social Responsibility in Selected Industrialized Countries

Introduction

So far, this book has concentrated on the US and UK. I have argued that corporate social responsibility (CSR) is increasing for a variety of reasons, not least because it makes economic sense for large transnational corporations (TNCs) in these countries to act in a socially responsible way. But is this mainly an English-speaking phenomenon? In the future, do TNCs, located in all industrialized countries, need to be more socially responsible than before? Will being socially responsible mean that it will be just that much harder to compete in the global market place? These questions, and how they are being tackled in some of the largest industrialized countries, are examined in this chapter.

The notion of CSR differs from country to country. Clearly, local cultures affect how consumers expect companies to behave, as does the response from and type of product sold by a company in a given country. Sometimes, culture and economics combine to produce different products. For instance, for many years visitors from Europe to the US were astonished at the size of their cars compared with their European equivalent. A wide, open country and cheap oil contributed to this, as did higher taxes on oil and the more confined space to which Europeans were accustomed. However, some convergence can be seen as the environmental lobby presses for less gas-guzzling cars and congestion increases. In fact, the astonishing convergence in the look of cars today across countries compared with a decade or so ago attests to the rapid convergence of tastes and culture – the strange-looking Citroën Deux Chevaux or the Trabant are now, unromantically, confined to the past.[1]

In a similar way, the interpretation of social responsibility differs from country to country. The US is one of the leaders in applying corporate responsibility standards to its companies (but less so corporate *social* responsibility) as this is increasingly accompanied by a variety of awards being given for good practice. However, the gap between 'application' and 'observance' seems not to have closed as fast as it might appear from the outside. Enron's receipt of several awards in the environmental area did not overflow into the area of corporate governance, ethical behaviour or financial probity.

The UK also seems to have gone a fair way along the CSR path. There, as a result of the Thatcher revolution, business has been given prominence over the public sector for the first time since the 19th century. A plethora of institutions and networks have arisen to monitor and comment upon the ethical and social responsibility of business.

How does the situation look in other large industrialized countries regarding social responsibility? To answer this, I now look at Japan, Germany, France and Italy, as well as some of the smaller countries, such as Holland and Denmark.

Japan[2]

The Asian crises of 1997, 1998 and again in 2001–2002 have shaken Japan's institutions and its major companies to the core. The patronage of banks, supported by government, to the major companies has exposed major weaknesses in the operation of market practices. But does this mean that social responsibility will have to lessen so that Japan can compete better with its Asia neighbours? Will Japan be forced to downgrade its levels of social and labour care to compete with other countries in the region? When survival of a company is at stake in a period of lower growth or recession, the bottom line becomes even more important. Any such company will have to look hard at labour conditions and at its community projects around the world, and will start, or even increase, the relocation of production to lower labour-cost countries. This was the case in Japan during the mid 1970s as it responded to the early 1970s oil shock. Yet, it is precisely during these times that companies must look at a planetary bargain. Japan needs this to ensure that other industrialized market companies do not undercut its production costs by moving to the most exploitative and lower labour-cost countries of all.

Issues of social responsibility are not new in Japan. Although CSR is not as developed as in the US, for example, there has been a long tradition of specific aspects of CSR in Japan. For instance, during the 1960s, CSR issues in Japan were discussed in terms of labour–management conflicts, and by the 1970s concern changed to the issues of pollution and environmental protection. This was commensurate with the worldwide concern at that time, prompted by the Stockholm World Environment Conference of 1972. Despite Japan being seen from the outside as a lukewarm player, it was particularly concerned with the crowded conditions in its islands and about its fragile dependability on imported oil. The conference followed shortly after Japan's strongest economic boom, in 1970 (the Izanagi boom), since the nation had been created. Critical remarks were made, then, for the first time regarding the single-minded growth objective that Japanese corporations had profoundly believed in during the post-war period.

Japanese corporations took the brunt of internal criticisms, and these increased in their intensity in 1974 after a series of crises – the international monetary crisis, the food crisis, the oil shock and rampant inflation – led to the oil industry trying to ruin petroleum prices by withholding supply. Japanese corporations were quick in their attempts to deal with this by responding seriously and defining standards for proper management activities at various levels so that corporations could act in a more socially responsible manner. However, when the Japanese economy re-entered a period of slower growth after the oil crisis, corporate efforts to be more socially responsible gradually, but steadily, disappeared as corporations began to trim their own management.

The Japanese economy began to expand again in 1986, resulting in an economic boom (the Heisei boom) that was almost as big as the Izanagi. CSR then re-emerged, and this time – in addition to terms such as social responsibility – corporate contributions to society and the community were prominent and ushered in an upsurge in philanthropy. Many corporations created departments aimed specifically at such activities, and philanthropic activities were boosted by corporate councils (for example, support to local community art and culture activities) and a 1 per cent club. For example, the Toyota Motor Company formulated a corporate philosophy of open and fair corporate actions expressly to be seen as a corporate citizen who could be trusted internationally. And Canon Inc, which positioned itself as a leader in CSR within Japan, is one of the very few companies that has adopted its own global corporate code of conduct.[3] However, the code is only written in Japanese and has not been distributed to managers at overseas subsidiaries and subcontractors. Nevertheless, Japanese corporations have become more focused in their relations with local communities and with countries where they are located.

In addition, while, in the past, Japanese corporations pursued their goal of supplying good products cheaply, what was most strained (and continues to be) were the lives of Japanese citizens. Issues such as the excessive work hours, and the inefficiency of overtime work that was done just because others were working overtime, have resulted in desires for a shorter work life and an enriched family life. Large Japanese companies are gradually taking a hard look at these issues, as well as at the wider issues of CSR to other stakeholders.

Today, as Japan is again in a period of slower growth, CSR is likely to be put on the back burner once more. But what will this mean for the country's longer-term prosperity? The globalization of the world's economy may make this more difficult than before. Globalization not only means freer flows of capital, human beings and technology; it also means a rapid increase in information flow. It is more than possible that if Japanese corporations regress in their levels of social responsibility, then this could harm their global marketing position. Japanese cars or computers assembled in exploitative conditions, whether in Japan itself or, more likely, in poorer Asian countries, will not escape the inquisitive eye of the world's consumers. This will be aided and abetted by leading manufacturers in the US, who will seek to install a level playing field. Consequently, a planetary raising of the rules in which businesses conduct their global affairs will come about simply because of the increased globalization of information. It is unlikely, therefore, that Japanese corporations will, or even should, reduce their levels of social responsibility as they have done in the past.

Germany[4]

The same issue of globalization and cheaper production in other countries also confronts most, if not all, of the large TNCs based in Germany – for example, Siemens, BMW and Volkswagen. Higher labour costs and more labour market rigidities than those of their competitors have forced these companies to relocate their production to lower-labour cost countries. Germany is one of the most expensive countries in which to do business, followed by the US, Belgium, the UK and France – far ahead of low-cost countries such as China, Thailand, Hungary, Malaysia, Indonesia and South Africa, who came in the last places of the 30 or so countries analysed in 1998.[5]

Nevertheless, social responsibility is a key issue. Volkswagen, for instance, established a group works council in 1992 to arrive at a mutual understanding with its employees and their representatives concerning the company's restructuring process; this was caused by the early 1990s worldwide recession and ever-increasing competition in the auto industry.[6] The council provides information and early consultation on a number of issues, such as the securing of jobs and plant structures; productivity and cost structures; working conditions (working hours, wages and salaries, and job design); new production technologies; new forms of work organization; work safety; plant environment protection; the effects of political developments on the group; and so on. Consultation is particularly emphasized when cross-border transfers of production are planned.

Indeed, Germany has had a long history of social involvement by enterprises in society. This dates from the 19th century, when pure capitalism existed, while at the same time social reformers could be found not only in churches and the scientific community but within the business community. The two extremes were Ernst Abbé (1840–1905) and his company Carl Zeiss, which stood for profit-sharing, employees' representation, safety at work and a reduction in working hours, and Alfred Krupp (1812–1887), the armaments maker who set up medical insurance, a pension scheme and built 3277 flats for 16,700 employees.

Abbé reflected the more democratic side of German company life at that time, which respected employees as people of full value, while Krupp's attitude was anti-democratic, feudalistic and patriarchal. The latter attitude was more common and in line with the ideas of Bismarck, who established a social insurance system at the end of the 19th century but forbade worker associations.

The social system in Germany has survived World War I, runaway inflation during the 1920s, World War II, a reform of the monetary system in 1948 and the reunification of the two Germanies. After World War II, the concept of *Soziale Marktwirtschaft* (social market economy) was established. This combined elements of the capitalist economy with labour market regulations and a system of social security.

However, according to Britta Rudolph, in contemporary Germany, job-sharing exists between private enterprise and the state at all federal levels; but no extensive literature on voluntary initiatives exists, such as is visible in the CSR literature in the US or the UK, for instance. The social provisions offered by enterprises are, normally, either required by law or in accordance with union agreement but, nevertheless, are close to the 'cradle-to-grave' social care that was once only the preserve of communist states. These social provisions have brought home to Germany the urgency of the question of globalization probably more than to any other country in the West. Discussions about labour costs and fringe benefits have become more and more heated as enterprises threaten to cut jobs in Germany and to export them to foreign countries with lower wages.

One exception is Siemens who, in 2000, added a *Corporate Citizenship Report* as a third element, as well as its financial and environmental reporting.[7] Its slim volume is not as extensive as, for example, Camelot's social report, nor does it cover all of its stakeholders. Nevertheless, with 450,000 employees around the world, the report is a small step in the right direction.

When the unemployment rate in Europe passed 11 per cent during the early 1990s, work-sharing, particularly in Germany, moved to the top of the agenda. Germany still has one of the highest unemployment rates in Europe at around 9 per cent – below Italy and Spain, but slightly above France.[8,9] The idea, as in France in 1998, was to spread the available work to as many workers as possible. Volkswagen (VW), for instance, suggested the reduction of working hours or laying-off 30 per cent of its workforce. In October 1993, VW proposed to its workers in Germany a four-day week with commensurate pay reductions – down from five days. This was symptomatic of the response to the employment problem, and in VW's case was due not only to the European recession but also to the higher and higher levels of productivity required to survive in the car industry. VW reckoned that it would produce the same number of cars in 1994 as in 1993 (1.4 million), at the same time as a 11 to 15 per cent productivity increase and switching parts manufacture from inside Germany to cheaper producers outside. The need to hoard skilled labour in case of an upturn was the basis of VW's reasoning; but the need to reduce its workforce from 103,000 to 72,000 because of 'over-manning' was also crucial, as was its agreement with the government of Lower Saxony to maintain its workforce at 100,000.[10]

As an alternative to VW's request, Germany's economic minister at the time called for three months' unpaid vacation a year. But the trade unions, having long fought for a reduction in the number of hours worked, shuddered at the idea of taking an equivalent cut in pay. Change is nigh on the welfare front, as well. Germany has had a far-reaching public social and educational system for decades, so there was no need of support from enterprises. Today, the situation has changed, leading to schools and social services lacking funds to buy equipment and to pay staff.

Consumers in Germany are also very demanding and led the worldwide movement to ban carpet imports from countries such as Nepal and India, who were using child labour (see Chapter 10). Yet, there is no doubt that the social benefits in Germany need to be restructured to make Germany competitive, not only with the developing world but also with its partners in the European Union (EU). But where should this end? It cannot end at the levels of the working conditions of prisoners in China. Rather, what is required is a planetary bargain where reasonable levels of wages and social benefits are agreed. The idea should not be to bring Germany's conditions down to the lowest common denominator but to bring the world much closer to Germany's social provisions.

France

France's highly centralized and paternalistic state, where most large corporations are either wholly or partially state owned, has an approach to social responsibility almost completely different from that in any other country. Like Germany, social costs are very high Whereas in the UK, payroll taxes add 10 per cent to the wage bill, in France the government takes 45.5 per cent for health, social security and pensions. This leads to many workers resorting to the black economy. This is not just restricted to the big towns; many workers receiving unemployment pay also work as casual labour as waiters, cooks and ancillary staff, for example, in the vacation resorts scattered around France.

To avoid these hefty social charges, many companies have relocated to the UK, where social charges are lower – 150 French entrepreneurs attended a conference in July 1997 organized by the association La France Libre...d'Entreprendre, and 15 companies actually relocated in 1997. Already, the water company Générale des Eaux, petrochemicals producer Elf Aquitaine and chemical company Rhône Poulenc have their headquarters in the UK.[11] Most large private firms believe that they pay enough in taxes and social charges to the state for social responsibility to be a long way down on their list of business priorities. However, as noted in Chapter 4, a new institution has been set up by French trade unions and a number of companies to promote socially responsible investment and CSR activities: the Observatoire sur la Responsabilité Sociétale des Entreprises (ORSE). Furthermore, the French government has published a draft law for quoted companies in France to publish social and environmental reports. It is anticipated that the first results of the law will appear in company reporting in 2003.

Quasi state-owned firms, such as car manufacturer Renault, engage in socially responsible activities; but these are more an extension of the state's wishes than a corporate programme on social responsibility. For instance, Renault offers courses to young unqualified school-leavers for jobs in many industrial sectors. The courses are planned by cooperation between Renault and around 40 companies, not all publicly owned companies. However, its actions outside of France are less socially responsible – witness its closing, in 1997, of the highly efficient self-managed assembly line at Volvo in Sweden.

The issue of globalization is of major concern in France, with its high level of unemployment around 9 per cent and its relatively low rate of economic growth around 2 per cent (both as of mid 2002). Yet, the restructuring of industry in France has been extremely slow, leaving the government to pick up the losses of quasi state-owned companies, such as Air France and Crédit Lyonnais, or to finance deficits through the alternative taxation system of the high prices charged to consumers by the wholly state-owned companies, such as the Electricité de France (EDF) or France Telecom. Globalization through French eyes is to provide, via the state, the necessary rules for trading standards, the environment and social rights. As the former French socialist prime minister, Lionel Jospin, said: 'Globalization gives a new legitimacy to modern states.'[12]

The initiative by Jospin, when he was prime minister, to reduce unemployment through reducing working time to 35 hours per week led to widespread discussion. Most enterprises argue that such a provision will actually result in job losses because labour costs will rise and enterprises will employ less workers, not more.

The case for fewer hours is simple. Jospin assumed that there is a certain amount of output to produce and, hence, a certain total number of hours of work to be done each week. As there are unemployed people who are desperate to work, it would be much better to reduce the hours worked by each worker and increase the number of workers. This would allocate a given amount of work more fairly and efficiently. Unwanted leisure would be reduced, valued leisure would increase and unemployment would fall.

However, this assumes that output would be unaffected. In fact, numerous countervailing forces are at work. First, increases in productivity could mean that output would rise even as the number of hours reduces. Second, output could fall if the work-sharing procedure leads to a fall in unemployment because there is a direct link between unemployment and inflation. The government's knee-jerk response to rising inflation to date, now even further exacerbated by Euro currency rules, is immediately to raise the rate of interest, thus reducing economic activity and output and, consequently, increasing unemployment. Third, if productivity increases but the prices of products fall in real terms, then the firm is forced to reduce payments to its workers as they reduce their hours of work. Fourth, operating overhead costs per person employed are not much different if the person works a four-day or a five-day week. And it is probably true that reducing the workforce by 20 per cent instead of reducing the working time by 20 per cent will be cheaper for the firm. Thus, work-sharing might not be beneficial to unemployment.

Depending upon what happens to output and its price, the effect of shorter working hours is mixed. Shorter hours are advantageous to employers if output and prices do not fall. However, this means that wages must be proportionately reduced. Then employers profit from the extra productivity and can afford to have labour costs remain fixed at previous levels. This does not reduce the unemployment rate but, obviously, prevents it from rising, at least in the short term. Moreover, French trade unions are reluctant to accept wage cuts, and some insist that regular full-time workers whose weeks are cut to 35 hours or so keep their 40-hour pay and benefits. Furthermore, health costs and pensions costs to the enterprise are very much the same for shorter working weeks if employees depends upon their jobs for future security.

Probably the best outcome is for workers to accept temporary hours of work and wage reductions, with costs supported by government, if need be. The anticipation is that output will eventually rise and full-time working can be resumed. This, of course, assumes that the firm is in a cyclical position regarding output, and that the government is willing to pursue counter-cyclical policies. Workers must also take care to negotiate a return to full-time working once the good times return. However, if the firm's product is seen to be in long-term decline, then the worker's best bet is to use the extra hours liberated from short-time working to obtain some extra training. Governments could help by setting up a reconversion fund for this purpose.

An initiative by Jospin to keep Marks and Spencers in Paris in 2001 illustrated the strong paternal attitude of French society. Widely applauded in France, Jospin announced that the indemnity paid to employees on retrenchment should be doubled for companies with more than 1000 employees. This ruffled feathers at Marks and Spencer; but the long-term impact on France's possibility to attract foreign investment by large firms is likely to be negatively affected and will eventually lead to less growth and higher unemployment.

Abroad, French foreign investment has been protected either through its overseas policy of *départements et territoires d'outre-mer* (DOM-TOM), where countries such as French Guyana, Réunion and Guadeloupe are actually departments of France, or through its one-time support of some of the most corrupt and brutal dictators in Africa, such as Mobutu in

Zaire, Bokassa in the Central African Republic or Liamine Zéroual in Algeria. In the latter case, companies such as Elf Aquitaine, EDF or French mining concerns benefit from the government's blind eye and enjoy the profits earned from unprotected and exploited labour. This policy only slowly changed under Jospin and is likely to be put on the back shelf now that President Chirac, with his well-known sympathy for large corporations and with a hint of corruption, swept all before him in the 2002 presidential elections. A big reduction (the talk was of a 40 per cent cut) in the 8400 French troops permanently stationed in six African countries and the closure of two bases in the Central African Republic heralded the possibility of a new approach to France's involvement in the developing world.[13] Whether this will also lead to increases in CSR by French multinationals is still too early to say.

Do enterprises in France need to be more socially responsible to compete globally? Arguably, the level of social provision by enterprises is so high in France that more social responsibility at home is not necessary. On the other hand, CSR is not just about labour costs. It is the equitable treatment of all stakeholders. For instance, France has long abused its environment – clear-cutting trees in the Alps, leading to erosion despite laws banning the practice; dumping pollutants in lakes and streams; large pylons obscuring panoramic vistas; etc. The legendary French service falls down very quickly as tourist consumers in Paris are well aware, and the state enterprises still treat consumers as nuisances, with organizations such as Crédit Lyonnais and EDF running roughshod over consumers.

One of the major problems in France is that the provision of social services, from health to social security to personal insurance, is grossly inefficient, leading to high social costs for employers and employees alike. Enterprises are forced by law to use costly state-run service enterprises that provide all sorts of social care. French enterprises can continue to operate despite these high social costs and increasing globalization for at least three main reasons: first, through the protected nature of the French state (which is often illegal, though this is ignored in practice); second, because of the integration of the French 'empire' through its DOM-TOM states; and, third, through the fiercely patriotic spending patterns of French consumers. It is rare, for instance, to see foreign-made cars on French roads, and it is unusual to enter a French supermarket and find anything other than French products – for instance, wine. Protection is also carried out by French farmers – although illegal, the blocking of British lamb imports and beef or Spanish tomatoes at French ports of entry is legendary. Furthermore, there is hardly a consumer movement in France to object to the textile importer Printemps, for instance, using cheap labour in poor countries, as would increasingly be found in the US, the UK and now Germany. It is to be expected, as France further converges with its European partners, that more and more questions will be asked about France's social responsibility outside of its shores.

Italy[14]

The level of social responsibility in Italy is difficult to judge because no overall data is available. The industrial system in Italy has, historically, been characterized by the predominance of the state. The largest Italian companies, such as Ente Nazionale Idrocarburi (ENI), petroleum company Agip's holding group, ENEL (electricity), IRI-STET (telecommunications), ANSALDO (electromechanical) and Alitalia (air travel) are owned and managed by the government.

The impact of globalization has forced Italian entrepreneurs to re-examine national practices. During the 1990s, the evident inefficiency of nationalized companies, in comparison with foreign competitors, was increasingly recognized by the public, and this has forced the issue of privatization onto the political agenda. The debate on whether and how to privatize national companies, especially when they produce and/or offer public utilities, has played (and is still playing) a central role in the political arena, with the result that the privatization issue in Italy has become a long drawn-out affair and remains, as yet, unrealized. Nevertheless, in 1996 the first privatization began (of ENI), and the offer to the public of the company's shares, was very successful.

Another driving factor towards privatization and, in a broader sense, towards the reorganization of the corporate sector, has been the increasing unemployment experienced during the 1990s. Given the unbalanced structure of the Italian economy, with most industrial and commercial activities concentrated in the northern regions, there is a great difference between these and the south.

Moreover, due to the centralized structure of the economy, socially responsible initiatives in Italy have not often been associated with particular entrepreneurs; rather, they have been the result of public debate and negotiation with the interested social partners. Trade unions, in particular, have played a central role though a widely diffused negotiation process with company managers and government representatives. Thus, in most cases, such as in company downsizing after mergers and acquisitions, or in a severe industrial crisis such as that experienced by the steel industry, the state was the major player in terms of socially responsible initiatives. These often took the form of early retirement programmes for employees who would have lost their jobs, or other forms of social benefits for workers. These policies contributed to a dramatic increase in public social expenditure, which – together with the old average age of the population – has resulted in a severe financial crisis of the Italian national institute for pension funds (INPS). Consequently, private involvement in socially responsible initiatives assumes an importance more crucial than ever before in today's Italy.

Despite the predominance of the state, a peculiar characteristic of the Italian industrial sector is the presence of a very few, but very important, family-owned companies. This is the case of the largest car producer FIAT

(Agnelli); the Benetton Group (clothing, restoration and Formula One racing team); Del Vecchio (the owner of Luxottica, the world leader in ice cream, quoted on the New York Stock Exchange, and the biggest tax-payers in Italy); Moratti (petroleum); Dioguardi (construction); Pirelli (rubber); Berlusconi (media); De Benedetti (founder of Olivetti, personal computers and telecommunications); Barilla (food); Marcucci (media); and Zegna (clothing).

It is difficult to find a comprehensive source of information about the social initiatives of these companies. However, some anecdotal evidence of these companies increasing their involvement in the social arena exists:

■ Benetton has sponsored several initiatives that foster young people in the arts, such as theatre and photography.
■ Zegna, a member of the Social Venture Network (SVN) Europe, has built a natural park (Oasi Zegna) near its founder's birthplace in Biella that is open to the public.
■ In 1994, the Dioguardi group's directors, anticipating a significant reduction in turnover, initially avoided laying off any of the group's employees by reaching an agreement with its labour unions and the state. The company negotiated 'contracts of solidarity' with all non-managerial employees. These foresaw a 10 per cent reduction in working hours and a commensurate reduction of pay, a portion of which was to be supplemented by the state.

The diffusion of corporate codes of ethics in the Italian business community is still of marginal relevance, though this is not the case for all of the major Italian enterprises – some have a written 'chart of values' (for example, ENI and Agip), and a written statement of principles for conducting business (for example, FIAT) is quite common. Nor is it the case for many Italian branches or affiliated companies of TNCs (such as IBM, Hewlett-Packard, Shell, Zeneca, Ciba and many others). The corporate code of ethics developed abroad by the head office is usually adopted, either in the original version or after being translated into Italian, and – in some cases – adapted for the Italian context. Nonetheless, an overview of the Italian business sector, as a whole, shows that the diffusion of corporate codes of ethics has had little incidence to date.

One significant example, however, is given by the experience of Glaxo Wellcome Italy (a company affiliated to the transnational parent company, Glaxo Wellcome) with more than 2000 employees. Since 1995, an integrated ethics programme (including training and the design of compliance structures) has been carried out in order to develop a corporate code of ethics. The code of ethics is being developed through a stakeholder approach that defines the company's social and ethical responsibility in its relations with customers, employees, shareholders, suppliers, partners, competitors, government agencies and local communities.

But the overall situation in Italy is far from the North American example, where around 90 per cent of the Fortune top 500 US companies have written ethical policies. This is mainly because, apart from the cultural differences between the European and the US contexts, the diffusion of corporate codes of ethics in the US has been strongly encouraged by a federal law – namely, the Federal Sentencing Guidelines, developed by the US Sentencing Commission. The presence of an effective corporate ethical programme is, in fact, considered good proof of the bona fides of corporate behaviour, and can allow a corporation to have a diminished fine in the case of misdemeanours. No such arrangement exists in Italy.

However, during the last few years the situation in Italy seems to have been changing. Shaken by the deep corruption scandals uncovered by the *mani pulite* ('clean hands') judicial investigation, Italian society has entered a new phase of critical re-examination and rethinking of the role of private corporations. The design of new rules so as to avoid collusion agreements between private businessmen, political representatives and public administrators has become a central point in the agenda of policy-makers.

Signs of this new climate can be seen from both the public (administration) and the private (corporation) side. A first, important, event was the 1994 government decision to introduce a 'code of conduct for public officials' that sets out the fundamental duties of any employee of the Italian public administration, if they are to behave ethically. Again, this development has a well-known precedent in the US, the Ethics in Government Act 1978 – the structure of which seems to have inspired the Italian legislators. After the introduction by law of this general code, the different organisms of the public administration are expected to adopt it and to make it more specific so as to reflect the ethical aspects connected to the nature and the scope of the services they provide to the community. To date, only two administrations seem to have followed this process – Regione Lombardia and Provincia di Vercelli.

A peculiar approach was also followed by some Italian companies during the 1970s in order to create what was called a 'social balance'. This was introduced as an extension of the usual financial accounting system, and was aimed at providing a monetary assessment of the social impact of corporate activities to the public. This approach was not widely adopted, probably because the interpretation of the data presented was too complicated for the public at large. More recently, during the 1990s, interest has been revived, with several companies – such as Coop (association of cooperative societies), Unipol (insurance) and the Italian railways (FS) – publishing a new type of social balance following the stakeholder approach. These have provided a more qualitative and readable set of information on the social performances of these companies. As such, they are much closer to social and ethical auditing than are social balances based solely upon monetary indicators.

Smaller European countries

The size of a country is no hindrance to social responsibility. Those considered here – namely, Denmark, the Netherlands, Switzerland and Ireland – are forced to interact on global markets because of their small domestic markets. Hence, these four countries have become some of the most open and efficient exporters in the world. At the same time, each of these countries has become known for high levels of social (and environmental) responsibility at home. Because of this, they are particularly keen to see a planetary bargain that does not favour the lowest common denominator.

Denmark

In Denmark, the social responsibility of enterprises is probably more developed than in the other three countries, although no one indicator shows this.[15] Since 1994, the ministry of social affairs has conducted a campaign entitled Our Common Concern – the Social Commitment of Companies. This is an attempt by the government to create a new strategy for Danish social policy to encourage companies to play a greater role. Consequently, many Danish companies have increasingly focused their attention on the social conditions connected with the operation of business. The New Partnership for Social Cohesion is an initiative of the ministry, and its publications form the basis for many of the country briefs presented here. The partnership starts from the observation that there are a number of business networks that collaborate on defining social responsibility – an estimate by SustainAbility Ltd counts 36 such business networks covering some 6000 companies.[16] The interest of the Danish government stems from its 'international obligation to offer its cooperation to develop...a new partnership for social cohesion'. Although not explicitly stated, this, in turn, presumably arises from its awareness that government on its own can only go so far in satisfying the public's social concerns. This interest initiated, in 1997, the setting up of the Copenhagen Centre (TCC). TCC strives to 'promote voluntary partnerships between business, government and civil society to provide opportunities for the less privileged to be self-supporting, active and productive citizens'.[17]

One of the more recent initiatives of the ministry has been the formation of a network of prominent company leaders who develop, and advise on, campaign initiatives. The network project's brochures cite three large Danish companies – Novo Nordisk, Grundfos and Pressalit – who are active in the network and have started many social initiatives in their own companies. A special feature of the new Danish partnership is the voluntary participation of enterprises and public authorities. The basic point of view of the Danish initiative is that enterprises, as well as other stakeholders in society, are dependent upon each other – and that they prosper by recognizing this dependency.[18] This way of looking at society creates scope for the social responsibility of enterprises; but it does not say anything about the scale of such social responsibility. This latter point has not been addressed in the Danish literature or elsewhere. It is essentially a normative question on ends rather than means, and is related to the quality of life; it is something many have struggled with but none have satisfactorily defined.

The Netherlands

In the Netherlands, the concern about social issues among the population is renowned. The Netherlands, along with Sweden, is one of the few countries worldwide that gives 1 per cent of its gross domestic product (GDP) for development aid and thereby obtains continual prestige, internationally, for its concern. The same is true regarding concern with social issues worldwide, although state initiatives, such as that seen in Denmark, have been confined to the environmental field, to date (for instance, the Dutch government's financial support to the World Conservation Union – IUCN – to move its European headquarters to Tilburg).

Nevertheless, enterprises have played a major role in social policy within the Netherlands for many decades. Together with the trade unions and government, they have determined, to a large extent, the evolution of social arrangements. Because of this, Einerhand believes that there was little room, or even necessity, for a more pronounced role of enterprises in the social field.[19] From World War II onwards, central agreements between government and its social partners dominated the playing field. But this has been decreasingly the case during the past ten years. National agreements are less binding than ever for the subsequent negotiations of social partners at company level. The talks between government and social partners may result in agreement, but the end result is determined at a decentralized level.

What about stakeholders, though? The system is rather rigid. For employees, there are three main ways in which enterprises play a role in arranging social benefits: first, through their role at a central level with the government and trade unions; second, through their role in negotiating trade agreements that cover about 80 per cent of all employees in the country; and, third, at company level. The last level exists for those companies not covered by trade agreements, where they are allowed to define benefits for employees themselves.

For local communities, initiatives are a result of agreements at company level – either agreements that have an effect on the local community or where there are specific initiatives. The Netherlands has a strong tradition of community support. For example, one company, Gist-Brocades (a bio-chemical company), saw that it was unable to help reduce unemployment directly because so many local people were poorly educated and, thus, unemployable. It therefore decided to offer 0.5 per cent of its total wage bill to projects for the long-term uneducated unemployed in the Delft region where it is located, with the aim of creating several hundred jobs.

For society at large, enterprises cooperate with the government to define the socio-economic policy of the country. Einerhand says that this 'influence cannot be underestimated'. For instance, part-time work was encouraged through the trade agreements to promote a better integration of women within the labour market. Arrangements were made so that part-time work was possible for *all* jobs in enterprises unless the interests of the enterprise would be damaged.

Internationally, one of the world's largest TNCs – the Dutch–UK corporation Royal Dutch Shell (see Chapter 5), based in Rotterdam – has been active in examining its social actions globally, and this initiative has been given extra impetus from the public scrutiny earned from the *Brent Spar* fiasco. To date, Dutch firms such as Shell and Philips have been known for their social responsibility at home – for instance, Shell runs the Shell Technology Enterprise Programme (STEP), which aims to help small firms solve practical problems by providing students to work on real projects during their school work-experience programmes. Under the programme, job opportunities for graduates in the small business sector are also identified. Each student is paid US$150 a week, usually funded partly by the host company and partly by the local training and enterprise council. In addition to tangible learning opportunities, STEP helps to build excellent links between business and local students.[20] In the UK, Shell, through its Better Britain Campaign, has a scheme for providing support for community-based environmental projects, now in its third decade, and in Germany *Jugendwerk der Deutsche Shell* is one of the main community initiatives. It plays a major role in youth research and has also been committed to road safety training for more than 40 years.[21]

Gradually, however, Dutch TNCs are looking at their international operations outside of the industrialized world, not only in the environmental sphere but also in the area of social responsibility. They have seen that consumers in the Netherlands simply will not accept exploitation of workers in poorer countries, especially children. But they have also seen that involving local communities in their operations internationally is good for business because it helps to develop a loyal and motivated local workforce.

Switzerland

Switzerland is known as the seat of financial capitalism and had, until recently, a reputation as a safe haven for capital. The fact that this safe haven was used by dictators such as Mobutu of Zaire and Marcos of the Philippines to hide their personal wealth, together with concerns during the late 1990s about the unclaimed bank accounts of Jews exterminated by the Germans in World War II, has left its worldwide reputation damaged. Yet, unlike neighbouring France, the Swiss have an enviable reputation on environmental regulation.

Migros, the nationwide supermarket chain, has an unspoilt and worldwide reputation for corporate responsibility and philanthropy. Through a 'cultural levy' placed upon the goods and services that Migros offers, it supports a wide variety of social causes:[22]

- *Alleviation of drug problems*: Migros's contribution to solving the drug problem was mainly in the form of financial support for projects connected with prevention, treatment and research.
- *Foreigners in Switzerland* aims to promote constructive cooperation with non-Swiss nationals working and living in the country.
- *Migros against Unemployment* aims to help tackle unemployment in Switzerland through a programme designed to create employment both within and outside of its operations.
- *Women Speak Up* is a course run by Migros to help put men and women on an equal footing by allowing female employees to receive training in speech and communication.
- *Quality in Social Work* was an initiative in which 350 participants from professions and institutions connected with social services accepted an invitation to three conferences on the theme of qualitative development of social services.
- *Health and Agility in Old Age* provided programmes focusing on nutrition, movement and relaxation in an 'Active Holiday Prospectus' for old people. The advisory service was also extended to, and aided, the Czech Republic.

However, ethical reflection in matters of investment is still embryonic, according to the Swiss Bank with the curious name of Banque Scandinavie en Suisse. This has an ethical investment fund and believes that CSR issues are at a similar stage as the musings on ecology were some 15 years ago. Today, the terms of ethical policy still depend largely on the management's sense of values; but more and more companies are intent on giving themselves a set of written rules of ethics that ensures socially responsible behaviour.

Previously, Nestlé a company of 230,000 employees and 12,000 products, with headquarters but very little else in Vevey near Montreux, was known for the slogan 'It kills babies' through a massive activist campaign aiming for Nestlé to promote breast-feeding in the developing world, instead of encouraging mothers to use its milk powder products. Stung by this, Nestlé has made huge efforts to change its image and has signed a business charter for sustainable development. It has also made halting steps toward the publication of a social report with its *Nestlé in the Community* publication that describes its philanthropic activities in 65 countries.[23]

Sustainable development is also an issue for Sandoz, which now attaches considerably more attention to environmental questions since it polluted the Rhine River some years ago – the Schweizerhalle catastrophe. However, according to the Swiss InfoCenter, a Swiss consultancy on corporate responsibility for investors, the Sandoz group has 'two different faces'.[24] On the one hand, it shows a progressive sensitivity for ecological issues; on the other, it has little to boast about on the social front. It is organized along strict hierarchic lines, it knows no strikes and is 'paternalistic...hardly ambitious in social partnership matters', says the InfoCenter. Recently, it joined with Ciba-Geigy to form the chemical giant Novartis. But little evidence of CSR emanates from its company reports to date, although there are plans to work towards a code of ethics and best practice. Curiously, of the nine Swiss enterprises examined in Chapter 9 with data from the InfoCenter, Novartis is ranked the highest. This suggests either that Novartis has cleaned up its image since it absorbed Ciba-Geigy, or else that it is simply the best of a poor bunch.

In June 2002, the Swiss Stock Exchange published a directive on corporate governance and, at the same time, the federal union of employers (La Fédération des Syndicats Patronaux Suisses) adopted a code of good conduct. Neither of these texts, however, had legal force and only applied to those companies quoted on the Swiss Stock Exchange who had to either apply or explain why they did not. Moreover, Swiss law applied to enterprises tends to protect majority shareholders and, to a lesser extent, minority shareholders. But nothing in the two texts published covered issues of stakeholder management as applied, for example, to workers, suppliers, civil society or the environment.[25]

Ireland

In Ireland, social initiatives by individual enterprises beyond what is an integral part of the employment contract are not widespread.[26] The social responsibility of enterprises in these areas is exercised through their representation in the social partnership mechanisms that exist at both national and local levels. At the national level, these are carried out through the National and Economic Social Council (NESC), formed in 1973 to advise the government on social and economic policy, and through the negotiation of the multi-annual national agreements on economic and social issues that have been continually negotiated since 1987. According to J S O'Connor of the NESC, much of the success of the Irish economy over the past decade can be attributed to the social partnership approach of 1987.

In addition, there is a wide range of locally based initiatives in the urban and rural areas in Ireland. While unemployment, particularly long-term unemployment, is the key motivating factor, there is, increasingly, a broader focus adopted in the local development effort. So, while social initiatives by individual enterprises in employment, education and welfare beyond what is integral to the employment contract are not typical in Ireland, employer representative bodies are, nonetheless, involved in social activities – both at a national level through social partnership mechanisms and at local level through support for, and participation in, local development initiatives.

In concluding this chapter, it is noteworthy that socially responsible initiatives are becoming increasingly widespread within the industrialized countries covered here. Steps outside of these countries to focus on wider international issues are slowly emerging. The governments themselves are beginning to be involved in the international social arena through the child labour initiative of the International Labour Organization (ILO) and, in the same organization, through international labour laws. Worldwide, TNCs are increasingly becoming involved in social issues through such bodies as the Caux Roundtable, the European Business Network for Social Cohesion (EBNSC), the Global Reporting Initiative (GRI), EU guidelines on CSR and the UN Global Compact, as well as through the large number of TNC business networks that have sprung up in the last five years or so. The experiences documented here show a considerable awareness of social responsibility issues within the countries considered. However, national-level indicators of the type proposed in Chapter 8 to measure different aspects of social responsibility are not generally available. Consequently, the discussion in this chapter has had to remain more at the anecdotal level than I would have liked.

Chapter 7

Frameworks to Measure Corporate Social Responsibility

Introduction

One of the tasks of this book is to identify a set of indicators that can be used to measure the different aspects of social responsibility of enterprises. Most of the work in this area to date has been in developing indicators within a social audit framework, or within screens designed to identify ethical investments. Before I present some of the theoretical work that has been carried out to underpin a set of indicators (in Chapter 8), and then attempt to apply these indicators in an empirical setting (in Chapter 9), I discuss, in this chapter, first, the social audit framework and, second, a number of the most prominent social screens.

The social audit framework

Social auditing (SA), according to the New Economics Foundation (NEF), is a process of defining, observing and reporting measures of the ethical behaviour and social impact of an organization in relation to its aims and those of its stakeholders. The methodology of SA has been developed further and given prominence in the UK by the NEF – who, itself, pioneered the application of social auditing to enterprises – and by Traidcraft, a small fair-trade organization with annual sales of around £6 million. Traidcraft published its first SA report in 1994, which was based on a consultation process with all of the stakeholder groups of the firm through questionnaires, one-to-one and group interviews, seminars and workshops.

SA is an approach to assess how a company's ethical and social aims, values and principles are implemented within the company procedures and actions, and SA attempts to take a comprehensive point of view. Through the SA process, an organization is able to set up its own indicators to assess the social performance achieved by the organization in the observed period (usually on a yearly basis). SA reports are published and validated by external institutions. A critical point of SA is benchmarking, which makes comparison between organizations and reference to best practices.

Accountability 1000

In 1996 the social audit activities of NEF were grouped under the umbrella of a new organization, the Institute for Social and Ethical Accountability (ISEA).[1] In November 1999 it launched AccountAbility 1000 (AA1000), and several large companies have referred to its use in their social reports (for example, British Airways (BA), The Co-operative Bank, Ford Motor Company, TXU Europe and Van City). One of the core components of AA1000 was stakeholder dialogue. However, many companies found difficulty in converting stakeholder dialogue into effective decision-making; therefore, the ISEA announced the launch of AA2000, in 2001, to provide more explicit guidance on stakeholder engagement and its assessment. Realizing that the new 'number' was confusing, AccountAbility went back to AA1000 and have since concentrated on revising and updating the instrument. AccountAbility now proposes to provide guidance on how to link to other corporate social responsibility (CSR) management tools that have been announced in recent years – such as the Global Reporting Initiative (GRI), the Sustainability: Integrated Guidelines for Management (SIGMA) Project, the Balanced Scorecard and other initiatives.[2]

AccountAbility has linked up with the GRI since the GRI is rapidly gaining ground (see below), and companies are becoming increasingly bemused at the number of standards and principles that are entering the arena. Which of the various standards or guidelines to use is confusing to many companies, especially as differences in the standards are often minor.

Ethical accounting statement

Similar to SA is the ethical accounting statement (EAS), which was developed at the Copenhagen Business School by the researchers Peter Pruzan and Ole Thyssen. It was first adopted by the SBN Bank, the seventh largest Danish bank, which published its first EAS in 1990.[3] Since then, roughly 50 private and public enterprises in Denmark have developed EASs. Like SA, the EAS is based upon the stakeholder approach. It provides measures of how well an organization lives up to the shared values it has committed itself to follow through an extensive analysis ('conversation process') of all the stakeholders' perspectives of the firm. EASs are published each year. The limits of an EAS are that it is not externally validated – although it is claimed that this is not needed in such a homogeneous and strong cultural context as exists in Danish society. The EAS approach also rejects any external bench-marking, arguing that this form of comparability is largely meaningless.

Global reporting initiative

A third type of SA is the social statement, which is common in the US and was originally developed with the company Ben & Jerry's. In the early days of the GRI, a distinguished person was invited to investigate any aspect of the company's activities and then to report as he or she wished. This approach fell into disrepute because it did not lead to the establishment of a systematic approach to social book-keeping, which is an evolving and important feature of the other two approaches.[4]

SA has been around for many years, particularly in the US, and, as Ackerman and Bauer noted in the mid 1970s:

> The origins, responsibility and credit for many of these emerging ideas are impossible to document. There is an invisible college of corporate staff, professionals, public accountants and academics who have been sharing and shaping ideas in recent years to the extent that the assignment of individual credit would probably be inappropriate even where it conceivably could be done.[5]

A structure for an SA was given by these two authors in the shape of a matrix. Here, a row represents one of the constituencies that we now call stakeholders (I have defined seven in Chapter 3) and a column represents one of the company's main activities (products, production, marketing, finance, facility location, research and development, new business development, government relations, and special programmes). In each of the cells there would be a verbal statement, quantified as much as possible, where the firm would seriously consider the consequences of its actions.[6] 'The ultimate social audit would be a matrix of this sort with all the entries in the cells completed – another mind-boggling proposition to contemplate,' say Ackerman and Bauer; but they also believe that concentration on these areas of interaction in the matrix between business and its stakeholders will 'not only prove useful in the long run for understanding the evolving corporate role, it will also be useful in the short run in considering immediate problems of corporate responsiveness'.

The GRI found that having its roots in the Coalition for Environmentally Responsible Economies (CERES) environmental principles has caused it to become one, if not *the*, standard for social, environmental and economic reporting. Interest in its principles and application is rapidly growing, as can be attested by a recent working group meeting in London where around 100 participants gathered from around the world to work out precise indicators so that, at a minimum, companies would know what to report.[7] The GRI was established in late 1997 to develop globally applicable guidelines for reporting on economic, environmental and social performance, initially for corporations and eventually for any business, governmental or non-governmental organization (NGO).

The GRI's reporting guidelines were released in March 1999. In 2002, the GRI established itself, with headquarters in Amsterdam, as a permanent, independent, international body with a multi-stakeholder governance structure. Its core mission is to maintain, enhance, and disseminate its guidelines through a process of ongoing consultation and stakeholder engagement. Specifically, the GRI's goals are to:

■ elevate sustainability reporting practices worldwide to a level equivalent to financial reporting;
■ design, disseminate and promote standardized reporting practices, core measurements and customized sector-specific measurements; and
■ ensure a permanent and effective institutional host to support such reporting practices worldwide.

On the basis of this vision, the United Nations Foundation awarded a US$3 million partnership grant to CERES and the United Nations Environment Programme (UNEP) to support GRI activities. To date, GRI claims to have around 80 companies from industrialized countries who have used the principles in one way or another. To ensure that other standards and principles are included (some might say, to ensure a take-over bid in the social reporting area), the GRI has included, on its steering group, members from each of the pre-eminent standard forming bodies – namely:

■ The Global Compact.
■ AA1000.
■ ISO14000.
■ Organisation for Economic Co-operation and Development (OECD) guidelines for multinational enterprises (MNEs).
■ Social Accountability 8000 (SA8000).
■ The Global Sullivan Principles.

Since the GRI found its roots in environmental reporting, the environment and the word 'sustainability' have been at the core of its efforts. However, in its published guidelines it has made halting steps to enter the economic and social spheres. Its measurement working group has embarked on an ambitious attempt to find a number of core indicators that corporations can adopt. These cover the three areas of economic, social and environment, which are further divided into three groups each covering, in the social area, issues such as labour rights, human rights and community development. The economic group is particularly interesting as it attempts to look at both the direct and indirect effects of economic and financial variables on a company's stakeholders.

The strength of the GRI is its attempt to include stakeholders from all walks of life in its deliberations. This strength is also its weakness. Its reporting and measurement guidelines appear to get longer and longer so as to accommodate all points of view; but they lack a succinct theory in which it could prioritize its concerns. The costs of implementing a full set of GRI guidelines and indicators for a company from scratch are likely to be significant. What happens, in practice, is that companies tend to select those parts of the GRI that they can quickly accomplish. Consequently, an aim of the GRI to produce comparable social reports between companies will be difficult to achieve.

But, at time of writing, there is no doubt that the GRI is currently the most widely encompassing framework to asses and measure CSR, of all that exist. Its attempt to devise a set of indicators so that companies can report on progress in meeting 'triple bottom line' (TBL) objectives is not without its critics, however.[8] Deloitte Touche have stated:

> *We do believe that the core indicators required by the '2002 Exposure Draft' are too voluminous and will discourage too many organizations from even attempting to report under the GRI guidelines. Further, we believe that the required boundaries of a sustainability report should not exceed the reporting entity's circle of control because it is unlikely that the reporting entity would have the ability to obtain the requisite information or determine its accuracy. Management may present supplementary, or additional, information on such matters, where relevant. We are concerned that the GRI is proceeding down a path of attempting to make a sustainability report be everything to everyone, rather than focusing on how the reporting entity's sustainability performance can be measured overall. While we recognize that the latter form of a sustainability report will not suit each and every stakeholder's perceived needs, we believe it will result in a far more meaningful presentation.[9]*

Nike, too, were critical but appreciated GRI's flexibility:

> *The depth of the questions is overwhelming at times; however, the flexibility allowed by the structure makes the GRI more digestible and tenable than most surveys. It can also serve as a useful catalyst in engaging internal leaders in substantive discussion around governance and triple bottom-line accountabilities.[10]*

A useful framework for considering codes of conduct is developed by Donna Wood and is one on which I have developed a number of indicators (Chapter 8 describes this framework in more detail). It is also multi-stakeholder in concept.[11] In this conceptual model, the following questions are asked: does the company have a clear statement of principles; is this followed by a number of processes to implement these principles; and what outputs can be measured? Thus, CSR is measured following a business organization's configuration into three levels – the triple-P approach to CSR:

1 Principles of social responsibility.
2 Processes of social responsiveness.
3 Products (or outcomes) as they relate to the firm's societal relationships.

These can then be further divided, naturally, into the principles, processes and outcomes for each stakeholder group. The GRI, in fact, implicitly uses this approach but gets a little confused by jumping in the TBL bed. That latter notion was developed by John Elkington in his innovative book *Cannibals with Forks* to describe his own process from the environmental field into the wider fields of social and economic considerations.[12] Given that GRI took its first steps in the environmental field since it grew out of the environmental CERES principles, it is not surprising that it is a little hamstrung by environmental considerations.

The TBL approach is simply too confusing, and intellectually suspect, as a basis for a code of conduct. The initial attraction, of course, is that TBL appears to neatly bring in concerns of the environment and society alongside the usual business notions of profitability and other economic concerns (the economic bottom line). However, the TBL concept suffers from, at least, four main difficulties. First, companies simply cannot put profitability on the same level as social and environmental concerns; a company cannot survive by either behaving socially or environmentally responsibly while making losses. Second, social and environmental benefits tend to be long term before impacting on stakeholder values. Third, TBL equates social with environmental aspects; social clearly encompasses environmental as one among many other concerns. Fourth, the notion of stakeholders is not necessarily defined in the TBL approach

Social Accountability 8000

The US Council on Economic Priorities (CEP) has also helped to extend the frontiers of SA further. It has formed the Council on Economic Priorities Accreditation Agency (CEPAA), now renamed Social Accountability International (SAI), which has developed a new international standard, SA8000, to which around 100 companies had been audited as of early 2002 in companies outside of the US.[13] The standard is based upon conventions of the International Labour Organization (ILO) and other major rights conventions.[14] It sets out auditable requirements on a broad range of issues – child labour, health and safety, freedom of association, right to collective bargaining, discrimination, disciplinary practices, working hours and remuneration (wages to meet basic needs). This standard takes a little further the idea of Ralph Estes and the Stakeholder Alliance on 'sunshine standards' for corporate reporting to stakeholders.[15] Estes believes that vital social responsibility information should be made available in each corporation's annual report to stakeholders. He cites Ben & Jerry's social report to its stakeholders as the best so far, with General Motors' (GM's) public interest report as a strong candidate for the worst example. The sunshine standards cover information needs for customers, employees, communities and society.

What is the difference between this initiative and the ILO standards, such as ILO Conventions 29 and 105 on forced and bonded labour, or ILO Convention 98 on the right of workers to collective bargaining? The difference is more in application than in content. Like the chief executive officer (CEO) proposals, adherence to ILO standards is purely voluntary; though many nations have signed the conventions, fewer have passed them into national laws. The ILO has never applied nor analysed standards to, and about, enterprises. This is because, to date, employers' organizations within the ILO form a powerful pressure group who has always resisted this (see Chapter 4). The ILO secretariat, as noted before, has also been reluctant to carry out independent research in this area, again because of pressure from its members, whether anticipated or actual. An independent body such as the CEP does not have to subscribe to such pressures and therefore will, eventually, be able to carry out independent verification of adherence to many of the things that the ILO and the United Nations (UN) promote but do not have the teeth to carry out. This is not the fault of the ILO or the UN per se; as international organizations, they have to balance the competing demands of all of the nations in the world with the trade union movement and employer organizations.

SA8000 is not without its critics either and has been criticized for shifting responsibility from multinational corporations to their suppliers, and for its reliance on auditors not specifically trained in auditing labour practices.[16]

Suggested cost-and-benefit framework

The disadvantage of SA, unlike the standard audit of a company, is that it does not focus on one or, at most, two figures.[17] The standard audit focuses on the profit-and-loss account of a company, which is relatively simple to grasp (it has a lot of detail that is not so simple to grasp); but the social audit cannot focus on just one or two indicators to judge the success or failure of a social audit. This raises the wider question of when enough is enough. In other words, how socially responsible does a company have to be before it is in an acceptable position of social responsibility? Obviously, it would be absurd for a company to, for instance, devote all of its profits to charity or allow all of its staff to work continually for the local community. There are, of course, two sides to this. The quantifiable side, for instance, deals with what percentage of profits goes to charity, and the qualitative side is concerned with issues such as how embedded in the company's ethos is the notion of social responsibility. SA is nowhere near addressing such questions. It also smacks of control, suspicion and criticism, as does, for instance, a normal company audit. Should social audits be compulsory? Moves are afoot to make this happen, with the French government prominent in its initiatives. Over time, there is not much doubt that other countries will also require social audits for companies headquartered in their country. Social audits help further the notion of a planetary bargain; but care in legislation must be taken to ensure that companies are not disadvantaged internationally. There is also the problem, of course, of which framework to adhere to.

More work is also required to assess the costs and benefits of investments in social responsibility. One way of addressing this could be through qualifying the contribution of social responsibility to the social capital of a firm.[18] Another way is to use a matrix of the type displayed here (see Table 7.1) and to quantify each of the individual contributions.[19] This forms part of the research programme at our centre for research.[20]

Ethical screens and rankings

Ethical screens are used by investment funds to decide whether or not to include a company in an investment portfolio. Normally, they exclude companies who fail certain tests – for instance, because they produce armaments. Thus, some of the indicators are binary – that is, does the company do something or not? Others provide a subjective judgement on a scale of 1–5. Rarely is quantitative data on an interval scale used (for example, the company gives x per cent of its pre-tax profits to communities).[21] At least five ranking or rating systems are widely known and have gained a degree of acceptability. These are the Fortune 500 Reputation Ranking, the CEP Screen, the Domini 400 Social Index (DSI), the Business Ethics 100 and the Dow Jones Sustainability Index (DJSI). They differ widely in intent and methodology. New ethical investment funds, and therefore screens, crop up all the time – the UK's FTSE4good described in Chapter 5 is an example of a recently launched screen that has risen to prominence (in the summer of 2001) and is widely quoted because both the reputable newspaper the *Financial Times* and the London Stock Exchange (LSE) are behind it.

Table 7.1 *CSR and profits: Likely benefits and costs*

Stakeholder group	Benefits	Costs
Directors	More independent non-executive directors	More meetings and briefings
Shareholders	Increased investment from ethically based pension funds	CSR premium on all company activities, such as increased reporting costs, more openness, etc
Managers	Better human resources (HR) policies lead to increased motivation	Increased training in ethics
	More awareness of ethical issues from focus-group sessions lead to more confidence about employees	Focus group sessions and reporting
Employees	Better HR polices lead to increased motivation	Inclusion of ethics training
	Good ethical conduct by superiors leads to improved productivity	More intra-company communications
	Less labour relations disputes Less strikes	
	Better working conditions	More effort on labour relations
	Good CSR company leads to easier recruitment of high fliers and young people	
	Reduced costs of recruitment	
Customers	Move to ethical consumption captured by company	Costs of goods may increase in the short term
	Less disputes	
	Advertising can cite CSR image	
Subcontractors/ suppliers	Better quality inputs	Cost of inputs may increase in the short term
	Less harmful effect on 'public image'	
Community	More willingness to accept new investments	Requires continual interaction with communities
	Improved public image	Will need to produce CSR report
		Will need to monitor internal activities
		Costs associated with human rights policy
Government	More confidence in company	Costs of adhering to new regulations will increase
	Fewer legal battles	
	No new potentially harmful legislation	
	More favourable trading regime	
	More willingness to accept expansion or downsizing	
Environment	Less legal battles	Investment in environmental damage control
	Improved public image	
	Contribution to sustainability of company	

The Fortune reputation ranking

Fortune magazine publishes its 'Corporate Reputation Survey' annually of 'America's most admired corporations'. This is based on an opinion poll of over 8000 senior executives, outside directors and financial analysts. More than 300 companies in 32 industries are included in the list. The Fortune survey measures such subjective attributes as:

- quality of management;
- quality of products;
- innovation;
- long-term investment value;
- financial soundness;
- ability to attract and retain talented people;
- responsibility to the community and environment; and
- wise use of corporate assets.

Multiple regression analysis is applied to the poll's data to obtain a reputation rating on a scale from 1 (lowest) to 10 (highest). Given that the poll's respondents are senior executives, outside directors and financial analysts, it is not surprising that 'quality of management' is considered the most important attribute of corporate reputation.

The primary advantage of this scale is that it serves as an opinion poll of senior decision-makers, and gives some clues as to their own biases and preferences. However, as a means of ranking *social performance*, it falls down. On this scale, an arms manufacturer can rank among the top five companies, even though the very nature of its business may exclude it from socially responsible investment portfolios. In a similar fashion, it is difficult to discern which is better, a firm with mediocre scores on all the measures or one with widely varying scores – for example, a very high financial performance and very low community performance.

The US Council on Economic Priorities' screens

The US Council on Economic Priorities' (CEP's) current screen research 9 evaluates nearly 700 US companies in ten issue areas, covering the environment, equal employment opportunity, employee relations, community involvement, weapons contracts and animal testing. In addition, 'extras' highlight such issues as nuclear power, product safety, tobacco production and sourcing guidelines. The CEP has produced a 'sin' list that highlights companies involved in tobacco, alcohol, nuclear and weapons-related activities. The CEP reports on these companies to its members, who may, or may not, use the information for investment decisions. It does not have an investment portfolio itself.

The CEP has also recently developed and applied indicators for 321 companies in the US, and its first screen, a social screen, is to be released in 'issue area format'. The screen provides both a quantitative and a qualitative analysis of different equal employment opportunities (EEOs). It has three main parts. One provides the number of employees disaggregated by sex, ethnicity and managerial status (board member, corporate officer, top 25 paid, officials and managers). The second covers whether it is mentioned in any of seven other rankings – *Working Mother* magazine's 100 best companies; does it have public release of EEO type data; in an equality's buyers' guide; non-discriminatory policy for sexual orientation; the Department of Labor (DOL) working women's honour roll; in *Hispanic* magazine's top 25 recruiters; in *Hispanic* magazine's top 75 companies. The third part provides grades on a five-point scale for the companies' responses to a number of questions, such as: does the company have special programmes for purchasing from minority or women company owners; or does the company provide diversity awareness training for all employees; or does the company recognize gay and lesbian employee groups? Some corporate managers may blink at a number of these questions, and wonder whether they are really necessary to run a socially responsible company. Indicators that concern more frequently required social data, such as social charges, paid maternity leave, hiring and firing policy, career development plans and salary scales, appear to be missing from the CEP's list.

The Domini 400 Social Index

Kinder, Lydenberg & Domini (KLD) have created perhaps the best database on companies (mainly US based) so as to construct the DSI. It is an index of 400 common company stocks based on their performance on multiple applications of the KLD 'social performance screens'. KLD's business earns its income by providing advice to investors who have an interest in investing partly on ethical concerns and partly on making a return on their investment.

The DSI is based on the idea that socially or ethically concerned investors will choose products and companies that have favourable social 'performance' (KLD's term) and adequate financial performance competitive with overall market performance. The advantages of this index are that it can help to influence (in terms of promoting socially responsible business decisions) institutional investors, such as pension plans. The administrators of such funds are *ethically* responsible with regard to CSR, but they are also *legally* responsible for sound financial decisions. Hence, an ethical decision must also be a financially wise decision.

KLD has constructed seven 'social screens'.[22] The establishment of these screens did not result from empirical research but is, rather, largely intuitive or derived from market research among investors who are deemed socially conscious. There are six screens in the system that allow for an actual weighted ranking to be given to a company, and one screen that is intended to simply eliminate companies from further consideration. Each of the six primary screens is divided into two sets of indicators: 'areas of concern', which are negative but not exclusionary, and 'areas of strength', which yield positive numerical rankings. Nominally, each screen ultimately provides a ranking of 0, 1 or 2 in each of the concern/strength areas. In reports issued by KLD on individual companies, these ratings are amplified in a narrative report that explains the bases for the rankings. If there is no indication of a numerical ranking, then the issue is essentially neutral for that firm. KLD does not publish the details of its own ranking system, or how it determined the 'weighting' of elements.

There are some significant omissions in the KLD approach. Corporate philanthropy is not given sufficient attention, nor is who decides on the amount or direction of gifts. While some criteria (1.5 per cent of pre-tax earnings) are provided, only the directionality (education, housing and so on) is given, and we have no idea of any practical outcomes of such giving. Under the 'employee relations' screen, unions, employee ownership, layoffs and hiring practices are covered; but actual salary level (in comparison, for example, with industry levels) is not mentioned. Nor is there any indicator that reflects empowerment of employees in the firm's decision-making. A firm who is screened might be located in an 'open shop' state, and thus union relations would receive no rating and salaries might be very low in comparison with the industry. This was, for example, the case with the textile industry in the southern US until unionization took place during the early 1960s.

A major omission is in the area of non-US operations. In 1994, the founders of KLD, Peter Kinder, Steven Lydenberg and Amy Domini, published their book *Investing for Good*.[23] There, they expanded upon their statement that 'data are less complete and more difficult to interpret', noting six restraints on providing adequate information to the international social investor, as expressed by the following questions:

- Do the words in the reports mean the same thing to me as they do to the issuer?
- Do the accounting categories and conventions correspond to US practice?
- Does the issuer's home country, its country of domicile, require it to report to securities holders at the same level that the US does?
- Will the reports indicate whether the company passes KLD's social screens?
- Do reliable external sources of information exist on the application of screens to the company?
- Are the screens that are applied in the US applied in the same way outside of the US?

KLD says that the answers to all these questions are 'no'. They go on to identify several international screening issues. Among these are human rights, operations in Northern Ireland and operations and investments in the People's Republic of China. They point out, however, that these are very difficult screens to shape and even more difficult to measure. They fall back from the possibility, for example, of using the criteria applied by Amnesty International for 'human rights and oppressive governments'; or the principles developed about whether and how a firm does business in a country who is popularly accepted as having an oppressive government, known as the MacBride Principles in Northern Ireland and the Sullivan Principles in South Africa. The potential danger here lies in the fact that the UK government would not accept that its activities in Northern Ireland were, at one time, akin to a 'repressive regime', or in the fact that South Africa is no longer an oppressive regime. To date, as seen with the difficulties faced by Andrew Young with Nike (see Chapter 5), and as will be seen with the controversy surrounding the use of child labour, these issues are not straightforward, and continue to be elusive and subjective for screens such as KLD.

By and large, the KLD indicators within the social screens fit into the corporate social performance (CSP) model (see Chapter 8) at the level of 'process' – the second level – which concerns policies and processes that flow, in turn, from an explicit or implicit set of social principles. In so doing, the KLD approach *implies* principles that are, or are not (to a greater or lesser degree) socially responsible. However, the indicators largely reflect the current attitudes of the investing community. These indicators appear to be fairly basic and representative; but, upon closer examination, there seem to be four problems.

First, other indicators could have been chosen to replace the ones used with an equal justification (or without justification). Second, as the screens remain at the *second* level of the CSP model, we are uncertain about the *outcomes* of any socially positive policies. Third, the *details* of measurement are not stated, nor do we understand why certain cut-off points were chosen. For example, an 'area of strength' in corporate giving is said to be higher than 1.5 per cent of pre-tax earnings. Ben & Jerry's Homemade, when operating as an individual company, gave 7.5 per cent of pre-tax earnings. Does this relatively larger share mean that Ben & Jerry's is *more* socially responsible? Fourth, each of the screens, and most indicators within each screen, that are applied appear to be given equal weighting.

KLD's 'areas of concern' carry the same problems; but a few more objectively measurable items are provided, such as 'fines over US$100,000'. Among the positive screens, there are many phrases such as 'strong union relations' that one assumes to be KLD's subjective judgement call and is meant to be accepted on faith in the rater.

KLD gathers the information for its database through two groups of sources. One is data that is publicly available and is taken from legally required information supplied to tax and regulatory agencies, as well as any other public information, such as newspapers and magazines – including, of course, corporate publications of all sorts. Secondly, KLD also polls the 400 companies in the DSI directly, both for the purpose of preparing individual firm reports and to give the firm the opportunity to review the report before it is published. This is the most significant database on social responsibility available. As such, it is a vital source of information to the researcher.

There is no doubt that the KLD/DSI work provides a large base for further research, as well as providing a valuable service to the investing community. The DSI index does not rate 400 companies 'from 1 through 400' on the basis of *social responsibility*; rather, it ranks them, as a whole, on *financial performance*, the second variable of interest to the ethical investor. Each company is given a rating based on its known performance under the screens used. The investor may then compare each company with its financial performance so as to arrive at an ethical portfolio. For the present, the success of KLD indicates the satisfaction of the investing community with its system.[24] And, as Steve Lydenberg wrote to me when I asked him about using the KLD indicators to rank companies on the basis of their social responsibility:

> *You're raising an important topic, near and dear to me. This is an area I've been working in and around now for more than 25 years and I have many (often contradictory) opinions on it. I'm not sure where to start. While at KLD I was instrumental in developing their profiling criteria [see the KLD Research & Analytics and Domini Social Investment websites, www.kld.com and www.domini.com]. This methodology isn't really a set of standards, but rather a practical way of presenting an objective snapshot of a company's CSR profile at a given moment. One of the questions you run into immediately is the difference between aspirational indicators and practical ones (also known as subjective and objective indicators). One thing I think is fair to say about indicators is that they are a means of defining corporations' proper relationship to society. The perception (and actuality) of the appropriateness of that relationship will vary from person to person, country to country, culture to culture, issue to issue, as well as over time. Consequently, I'm of the general position that a comprehensive, definitive set global CSR standards, as admirable as they might sound, are a bit of a red herring. If you believe that one global standard for CSR is achievable on all CSR issues everywhere, then constructing a comprehensive set of CSR standards makes sense. In my view, whoever has the political muscle will ultimately win that game. I'm not sure appropriateness will*

necessarily win out. Consequently, I'm not a fan of comprehensive global standards. However, minimal globally accepted standards on a limited number of issues do make sense (create a level playing field and then let variations thrive). I'm more of this philosophical inclination.[25]

Business Ethics

Business Ethics, an excellent US-based monthly magazine covering ethical issues, publishes on an annual basis a list of 100 of 'America's most profitable and socially responsible companies'.[26] To do this, they collect the names of more than 1000 public companies deemed socially responsible by authoritative sources on the subject – the CEP, KLD, Clean Yield and books such as *The 100 Best Companies to Work for in America*.[27] Their approach, in 1996, was eclectic. They weeded out firms who did not respond to a mail survey (to which 500 *did* respond in 1996), firms who gave information in less than three social fields, and also firms who had been non-profitable in the previous five years. Each company's social criteria were then given points on a scale of 1–10 and the result was averaged to find the company's rank. These individual scores were not documented, unfortunately; but *Business Ethics* did, and still does, present numerous indicators that are used as part of its ranking process. As well as indicators on profits, revenue, market capitalization and earnings per share, the social indicators are number of employees; percentage owning stock; percentage of pre-tax profit to charity; the Investor Responsibility Research Center's (IRRC's) tracked reduction in toxic emissions over 1988–1992; percentage of women on board; percentage of minorities on board; percentage of women employees; whether or not the firm employs an ethics officer; whether it has an ethics programme; whether it has gay partner benefits; whether it conducts sexual orientation training; how many jobs were cut within the past year; the CEO's pay; and the CEO's bonus.

Thus, no theory underlined the choice of indicators at the time. *Business Ethics* essentially made do with what it could find. In the event, its ten top-rated companies in 1996 were:

1   St Paul Companies.
2   Honeywell Inc.
3   Ben & Jerry's.
4   Fuller (HB) Company.
5   Adolph Coors Co.
6   TRW Inc.
7   Northern States Power Co.
8   Frontier Corp.
9   Becton Dickinson & Co.
10 Bell Atlantic.

By 2002, *Business Ethics* changed its methodology or, rather, developed a much improved one that might help to explain why only one of the top ten in the 1996 list figured in even the top 100 companies in the 2002 list. The top-rated companies in 2002 were:

1   IBM.
2   Hewlett Packard.
3   Fannie Mae.
4   St Paul Companies.
5   Procter and Gamble.
6   Motorola.
7   Cummins Engine.
8   Herman Miller.
9   General Mills Inc.
10 Avon products.

The 2002 methodology was developed by Samuel Graves and Sandra Waddock of Boston University, along with *Business Ethic's* editor Marjorie Kelly. Briefly, the essence of their definition of corporate citizenship (they don't like the phrase CSR) is based upon seven measures, reflecting quality of service to seven stakeholder groups: stockholders; community; minorities and women; employees; environment; non-US stakeholders; and customers. All data cover the three-year period of 1998–2000. Stockholder data represents a three-year average of total return to shareholders (capital gains plus dividends), using figures from the Center for Research in Security Prices (CRSP), Standard & Poor's (S&P's) statistical service COMPUSTAT and Morningstar. Any companies with losses in 2000 were eliminated. Social data came from KLD Research & Analytics in Boston, using their six social categories as described above. Since all seven variables have different scales, they were standardized. In the final step, an unweighted average of the seven measures is taken to yield a single score for each company. The fact that the scale is unweighted means that all stakeholders have equal status.

    After initial rankings are established, database search of news sources on each company is made to look for significant scandals or improprieties not detected in the KLD data. A handful of companies are dropped.

Dow Jones Sustainability Index (DJSI)

This index was launched by a small company, Sustainability Asset Management Group (SAM), based in Zurich at the end of 1999.[28] It was established to track the performance of companies who lead the field in terms of corporate sustainability. All indexes of the DJSI family are assessed according to the same corporate sustainability methodology and respective criteria. The global indexes, the Dow Jones Sustainability World

Indexes (DJSI World), consist of a composite index and five narrower, specialized indexes, excluding companies who generate revenue from alcohol, tobacco, gambling, armaments and firearms or all of these industries. A set of European indexes, the Dow Jones STOXX Sustainability Indexes (DJSI STOXX), was launched in 2001.

The DJSI is a true index in the sense that it is an interval-scaled number based upon a methodology that allocates scores to a number of attributes of a given company. FTSE4good, for instance, is an index of share price performance of the companies who are included in the screen. Consequently, FTSE4good is not a 'true' index of sustainability or CSR. Thus, DJSI can rank companies according to SAM's perception of a companies sustainability – what I call sustainability** that includes social, economic and environmental criteria (see Chapter 3).

Its economic criteria covers the organizational structure, planning processes and governance of a company, and also how a company adapts to the changing demands, sustainability trends and macro-economic driving forces. Its environmental criteria cover the environmental management and performance of a company. These criteria reflect a company's efforts to reduce and avoid environmental pollution while, at the same time, benefiting from the new developments and technologies aimed at reducing resource use and environmental impacts. Its social criteria cover both internal (employee relations, labour practices) and external (stakeholder, community relations) aspects. Social criteria are based on worldwide minimum standards and best practices. How companies deal with human rights issues, internally, in their supply chain and in the communities in which they operate is also taken into account.

To create DJSI, SAM uses a mixture of company-supplied questionnaires, data gleaned from company reports and 'qualitative' judgement. This latter input means that the DJSIs are not completely 'objective' assessments, although SAM allows Price-Waterhouse Coopers to assess its judgements. Nevertheless, the DJSIs, along with the *Business Ethics* assessments described above, are probably the best indices around at the moment that give a guide to the level of CSR of the top companies.

The DJSI, and now *Business Ethics*, both come close to the suggestions made in the earlier edition of this book on how to create an index of CSR. The other above-mentioned organizations only have a fuzzy conceptual basis for their work. Without a conceptual framework, this means that the choice of indicators is ad hoc. What should be included and what should be excluded? What, in fact, happens is that indicators are included for which data is readily available. This data is available because of some previous, now forgotten, conceptual framework, such as 'What the heck should I do about all these women who say they never receive promotion', rather than a serious attempt to decide what and why one wants to measure something. Neither the market leader in social screens – KLD – nor the upcoming leader in indicator measurement – the GRI – has conceptual frameworks. Consequently, Chapter 8 looks in more detail at some of the more theoretical academic literature, uses this to decide upon a conceptual framework and then develops a set of indicators to coincide with this framework or model.

Chapter 8

How Best To Measure What Is Corporate Social Responsibility?

Introduction

What indicators could be used to measure what is meant by corporate social responsibility (CSR)? It is easier to devise indicators that measure some aspect of CSR than to conclude that this particular set of indicators describes what is actually meant by a socially responsible company, and that high scores on each of these indicators thereby defines when a corporation is socially responsible. These questions have been discussed in what could be termed the 'academic literature' for many decades, and the research has been more extensive in the US than elsewhere. The debate continues because no general agreement exists on the indicators to be used, their measurement, or what their levels should be. This chapter samples some of the literature that seeks to define and measure the dimensions of what is meant by a socially responsible enterprise. It then uses the theory developed to present a set of indicators. In Chapter 9, these indicators are applied empirically.

Range of literature

The academic field in which this topic lies was largely known as 'social issues in management' (SIM). (It is also increasingly known as 'business ethics' or 'corporate social responsibility' and, more recently, 'business in society'). SIM studies range from pure philosophy to detailed and documented empirical studies of some particular element of social responsibility. There is a consensus that a business is a social organization with a clear objective of earning a profit from its activities through the activity of interdependent elements. Each element consists of people and systems directed towards profitability. Business also maintains external relationships with its customers, its suppliers and society. These elements affect all players and determine the character of the relationships, as well as the outcomes. The total process is a system and consists of three main elements:

1   *Ethical principles* exist that govern the tactical and strategic decision-making of the enterprise. These principals may be published, or may exist only in the behaviours of the business.
2   *Mechanisms* within the enterprise put the principles into action. They may be as simple as a sales organization which acts purely upon the principle of profit.
3   *Outcomes* occur as business is conducted. These are the result of the application of ethical principles (whether published or not) to daily operations.

Legitimacy of the study of CSR

US scholars in the SIM field have been concerned about how much social responsibility there should be in an enterprise, given that it is a social entity, as well as a profit-making one. In 1975, Preston and Post suggested an approach that helped to establish the legitimacy of the field.[1] Business had previously been assumed to be an independent social force, which interacted with other social forces but was not influenced by them. Preston and Post pointed out that all social systems 'penetrate' and mutually affect one another. Employees, for example, do not exist wholly within a business, but also represent the external world and bring their own skills, understandings, prejudices and limitations to the workplace. Similarly, a manufacturing business *buys* certain raw materials, but freely 'uses' air and water in its processes. Practices, for instance, that take vast amounts of water from general usage or that emit residue into the atmosphere penetrate other aspects of society and give society the legitimate right to examine the role of business in society.

Carroll on the hierarchy of social responsibilities

Carroll added a further clarification by suggesting that there was a hierarchy of responsibilities, each of which had to be satisfied in decision-making.[2] Carroll's model started with *economic* performance at the base of a pyramid of CSR. At the same time, business is expected to obey the law. The next level is business's responsibility to be ethical. Finally, business is expected to be a good corporate citizen, and this is satisfied through philanthropic responsibility. Total CSR entails the simultaneous fulfilment of these four responsibilities. So far, this seems very esoteric; however, in a practical application, similar to that of Carroll's model, GrandMet (now merged into Diageo) presented a pyramid of responsibilities under the title of *The Company in Society* in their 1997 corporate citizenship report.[3] This was included to illustrate how the different segments of the company relate to, and support, each other. The base of the period was called 'the business basics'; the next higher level was 'commercial initiatives'. Then came 'social investments' and the apex was labelled 'charity'.

Wood's pyramid of social responsibility

Wood and Jones saw two main problems with Carroll's pyramid (and similarly GrandMet's pyramid):[4]

1   Carroll saw business only as an economic institution.
2   Carroll believed that a firm's first responsibility is to make a profit.

A business enterprise is not only an economic institution, but also a social, political, legal and cultural entity. Carroll's second level of principles rests entirely upon the first. Carroll – Wood and Jones believed – confused the individual business with the *institution* of business. An individual business may have profit as its primary responsibility in order to survive; but the institution of business will remain and other responsibilities must be fulfilled in order to legitimize the institution.

In her book *Business and Society*, Wood argued for an inversion of Carroll's pyramid.[5] She felt that businesses do not make decisions as faceless entities; rather, *individuals* within the organization make choices and take decisions. It is these individuals who exercise managerial discretion toward (or away from) socially responsible outcomes. She states that the *first* responsibility of a socially responsible enterprise (SRE) is to support the ethical decision-making of its members. Wood sees the ethical principles of the general society as the next level of responsibility. Here, ethics define the balance between the self-interest of the SRE and the collective good of society. Having fulfilled these responsibilities, the firm is then bound to obey the law and only then to make a profit. This final, top layer of Wood's version of Carroll's pyramid can only be approached when the institution of business has established its legitimacy through its attention to the three lower layers. However, Carroll (and GrandMet) both had philanthropy at the pinnacle of the pyramid, so Wood presumably meant a much wider base of social responsibility than only philanthropy. Nevertheless, a business cannot be solely socially responsible and ignore the economics of business – in my opinion, the base of the pyramid should be both social responsibility and economics intertwined. The environment should also be included – but as one of the stakeholders, not, as so many have done, as the key building block.

Social responsiveness

Frederick, following Ackerman and Bauer, added a new dimension to the development of a model of an SRE – namely, *responsiveness*.[6,7] In Chapter

1, social responsiveness was defined as the capacity of the corporation to *respond* to social issues. As CSR had already claimed the acronym CSR, Frederick referred to corporate social *responsiveness* as CSR$_2$.

Frederick observed that neither Preston and Post's nor Carroll's models offered a means by which a business's *fulfilment* of its social responsibilities could be measured. They proposed a conceptual shift to look at the *responsiveness* of business to social issues and sought to classify such responses as *reactive, defensive* or *responsive*. Thus, a wholly different layer of analysis was added to simple responsibility within the general domain of ethical principles – a consideration of *action* was added.

Corporate social performance (CSP)

Wartick and Cochran took Carroll's pyramid as inverted by Wood as the top 'layer' of a model that consisted of *principles* (top layer) and *processes* (the middle layer, seen as reactive, defensive, responsive and interactive), and added *performance*, as indicated by programmes and policies as the *measurable* layer.[8] They saw what a company actually *did* – as the result of its social responsibility – as the empirically observable elements of their model. The Wartick and Cochran model thus took ethical governance in the form of principles, added responsiveness as directionality, and arrived at *outcomes* of socially responsible actions as the result of those actions.

Thus, by 1985, a number of studies had defined an area of interest in which indicators of social responsibility might be developed. The concept, then, was that a business firm was an economic, social and cultural organization who operated within many relationships within the larger society. Because of these interdependent relationships, a business was obligated to act in concert with general and specific ethical concerns. These actions would result in observable outcomes, and it was these outcomes that determined relative social responsibility.

Measuring social performance: The CSP model

Preston and Post focused interest on a firm's ability to *respond* to social issues, corporate social *responsiveness* or CSR$_2$, as it was named by Frederick (the '$_2$' indicating *responsiveness* rather than *responsibility*). Thus, several essential ingredients of a social responsibility model now existed. Preston and Post had suggested a basis for the *legitimacy* of society's right to expect certain conduct from business; Carroll had defined four essential elements of corporate *responsibility*, and had added an entirely new dimension concerning the ability of business to *respond* to social issues.

But Wood recognized that neither motivating principle nor 'responsiveness' lent itself to measurement, nor did either one take full cognisance of the roles of the stakeholders. Wood sought a model that would include the outcomes of social responsiveness as actual *indicators* of corporate social *performance* (CSP). In 1991, Wood defined CSP as 'a business organization's configuration of *principles* of social responsibility, processes of social responsiveness and *observable outcomes or products as they relate to the firm's societal relationships*' – what I call the 3-P model of principles, processes and products (outcomes). The three levels of this model are summarized in Table 8.1. The following sections take each of these levels in turn.

Table 8.1 *Wood's CSP model*

Principles of social responsibility		
Legitimacy	Public responsibility	Managerial discretion
Processes of social responsibility		
Environmental scanning	Stakeholder management	Issues management
Products or Outcomes		
Internal stakeholder effects	External stakeholder effects	External institutional effects

Level 1: *Principles* of social responsibility

The *level* of application of this principle is institutional and is based on a firm's basic obligations as a business organization. Its value is that it defines the institutional relationship between business and society, and specifies what is expected of any business.[9] This level of the CSP model itself contains three major *elements*, as follows:

1 *Legitimacy* concerns business as a social institution and frames the analytical view of the inter-relationship of business and society – sometimes known as its licence to operate or its set of values.
2 *Public responsibility* concerns the individual firm and its processes and outcomes within the framework of its own principles, in terms of what it actually does.
3 *Managerial discretion*: managers and other organizational members are moral actors. Within every domain of CSR, they are obliged to exercise such discretion as is available to them to achieve socially responsible outcomes.

Level 2: *Processes* of social responsibility

CSR_2 is a business's capacity to respond to social pressures. This suggests the ability of a business organization to survive by adapting to its business environment. To do so, it must know as much as possible about this environment, be capable of analysing its data and must react to the results of this analysis. But the environment of business is not static; it is a complex and ever-changing set of circumstances, encompassing complicated 'interpenetrations' of social systems. The ability to successfully scan, interpret and react to the business environment requires equally complex mechanisms. Three such elements have been identified as basic elements of this level of the CSP model:

1   *Environmental scanning* indicates the information-gathering arm of the business and the transmission of the gathered information throughout the organization, with its ultimate use in forward planning.
2   *Stakeholder management* refers to mapping the relationships of stakeholders to the firm (and among each other), while seeking to balance and meet legitimate concerns as a prerequisite of any measurement process.
3   *Issues management* concerns those policies to be developed in order to address social issues. Having identified the motivating principles of a firm and having determined the identities, relationships and power of stakeholders, the researcher now turns to the issues that concern stakeholders. The researcher is aware of 'social problems that may exist objectively but may become issues: requiring managerial attention when they are defined as being problematic to society, or to an institution within society by a group of actors, or to stakeholders capable of influencing either governmental action or company policies'.[10]

Level 3: *Outcomes or products*

The issues of measurement are most concerned with the third level of the CSP model. Programmes, and the behavioural outcomes of motivating principles, can be significant only if they are measured in terms of the stakeholders they affect. To determine if 'CSP makes a difference', all of the stakeholders relevant to an issue or complex of issues must be included in any assessment of performance:

■   *Internal stakeholder effects* are those that affect stakeholders *within* the firm. An examination of these might show how a corporate code of ethics affects the day-to-day decision-making of the firm with reference to social responsibility. Similarly, it might be concerned with the positive or negative effects of corporate hiring and employee benefits' practices.

■ *External stakeholder effects* concern the impact of corporate actions on persons or groups outside of the firm. These might involve such things as the negative effects of a product recall, the positive effects of community-related corporate philanthropy, or – assuming the natural environment as a stakeholder – the effects of toxic waste disposal.

■ *External institutional effects* refer to the effects upon the larger *institution* of business rather than on any particular stakeholder group. For example, several environmental disasters made the public aware of the effect of business decisions on the general public. This new awareness brought about pressure for environmental regulation, which then affected the entire institution of business, rather than one specific firm.

Applying the model: An example

One example of the way in which the model might be applied can be seen by looking more closely at Ben & Jerry's Homemade Ice Cream (now part of Unilever). The company's founder, Ben Cohen, articulated one aspect of the *ethical principles* of the firm as follows:

> *Businesses tend to exploit communities and their workers, and that wasn't the way I thought the game should be played. I thought it should be the opposite – that business had a responsibility to give back to the community; that because the business is allowed to be there in the first place, the business ought to support the community. What we're finding is that when you support the community, the community supports you back.*[11]

This is a clear statement of principles that belongs in the first level of the CSP model. As stated, the principles fulfil both the institutional element (they act to legitimize the institution of business) and the discretionary element (they direct the firm in a socially responsible path), and go well beyond any legal requirements.

At the level of *processes of social responsiveness*, Ben & Jerry's social issues' scanning is accomplished through a number of mechanisms, ranging from direct community involvement through newsletters to special events sponsored by the company. The effectiveness of the scanning and issues management mechanisms can be seen in their funding of organizations as diverse as the Native American Community Board in South Dakota to the Central Massachusetts Safe Energy Project. Clear linkages can be seen, extending from the realm of principle toward corporate action.

One specific *outcome (or product)* of Ben & Jerry's concern for community welfare is carried out through its purchasing policies. To bake its brownies, the company calls on the Greystone Bakery in Yonkers, New

York, a firm that uses its profits to house the homeless and train them as bakers. This outcome is very specific and wholly measurable in a number of ways. One could simply measure the number of homeless people employed by the bakery and the number of trained bakers graduated by the programme. One might also look at how many are still employed at the bakery or some other place as bakers. There is a clear causal linkage back through corporate mechanisms to ethical principles, and the analytical framework can be seen to function. Further research could be done at Ben & Jerry's to cross-relate different elements and their indicators so as to determine how, for example, profitability is affected by the 7.5 per cent share of pre-tax earnings given by Ben & Jerry's to philanthropic purposes. Conversely, one might take a proposed indicator, such as 'outcomes of community involvement', and examine its statistical relationships to other indicators in other elements.

The stakeholders in this process are first *external* to the company, and are the homeless who take part in the training programme. A second group of stakeholders can be identified as the community from which the homeless are taken. Clearly, the bakery itself profits as a supplier to Ben & Jerry's, and it, in turn, provides benefits to the stakeholders, which are possible because of their business with Ben & Jerry's. As one aspect of a very successful social programme, this also benefits shareholders as the success of the firm grows.

Combining the model, indicators and measures

I have, on the basis of Wood's and others' theoretical framework, defined nine elements of an analytical framework through which to view the dimensions and relationships of an SRE. These are as follows.

On the level of *principles*:

■ legitimacy;
■ public responsibility;
■ managerial discretion.

On the level of *processes*:

■ environmental scanning;
■ stakeholder management;
■ issues management.

On the level of *outcomes or products*:

- internal stakeholder effects;
- external stakeholder effects;
- external institutional effects.

I next use the elements of this model to extract and classify a number of additional indicators of social responsibility as related to each element of the model. I have used the definition of stakeholders that was developed in Chapter 2. Table 8.2 places elements of the model, common characteristics of business and potential indicators into an analytical framework similar to that of the CSP model. The table contains three columns. The first is the model listed as above; the second is the sort of concrete indicator or action that the firm has taken; and the third column contains an example of a precise measure that could be used to quantify the indicator. For instance, the indicator of legitimacy is whether the firm has a code of ethics, while its measure is whether it has been published or distributed to employees, or whether an independent group monitors its application. Clearly, the measurement tells us very little about what is in the code of ethics, and as such is weak. However, if one complicates the table too much, then it becomes difficult – if not impossible – to apply in practice, given the present state of data availability.

Levels 1 and 2 of the model concern subjective issues. The objective judgement of the degree to which a certain code of ethics is socially responsible is very difficult, and must itself be the topic of research. I suggest that at levels 1 and 2 of the model we are (at this stage) largely concerned with the simple existence of a published code of ethics. This appears to be a prerequisite of successive levels of the model. All firms have some code of ethics. This may be as simple as a sales manager explaining how to pressure prospective car buyers. But it only becomes available to stakeholders and researchers if it is *published*, and *training* in it puts it into practice. Indicators at these first two levels are necessarily general because only *outcomes* (level 3) are more empirically measurable.

So much for theory. What happens when I try and put this theoretical framework into practice? This is what I look at in Chapter 9 using illustrative data from the 25 largest UK companies.

Table 8.2 *Suggested elements, indicators and measures*[12]

Element of SRE model	Stakeholder groups (assumed)	Indicator	Measure
Level 1: principles of social responsibility			
Legitimacy		Code of ethics	Published?
		Code of ethics	Distributed to employees?
		Code of ethics	Independent group does monitoring?
Public responsibility		Litigation involving corporate law-breaking	Amount, size?
		Fines resulting from illegal activities	Amount?
		Contribution to innovation	R&D expenditure
		Job creation	Number of net jobs created
Managerial discretion		Code of ethics	Managers and employees trained?
		Managers convicted of illegal activities	Number, amount?
Level 2: processes of social responsibility			
Environmental scanning		Mechanism to review social issues relevant to firm	Exists?
Stakeholder management		Analytical body for social issues as integral part of policy-making	Exists?
		Social audit exists?	
		Ethical accounting statement exists?	
Issues management		Policies made on basis of analysis of social issues	Firm's regulations and policies
Level 3: outcomes (products) of social responsibility			
Internal stakeholder effects	Owners	Profitability/value	Share value, return on investment, etc
		Corporate irresponsibility or illegal activity	Fines, number of product recalls, pollution performance measured against some industry standard
		Community welfare	Amount of giving, programmes as percentage of earnings
		Corporate philanthropy	Amount of pre-tax giving as percentage of earnings
		Code of ethics	Published, distributed, trained

Managers	Code of ethics	Trained in code of ethics and apply in demonstrable and measurable ways
		Rank of manager responsible for applying code
Employees	Union/staff relations	Evidence of controversy, good relations
	Safety issues	Litigation, fines
	Pay, pensions and benefits	Relative ranking to similar firms (measuring percentage spent on employee benefits, programmes, etc)
	Layoffs	Percentage, frequency, individuals chosen
	Employee ownership	Percentage
	Women and minorities policies	Existence, rank with similar firms, litigation and fines
External stakeholder effects	Customers/ consumers	Code of ethics	Evidence of application to products or services
	Product recalls	Absolute number, seriousness demonstrated by litigation or fines, percentage of total production
	Litigation	Amount of fraud, price fixing, anti-trust suits
	Public product or service controversy	Seriousness, frequency
	False advertising	Litigation, fines
Natural environment	Pollution	Performance against index, litigation, fines
	Toxic waste	Performance against index, litigation, fines
	Recycling and use of recycled products	Percentages
	Use of eco-label on products?	Yes/no
Community	Corporate-giving to community programmes	Amount, percentage
	Direct involvement in community programmes	Number, outcomes, costs, benefits
	Community controversy or litigation	Number, seriousness, outcomes
Suppliers	Firm's code of ethics	Applied to all suppliers
	Supplier's code of ethics	Applied
	Litigation/fines	Number, amount, outcomes
	Public controversy	Amount, outcome
External institutional effects	Business as a social institution	Code of ethics	Published and applied
	Generic litigation	Amounts, number, outcomes
	Class action suits	Amounts, type, number, outcomes
	Public policy and legislation improved due to pressure from corporation	Yes/no

Chapter 9

Empirical Application of Corporate Social Responsibility Indicators

Introduction

The indicators suggested in Chapter 8 are much easier to present than to collect for many companies at once. My original aim, in 1992, was to rank the Fortune 500 largest companies in the world from 1 to 500 in terms of social responsibility. My idea, at the time, was simply to raise the issue of corporate social responsibility (CSR) so that corporations would compete to provide more social responsibility; otherwise, they would be punished by consumers and shareholders. The work was to mirror the human development index (HDI) of the United Nations Development Programme (UNDP) that serves to rank nations on how well they perform in terms of social development. My critics at the time thought that I was excessively naive to embark on such work. But, since the publication of the first edition of this book, we have seen a growth in measurement systems and rankings – the main ones were described in Chapter 7. Perhaps the closest to my earlier model is the Dow Jones Sustainability Index (DJSI) that is growing in influence and applicability. However, even the DJSI only covers the top 10 per cent of Fortune 500 companies. My own work, that I present here, proved more time consuming than I had anticipated, and so I restricted my first attempt to do this to the UK's largest companies. This work forms the basis of this chapter.

Interested readers may like to see where their company fits in my scheme of things. A subset of my indicators, following the theory developed in the previous chapter, has been turned into 20 questions and is available on my company's website.[1] I call this the Corporate Responsibility Index through Internet Consultation of Stakeholders (CRITICS), which is a questionnaire that allows people who are inside or outside of corporations or institutions to rapidly self-assess the CSR of these corporations or institutions. A score is given between 0–1, and the more socially responsible your institution, the higher your score. To date, of the hundreds of replies received, the highest score has been achieved by Shell, with institutions such as the United Nations (UN) and its Global Compact coming along way behind!

Research

When researching data for the largest companies in the world, from the US to Europe to Oceania, I often heard that data must be available or that such and such a group had produced an identical set of data. Clearly, if one focused just on one company for a sufficient time that also included interviews with key individuals, then it would be possible to obtain a substantial part of the required data – though probably not all. However, face-to-face interviews are expensive. Another alternative is a mail-distributed questionnaire; but it is well known that responses are poor, even assuming that one can find the appropriate individual to address. The internet also proved a failure: so much qualitative data pointing you in the direction of yet more qualitative data. Our searches at the time, with the exception of the work by *Business Ethics* for the US (see Chapter 7), failed to find any quantitative data for many companies at once covering indices of social responsibility. The situation has improved a little since my exploration in 1997. Kinder, Lydenberg & Domini (KLD) now publish their data for the largest US companies and it is available for a fee. The DJSI data is not publicly available and the Global Reporting Initiative (GRI) work is only in its early stages.

To limit my original research, I decided to reduce data search and analysis to the 100 largest UK companies. As this list is mainly for illustrative purposes, I only present the data for the biggest 25 companies in the UK.

Measuring the 'biggest' company is not straightforward, either. Should market capitalization, turnover, pre-tax profit, number of employees or capital employed be the criteria used? For instance, a large company such as Eurotunnel had, in 1996, about £11 billion of capital employed; yet, it also had only 2302 employees, a loss of £386,887, a turnover of only £30 million and a market capitalization of £3 million. This may be compared with British Petroleum (BP), for instance, which had figures of £20 billion capital, 66,550 employees, pre-tax profits of £2.2 billion, a turnover of £33 billion and capitalized at £19 billion. I chose capital employed, partly because this figure is less changeable from year to year and partly, or primarily, because *The Times* uses this to determine its top 100 companies in the UK.

The list, therefore, in Table 9.2, gives the 25 largest UK companies by capital employed. It can be seen that the biggest UK company at the time was British Gas, with a capital employed of £24.6 billion, followed by BP and Hong Kong and Shanghai Banking Corporation (HSBC) Holdings. In the top 25, seven are financial or banking companies; four are energy related; three are brewers or distillers; two are in the transport business; two more are in the communications area; and a further two are in chemical and drug-related industries. There are also conglomerates and mining, tobacco, media and property companies. The energy and financial companies tend to be in the top part of the list; but no other particular pattern emerges. Most noteworthy is that traditional manufacturing industries, such as cars, steel, textiles and so on, are all missing. This is the status of the UK today, which is increasingly becoming a service-orientated country where traditional industrial production (if it is done at all) is conducted by the overseas holdings of the financial companies.

What is the point of obtaining a selection of indicators, scaling them and then ranking them? In a sense, this is self-evident; quantifying phenomena provides a more precise view of what we are talking about. It also helps to judge which company is more socially responsible than another. But why should this matter if all companies are more or less equally socially responsible? The point is that there is large variation between the different companies. And, as the argument in this book goes, if the private sector is to take on more of the social tasks that governments simply will not pay for in the future, then we want to know who these companies are and what sorts of things they do. Providing a ranking of companies depends, of course, upon the indicators chosen and their availability. I have tried to choose the indicators according to what theory exists to measure CSR, using the frameworks set up by Donna Wood and her colleagues in the US (see Chapter 8). Yet, as we shall see, not all of the data is available, and choices of a pragmatic nature have had to be made.

The main advantage of a composite indicator and a composite ranking are that they synthesize in an easily understood manner a complex set of underlying phenomena. Hopefully, too, such a treatment can serve as a sort of Trojan horse, by which interest is stimulated enough for people to wish to delve more deeply into the theory and data underlying the composite indicator and ranking. This is exactly what happened to the UNDP's human development index of countries. Results indicating that one country performed better than others was of interest for all countries. I was once invited by the UN to adjudicate, as an independent analyst, on why Morocco had performed so badly. King Hassan sent his minister of finance to New York to check the UN's data. He found errors, which led Morocco to collect a new set of data on its most recent social and economic status. Morocco's ranking was eventually revised; unfortunately, the new rating did not satisfy the king, who promptly sacked his minister on his return from New York!

Theory and practice

Table 9.1 shows the indicator set that the theory led me to develop (first column) and what I eventually used in practice (second column).

It can be seen that of the 47 categories of indicators that the theory led me to identify, only 19 were found in practice in the UK – a country who is as open as any in the world, with the possible exception of the US. Even

Table 9.1 *Elements, indicators and measures: Theory and practice*

Indicator suggested from theory	Indicator used in practice for UK list
Code of ethics published?	Subscribed to Cadbury Code of ethics?
Code of ethics distributed to employees?	*
Code of ethics monitored independently?	Code monitored independently?
Litigation involving corporate law-breaking	*
Fines resulting from illegal activities	*
Contribution to innovation	*
Job creation	*
Job creation (scaled 1-5, where 1 = poor; 5 = very good)	
Trained in code of ethics	Cadbury Code?
Managers convicted of illegal activities	*
Mechanism to review social issues relevant to firm	*
Analytical body for social issues as integral part of policy-making	*
Social audit exists?	*
Ethical accounting statement exists?	*
Policies made on basis of analysis of social issues	^
Profitability/value	Available
Corporate irresponsibility or illegal activity	*
Community welfare	Member of Business in the Community?
Corporate philanthropy	Amount given to charity as percentage of pre-tax earnings
Code of ethics for owners	Cadbury Code?
Code of ethics for managers	Cadbury Code?
Union/staff relations	Composite index used from *The 100 Best UK Companies To Work For* (index based on pay, benefits, communications, training, career development, morale on scale average, good, very good, excellent, superb)
Safety issues	
Pay, pensions and benefits	
Layoffs	
Employee ownership	
Women's and minorities' policies	
Code of ethics applied to products	Cadbury Code
Product recalls	*
Litigation	*
Public product or service controversy	*
False advertising	Number of complaints to Advertising Standards Authority (ASA)
Pollution	Index of corporate environmental engagement used (index based on whether a company has an environmental management system; published environmental targets;
Toxic waste	
Recycling and use of recycled products	
Use of eco-label on products?	

	Green procurement programme; board member responsible for the environment)
Corporate giving to community programmes	Member of Business in the Community?
Direct involvement in community programmes	Amount given to charity as percentage of pre-tax earnings; member of UK Per Cent Club?
Community controversy or litigation	*
Firm's code of ethics	Cadbury Code?
Supplier's code of ethics	Supplier code of ethics? (scale: 0 =
Litigation/fines	no; 0.5 = weak; 1 = yes)
Public controversy	*
Code of ethics published?	Cadbury Code?
Generic litigation	*
Class action suits	*
Public policy and legislation improved due to pressure from corporation	*

Note: * = little or nothing available for top 100 UK companies.

then, the indicators that were available covered mainly 'subjective' impressions. For instance, *The 100 Best UK Companies to Work For* index gave a scale of 'average' to 'superb'; but nowhere does it define a methodology to calculate these scales. Presumably, the book's authors used their own judgement. As mentioned before, it would be possible to improve the coverage by concentrating on one company for a period of time and working with key individuals within the company. Alternatively, more detailed compliance principles could be worked out with, for instance, the London Stock Exchange (LSE) or the work of the GRI. This would allow data to become more readily available.

Type of data available and sources used

Data was obtained from a wide variety of published sources – for example, company reports, newspaper articles, the internet, books and published articles. Sources for each of the data are given in the Appendix to this chapter.

Do these data refer to the UK's or the companies' global practices? As can be seen, the indicators largely refer to operations in the UK itself, although the ranking of the largest company depends upon worldwide capital employed. Can we say that being socially responsible in the UK also means being socially responsible elsewhere? The KLD screens, for instance, apply a methodology that KLD call the 'bellwether' approach.[2] KLD say that in the Middle Ages, shepherds simplified finding their flocks by putting a bell on the leading sheep – the bellwether – and its companions followed. Find the bellwether and find the flock. They go on to say that:

> *...experience has shown that a combination of bellwether issues indicate companies' overall performance in a screening area. For instance, a company's relations with its unionized workers often reflects its record, generally, on employee and employment issues.*

Generally, one might expect this to be true. However, the largest companies' dealings with less developed countries do not always follow this maxim – presumably, out of sight out, of mind. The case of Rio Tinto Zinc (RTZ) is just one recent example (see Table 9.3). It appears as number 4 in our rankings of social responsibility. Yet, according to an article in the *Guardian* (July 1997), perhaps its CSR score should be much lower than its 'bellwether' score would suggest.[3]

A Scottish engineer developed throat cancer after working in the RTZ-owned Rossing mine in Namibia. He was exposed to high levels of radioactive uranium and silica dust, and had his larynx removed in 1986. The engineer repaired machinery day and night while giant granite boulders containing radioactive uranium were tipped into nearby ore crushers. He insists that he was never given a face mask, nor were fellow Namibians who worked there with him. He brought his case to the UK House of Lords in London and hopes to win his case against RTZ. This illustrates that RTZ, although its bellwether gave it high rankings in our CSR scale, may well have received lower scores if its overseas holdings or subsidiaries had been included. A further point is also worth making – namely, that the case was heard and judged in London because the Law Lords held that the case could not be properly tried in Namibia since the required highly professional representation, from legal and scientific experts, was not available there. This ground-breaking judgement, according to the *Guardian*, showed that the world's largest mining company could be sued by employees for negligence in London for injuries received thousands of kilometres away. The point is that the decision opens the door for other multinationals with headquarters in London to be sued for actions of their overseas subsidiaries. But the consequences are complicated because, as an RTZ spokesman said:

> *The Lords' decision has only to do with where the case should be heard, and not on its merits; and while RTZ had every sympathy with the engineer, as far as we are concerned, and as far as we know, his condition has nothing to do with his employment in Namibia.*

In 1996, RTZ was involved in a dispute with Aboriginal leaders in Australia over the proposed Century Zinc project, after it was accused of trying to undermine Aboriginal land rights legislation. RTZ was also criticized during the same year by the World Development Movement for spending US$500million to expand the Grasberg mine in West Papua (Irian

Table 9.2 *Ranking of top 25 UK companies in terms of how socially responsible they are*

Rank in size (capital employed)	Still in FTSE 100?	Sector	Company name	Job create scale 1 to 5	Cadbury comply ?	Inde- pendent audit
1	1	Energy	British Gas	1	1	0
2	1	Energy	British Petroleum	3	1	1
3	1	Banking	HSBC Holdings Midland	4	1	0
4	1	Energy	Shell Transport and Trading	3	1	0
5	1	Finance	Abbey National	5	0	0
6	1	Communication	British Telecom Communications	2	1	0
7	1	Conglomerate	Hanson	2	1	0
8	1	Banking	NatWest	2	1	0
9	1	Banking	Barclays	3	1	0
10	0	Finance	Salomon Brothers Europe	3	0	0
11	0	Transport	Eurotunnel Group	3	0	0
12	1	Media	News International	3	0	0
13	0	Energy	Nuclear Electric	3	1	0
14	1	Tobacco	BAT Industries	3	1	0
15	1	Banking	Lloyds–TSB	3	1	0
16	1	Brewing	Grand Metropolitan	4	1	0
17	1	Chemicals	ICI–Zeneca	3	1	0
18	1	Communication	Cable and Wireless	3	1	0
19	1	Chemicals	Glaxo Wellcome	4	1	0
20	1	Transport	British Airways	4	1	0
21	1	Brewing	Guinness	4	1	0
22	1	Property	Land Securities	4	1	0
23	0	Finance	Halifax	3	0	0
24	1	Brewing	Bass (Britvic)	4	1	0
25	1	Mining	Rio Tinto Zinc	4	1	1

Notes on transformation:

1 Job create (scale 1–5)	Per cent jobs created as per cent of previous year, scale from lowest to highest per cent (–22 to +14), divided into five ranges and given 1–5 depending upon range occupied (missing values assigned an average, ie 3)
2 Cadbury comply?	Compliance with Cadbury Code: yes = 1; no = 0 (no missing values)
3 Independent audit?	1 = yes; 0 = no or no information
4 Charity contributors (scale 1–5)	Per cent use of profit on scale 0.08–0.48 put in range of 5; highest given 5. If negative profits, then given the score 4. Dates around 1996 used
5 Best Company?	Using the six indicators of the book and then a five-point scale in the book, with 5 the best. If not in the book, then given one point less than the lowest score recorded
6 ASA Complaints upheld	Number of complaints: 0 = score of 5; 1 = 4; 2 = 3; 3 = 2; 3+ = 1. No mention, then score of 5 given

Charity contributions scale 1 to 5	Best company	ASA complaints upheld	Business in the Community?	UK Per Cent Club?	Index of CEE	Supplier: own code	Scaled total	CSR rank
3	13	5	1	1	3	1	0.69	12
1	18	4	1	0	4	0.75	0.69	12
1	13	5	1	1	3.5	0.75	0.70	8
5	16	4	1	0	5	1	0.70	8
1	13	3	1	0	2	0.75	0.45	22
1	19	3	1	1	5	1	0.70	8
1	13	5	1	0	4	0.5	0.54	18
2	17	4	1	1	5	1	0.73	5
2	13	3	1	1	2	1	0.65	15
4	13	5	0	0	3.5	0.75	0.44	23
4	13	4	1	1	3.5	0.75	0.62	16
3	14	1	0	0	3.5	0.75	0.34	25
1	13	5	1	1	3.5	0.75	0.68	14
1	13	5	1	1	4	1	0.71	7
3	13	3	1	1	3.5	1	0.70	8
4	13	5	1	1	4	0.75	0.77	3
1	21	5	1	0	5	0.5	0.61	17
1	13	5	0	1	2	0	0.47	24
3	21	5	1	1	3	1	0.78	2
1	15	3	1	1	5	1	0.72	6
5	24	5	1	1	3	0.75	0.81	1
1	13	5	1	0	1	1	0.57	20
2	16	3	1	0	3.5	0.75	0.47	20
2	14	3	1	0	1	0.75	0.53	19
1	13	5	1	1	5	0	0.75	4

7 Business in the Community?	Member = 1; not member = 0 (no missing values)
8 UK Per Cent Club?	Member = 1; not member = 0 (no missing values)
9 Index of CEE	Scores used in reverse order to those of the Index of Corporate Environmental Engagement (CEE) so that 5 = best. Missing values given average score of 3.5
10 Supplier: own code	Based on company reports, if company says that it has a code, including a set time or adherence to Confederation of Business Industries (CBI) code, then score of 1 given; vagueness or no set time is given score of 0.5; score of 0 is given for those who admit that they have no code. Missing values given an average score of 0.75
Total	Straight total of scores
11 Scaled total (CSR score)	Scores divided by maximum minus minimum value of each indicator, summed and divided by 10 (10 = number of indicators)
12 Rank	Ranked from 1–25 on basis of scaled average totals

Jaya) Indonesia against the wishes of the indigenous population and amidst continuing allegations of environmental damage and human-rights abuses.[4]

The data and manipulations

The data and rankings are given in Table 9.2 and summarized in Table 9.3. The footnotes show the manipulations that were involved in arriving at the scaled total or index of social responsibility. Essentially, this places each indicator on the same scale of 0–1 through dividing by the range (that is, the maximum minus the minimum possible figure), adding the results together and giving the average. This means that each of the selected indicators is given equal weights. This is the simplest way to go about the issue. Another would be to give increased weights to those indicators that themselves are composite indicators. This, however, would weight the CSR scores too closely to existing scales, and give lesser weight to those newer indicators included here. Another variation would be – given the importance of a code of ethics and its monitoring in the theoretical discussion of Chapter 8 – to give increased weights to these two indicators. This has been rejected, given the small variation in both these indicators, which, in other words, means that nearly all the companies subscribe to the Cadbury Code, but hardly any have independent auditing of compliance with the code.

Yet another approach could be to group the indicators into stakeholder relationships (customers, employees, shareholders, suppliers, community, environment). Then, for a 'true balanced stakeholder view' each of these six dimension should have equal weight in the total score.[5] This model is implicit in the indicators retained – Table 8.2 identifies indicators for each stakeholder group but the 'Nisbet' model does not cover all three levels of the corporate social performance (CSP) model as I do.

The results and their interpretation

The most socially responsible of the largest 25 companies operating in the UK at the time the measurements were taken was Guinness, the highly successful international drinks company who produces some of the world's distinctive brands, such as Johnnie Walker, Bell's and Dewar's Scotch whiskies, Gordon's and Tanqueray gins and the famous Guinness stout. It is also a major shareholder in Moet Hennessy, the famous French wines and spirits house. Guinness has since merged with GrandMet (number 3 in my list) to form Diageo, which itself continues a high CSR tradition, as the corporate citizenship part of its 2001 revamped website illustrates.[6]

At the time, Guinness employed around 25,000 individuals worldwide, including 6000 in the UK, and trades across 140 countries. According to

Table 9.3 *Final rankings*

Sector	Company name	CSR rank
Brewing	Guinness	1
Chemicals	Glaxo Wellcome	2
Brewing	Grand Metropolitan	3
Mining	RTZ	4
Banking	NatWest	5
Transport	British Airways	6
Tobacco	BAT Industries	7
Banking	HSBC Holdings – Midland	8
Energy	Shell Transport and Trading	9
Communications	British Telecommunications	10
Banking	Lloyds–TSB	11
Energy	British Gas	12
Energy	British Petroleum	13
Energy	Nuclear Electric	14
Banking	Barclays	15
Transport	Eurotunnel Group	16
Chemicals	ICI–Zeneca	17
Conglomerate	Hanson	18
Brewing	Bass (Britvic)	19
Property	Land Securities	20
Finance	Halifax	21
Finance	Abbey National	22
Finance	Salomon Brothers Europe	23
Communications	Cable and Wireless	24
Media	News International	25

The 100 Best UK Companies To Work For, Guinness had superb pay and training, and excellent benefits, career development and morale for its workforce. It gave generously to charities, was active in Business in the Community and was a member of the Per Cent Club, in which adherents tie their level of giving to a predetermined percentage of the company's pre-tax profits or dividends. For example, Guinness gave US$100,000 to the UNDP in 1996 to help it develop an improved design for water pumps in villages in developing countries.

Guinness came less high on environmental grounds. It had only an average score in the Index of Corporate Environmental Engagement (CEE), an index on corporate environmental life published by the non-profit organization Business in the Environment (BIE). It is based on ten questions that range from whether a company has an environmental management system, published environmental targets or a 'Green' procurement programme, to whether it has a board member responsible for the environment. Companies are given a score of 1–5, depending upon an analysis of their responses to the ten questions. Yet, the index complies with the Cadbury Code – the code of best practice recommended by the

Cadbury Commission on the Financial Aspects of Corporate Governance, although no evidence is available that this compliance is subject to independent monitoring. Indeed, there are fears that the Cadbury Code may well be weakened.[7] The code was originally set up after the scandals associated with Maxwell and Polly Peck (the former absconded with pension funds, and the latter's managing director went where the law could not catch him to Cyprus). It originally sought to put in place measures to prevent public companies from falling under the absolute control of a fraudulent individual. Many of Cadbury's recommendations, such as splitting the role of chairman and chief executive and appointing at least three non-executive directors, are now largely accepted practice (again, according to the *Observer*).

Guinness being in number 1 spot raises the vexed question of the type of product that companies market. In many social investment screens, the sale of alcohol, tobacco, armaments, chemicals for making nerve gas and so on is a justification for excluding them. (The author, who adores wine but neither smokes nor has a high regard for armies, differs in his values from others.) Product type is not included in the theoretical indicators or in the indicators chosen for our CSR index. What is one person's meat is another one's poison. For instance, vegetarians would veto the eating of any slaughtered animal, but will eat plants, which some say also have a personality. Furthermore, many financial companies support, indirectly, the purchase of arms. Consequently, any choice of a product list for inclusion or exclusion depends very much upon the social and cultural values of the person or society purchasing the product. (The author would draw the line at including a company as socially responsible who dealt in the arms trade; but his other prejudices are conducted on the shop floor through his purchases because he doesn't believe that all of his prejudices should influence others unless they are in possession of the complete facts.) Books or reports, such as *Shopping for a Better World*, with its basic idea of providing a 'quick and easy guide to socially responsible shopping', help to inform consumers on their rights.[8] Although, unfortunately, this book was never re-issued after 1991, its US counterpart, published by Council on Economic Priorities (CEP), is doing better; but neither editions are in regular use by consumers. Indeed, consumers in other parts of the world are much less well informed than those in the UK and US, and it will be many decades before the aphorism 'Let the buyer beware' can be fairly adopted worldwide.

At 2, 3, 4 and 5 in our list of CSRs (see Table 9.3) come Glaxo Wellcome (the world's largest pharmaceutical company), Grand Metropolitan (brewing and hotels), RTZ (mining) and the NatWest Group (banking and financial services), respectively. Last in the list comes News International, owned by Rupert Murdoch, the Australian entrepreneur, just below Cable and Wireless.

No particular groupings by type of industry emerge. Financial companies, for instance, are grouped at the foot of the table, but no golden law says that they are particularly bad regarding social responsibility – for instance, NatWest financial group is at 5 in the ratings. Indeed, NatWest actively encourages its staff to get involved in community projects.[9] The encouragement comes in the form of what NatWest calls Community Action Awards. These reward employees' work by making cash donations to their voluntary organizations. The company backs around 3800 staff with such awards. For one NatWest employee, the scheme led to her appointment as chairman of the governors of a primary school in West London after she found herself working closely with the school's head teacher to raise standards after a negative report from a school inspector.

On the other hand, energy companies could do more, it would appear, with none appearing higher than 8 in the table and all being grouped around 8–14. Shell, for instance, has suffered badly in the past decade with its *Brent Spar* fiasco (the abandoned attempt to ditch an oil rig in the deep waters of the Atlantic, opposed somewhat flashily but carelessly by Greenpeace), and its harsh neglect of the effects of oil-related pollution on the Ogoni people in Nigeria. This latter incident led to an even poorer public image, resulting from its 'do nothing' stance in the case of Ken Saro-Wiwa, the Ogoni people's leader who was subsequently executed by the Nigerian government (his cause having been strongly supported by The Body Shop but not picked up until too late by the media).

Public image and CSR ranking

In the UK's Market and Opinion Research International's (MORI's) 1996 survey, reported in Chapter 5, respondents were asked about their perceptions of current social responsibility in comparison with their expectations of what should be done. MORI found that the public's expectation of responsibilities differed by sector of activity. I further used MORI's scores to look at the public's expectations of social responsibility for 14 of the 25 largest UK companies for which MORI had data in its survey. The results are given in Tables 9.4 and 9.5.

Glaxo Wellcome came number 2 in my ranking of firms, and 24 per cent of the public thought that it took its responsibility seriously according to the MORI survey, which explains why only 7 per cent thought it should make more effort to take its responsibility seriously. British Telecommunications (BT) was relatively highly placed in my CSR rankings (number 8), and it received the highest score of the 14 MORI companies in my table, with 38 per cent of the public believing that it takes its social responsibilities seriously, while 10 per cent thought that it could do more.

The activity sector problem is clearly indicated. RTZ is in a 'dirty' industry where negative publicity can quickly arise – dangerous working conditions, polluting dust, environmental damage, poor working conditions in the developing world and so on. Yet, RTZ comes out well at number 4 among the 25 biggest UK companies in terms of being a socially

Table 9.4 *The author's CSR rankings compared with public perceptions*

Company	CSR ranking	Take social responsibility (SR) seriously? (per cent)*	Should take SR more seriously? (per cent)*
Glaxo Wellcome	2	24	7
Grand Metropolitan	3	2	4
RTZ	4	0	4
NatWest	5	12	9
HSBC Holdings	8	16	8
Shell Transport and Trading	8	30	16
British Telecommunications	8	38	10
Lloyds–TSB	8	17	8
British Gas	12	23	22
British Petroleum	12	29	13
Barclays	15	10	11
ICI–Zeneca	17	37	12
Halifax	20	28	5
Abbey National	22	22	6

Source: * adapted from MORI (1996) (see Chapter 5, 'MORI study of consumers about corporate social responsibility')

responsible enterprise (SRE). However, in the public's mind, it has a lot of work to do – no one in the sample saw RTZ as currently taking its responsibilities seriously. It is surprising that only 4 per cent of respondents thought that RTZ should take its social responsibility more seriously.

Did the public's appreciation, in general, of the extent to which they believed the companies were socially responsible match up to the observed statistics that led to my rankings? Table 9.5 gives an idea of the answer, using correlation coefficients (a positive score of 1 indicates that the two items are highly correlated, while a score of 0 suggests that they are not correlated at all). In the event, the correlation showed that the higher the ranking, the better the score for both questions asked! This demonstrates that of the companies considered, those who did well in terms of actually being socially responsible in my ranking are not seen to be socially responsible in the public's mind, according to MORI. Alternatively, it could just suggest that the name recognition for the companies lower down on my CSR ranking is higher than for those at the top – that is, GrandMet, RTZ and NatWest are lesser known than Shell, BT, Imperial Chemical Industries (ICI) and the (former) building societies Halifax and Abbey National.

Table 9.5 *Correlation coefficients*

	CSR ranking	Takes social responsibility (SR) seriously?	Should take SR more seriously?
CSR ranking	1.00	0.42	0.45
Takes SR seriously?		1.00	0.14
Should take SR more seriously?			1.00

How does CSR ranking affect financial performance?

This question has attracted considerable interest since the first edition of this book.[10] However, available research on this key topic is strongly limited by the paucity of existing data. Yet, there is a belief that there is a positive link between social and financial performance, especially when looking at the increased relevance of intangible assets such as reputation and knowledge networks. These turn into a source of market value and competitive advantage. Furthermore, the belief is that CSR is not simply an ethical add-on to existing business, but is part and parcel of corporate strategy itself. The adoption of CSR as a central component of corporate strategy will, it is intended, eventually lead to both a prosperous company and a prosperous society.

The simplest way to test the proposition of the link between CSR and financial performance is to look at the correlation between a company's level of CSR, as measured by my CSR index, and how well this serves as a predictor of its share price. This is what I do in the rest of this section. However, this exercise suffers from at least five problems. First, it is well known that share prices are diabolically difficult to predict – hence, my exercise, even if showing an excellent correlation, could just be a fluke. Second, the share price does not necessarily indicate the financial viability of a company. The excessive stock market valuations of the so-called 'dot-coms', followed by many bankruptcies, is a recent example of this. Third, there are many and perhaps better indications of financial viability than share price – economic value added (EVA) is one that is increasingly used. Fourth, my CSR measure is only a proxy for CSR since all data was not available; even then, my CSR theory will have doubters. Fifth, correlation does not indicate causation – if more storks are flying around and there happen to be more babies born, this does not mean the storks were in any way involved in the birth of the babies!

Nevertheless, these caveats aside, an exercise linking my CSR ranking to share price performance is interesting for its own sake. Most of my data used to estimate the CSR rankings was collected in 1996. The results on whether CSR affects share price are given in Table 9.6 and are respresented

Table 9.6 *Share price change versus CSR ranking*

Company	CSR ranking	Share price change, 1994–1996 (per cent)
Guinness[21]	1	1.67
Glaxo Wellcome[19]	2	43.20
Grand Metropolitan[16]	3	12.78
RTZ[25]	4	13.24
NatWest[8]	5	33.37
British Airways[20]	6	69.61
BAT Industries[14]	7	12.28
British Telecommunications[6]	8	4.50
Shell Transport and Trading[4]	8	45.34
HSBC Holdings–Midland[3]	8	84.85
British Gas[1]	12	−28.51
British Petroleum[2]	12	64.63
Barclays[9]	15	63.88
Eurotunnel Group[11]	16	−72.18
ICI–Zeneca[17]	17	2.60
Hanson[7]	18	−41.02
Bass[24]	19	59.57
Land Securities[22]	20	24.83
Abbey National[5]	22	77.70
Cable and Wireless[18]	24	29.12
News International[12]	25	103.51
Correlation coefficient		0.13
FTSE change over 1994–1996		28.7

Notes: Number in brackets indicates size ranking by capital employed for the 25 biggest companies. Some companies are excluded, such as Halifax which was not a publicly quoted company in 1995, leaving 21 companies that can be studied.

graphically in Figure 9.1. A weak positive correlation is seen between my CSR ranking and the percentage change in share price over the period end 1994–end 1996; in other words, this means that a high CSR ranking is slightly worse for a company's share price than a low one. Over end 1994–end 1996, the FTSE 100 share index rose by 28.7 per cent. Eleven of the 25 biggest UK firms saw their share price rise by more than this.

Of the three companies who saw their share price fall, all were in the lower half of the rankings. The data also shows that a company's CSR ranking does not affect its share price significantly – this can be seen through noting that the top ten ranked companies have all recorded positive share price gains over the period. High share price gains significantly higher than the FTSE 100 average rise were seen by HSBC Holdings (ranked CSR number 8, with a share price rise of 84.4 per cent), Glaxo Wellcome (ranked number 2, with a share price gain of 43.2 per cent) and British Airways (ranked number 6, with a share price gain of 69.6 per cent).

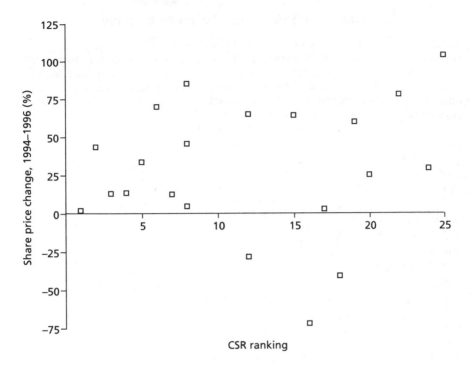

Figure 9.1 *Share price change versus CSR rank*

Of course, the results do not imply that being an SRE is both a necessary and sufficient condition for having a good performance on the stock market. This is shown by the fact that our top-ranked SRE, Guinness, recorded only a 1.7 per cent gain over the period compared with the FTSE 100 average rise. It is also demonstrated by the fact that the company who did worst in the rankings – News International – actually had the largest share price rise. Clearly, the public's purchasing of shares is still not greatly affected, as yet, by the companies' level of social responsibility. However, one conclusion stands out, and that is that CSR ranking does not necessarily badly affect a company's share price. Of course, some may argue that a company could have had an even better share price had it not been so socially responsible; but this is not possible to tell for individual companies, because one would need a control group of non-SREs and SREs for the same company during the same period.

An Application in Switzerland

Based upon my framework for indicators, Marianne Sorg, formerly of the InfoCenter in Switzerland, tried to find data for the largest Swiss companies. For Switzerland, she notes, 'the Wood model is a very

Table 9.7 *CSR indicator list for Switzerland*

Nationally or internationally established codes of ethics: do not exist
Nationally or internationally established codes for environmental protection:
* ICC Charter (business charter for sustainable development, launched by the International Chamber of Commerce, or ICC) or United Nations Environment Programme (UNEP) declarations for sustainable development (launched for banks and insurance companies) (ICC/UNEP)
* Membership of OEBU (Swiss association for ecological awareness in management)
Employees
* Existence of corporate social policy and guidelines (Empl1)
Net job creation without acquisitions (Empl2)
Share of permanent employees under permanent contract (Empl3)
Turnover increase per employee (Empl4)
Average expenditure per employee (Empl5)
* Participation on profit (Empl6)
* Employee shares (Empl7)
  Safety audits (Empl8)
  Women employed versus women in upper management (Empl9)
* Equal opportunities promotion programmes (Empl10)
Customers/Consumers
* Corporate guidelines for marketing practices or anti-corruption directives (Cust1)
Marketing expenditure as percentage of sales (Cust2)
Number of rule-breaking actions with regard to codes or legislation for advertising practices (Cust3)
Suppliers
* Ethical guidelines in purchasing policy (Sup1)
Owners
Annual financial statements according to International Accounting Standards Committee (IASC) guidelines or European Union (EU) standards (Own1)
Percentage of voting securities in share capital (Own2)
FuW-rating (rating for Swiss companies regarding the criteria of 'transparency' and 'relations with shareholders' (Own3)
Community
Corporate giving in percentage of profit (Com1)
* Direct involvement in community programmes (welfare, culture and sport, research and education) (Com2)
Developing countries
Investment in developing countries versus sales in developing countries (Dcs1)
* Direct involvement in development aid programmes (Dcs2)
Number of R&D units versus number of production sites in developing countries (Dcs3)
Natural Environment
* Existence of a corporate environmental concept (Env 1)
* Advanced implementation of environmental management instruments (Env 2)
* Environmental audits (Env 3)
Total amount of environmental liability fines (Env 4)

Note: * = included in the ranking calculation

Table 9.8 CSR indicators for selected companies in Switzerland

Company	Sector	Turnover (US$ billion)	Year	ICCI/ UNEP	OEBU	Empl 1	Empl 6	Empl 7	Empl 10	Cust1	Sup1	Com2	Dcs2	Env2	Env2	Env3	Score	Rank
Novartis	Chemicals		1997	1	1	0.33	0.11	1	1	1	0	1	1	1	1	1	0.80	1
Roche	Pharmaceuticals	8.8	1992	1	1	0	1	0	1	1	0	1	1	1	1	1	0.77	2
ABB	Electro	3.9	1994	1	0	0	0	1	1	0	0	0	1	1	0	1	0.46	7
Swissair	Transport	4.4	1994	1	1	1	0	0	1	0	0	1	0.75	1	1	1	0.60	5
Nestlé	Food	39	1994	1	1	0	0	0.56	1	1	0	0.29	1	0	0	0	0.53	6
Rieter	Machines	1.3	1995	0	0	0	0	1	0	0	0	0.29	0.29	0	0	1	0.18	8
Swiss Re	Re-insurance	8.8	1995	1	1	1	0	0	1	1	0	0	0	1	1	1	0.62	4
Zürich	Insurance	18.1	1995	0	0	0	0	1	0	0	1	0	0	0	0	0	0.15	9
Winterthur	Insurance	15.3	1995	1	0	1	0	1	1	1	0	1	0	1	1	1	0.69	3

Note: 1 = yes; 0 = no.

interesting approach; it gives a more sophisticated structure to the criteriology compared with most of the existing models used in practice. But it also requires the definition of more and new indicators.'[11] She further remarks that in Switzerland you cannot profit from studies such as *The 100 Best UK Companies To Work For* or from environmental indices. Nobody has yet performed broad, empirical research on social or environmental factors that would allow companies to be compared with each other. InfoCenter is the pioneer in Switzerland; but it has a very demanding and holistic approach and has not advanced very far. Nevertheless, Sorg was available to use InfoCenter files and came up with the list of indicators and some data that she says were selected upon the basis of 'research done in a short time and with little costs' – these I list in Table 9.7.

Sorg found data for most of the indicators listed. To create a ranking, I used only those indicators for the nine biggest Swiss companies for which I had data for at least seven of the indicators. The data are binary (1 = yes; 0 = no), and I give them for the 13 indicators selected in this way in Table 9.8. The rankings are calculated simply by putting average scores for the (few) missing values and the averaging across the 13 indicators displayed. This gives the rankings displayed in Table 9.8. First is the chemical giant Novartis, followed by another huge chemical conglomerate, Hoffman La Roche. Third comes the insurance company Winterthur, followed by another (re)insurance company, Swiss Re, then Swissair, Nestlé, ABB, Rieter and the Zürich insurance company.

Appendix: Definitions and sources of indicators of relevance[12]

Indicators actually used are denoted by an asterisk.

*Member of Business in the Community

Founded in 1982, Business in the Community (BitC), non-profit organization, aims to make community involvement a natural part of successful business practice, and to increase the quality and extent of business activity in the community. (Source: BitC, 44 Baker Street, London.)

Race for Opportunity

These are all, as part of BitC, members of the Commission for Racial Equality and deal with, respectively, racial equality, sexual equality and community involvement. Racial equality is said to be good for business, for communities and for the nation. (Source: BitC, 44 Baker Street, London.)

Opportunity 2000

This is a campaign to increase the quality and quantity of women's work. Members offer a variety of benefits to some or all of their employees, ranging from flexible hours, equal pay for work of equal value and job-sharing, to ongoing training programmes and regular reviews or appraisals. It currently has 300 company and institutional members. It is also a programme of BitC. (Source: BitC, 44 Baker Street, London.)

*Index of Corporate Environmental Engagement (CEE)

This is intended as an annual feature of corporate life published by BitC. It is based on ten questions that range from whether a company has an environmental management system, published environmental targets or a 'Green' procurement programme, to whether it has a board member responsible for the environment. Companies are given a score of 1–5, depending upon an analysis of their responses to the ten questions. It is also a programme of BitC. (Sources: *Financial Times*, 'Polluting Industries Marked by Index', 18 November 1996, and BitC, 44 Baker Street, London.)

Investors in People

Being recognized as a company Investor in People broadly means accepting a standard that commits to investing in people in order to achieve business goals; planning how to achieve these goals; taking action to develop the necessary skills; and evaluating training outcomes. (Source: Investors in People, www.iipuk.co.uk.)

*Member of UK Per Cent Club

The idea is that members tie their level of giving to a pre-determined percentage of UK pre-tax profits. The aim of the Per Cent Club is to promote increased levels of support by the private sector both for charities, generally, and also for the social issues that most concern businesses and the local communities within which the companies operate. This is also a programme of BitC. (Source: Per Cent Club, 44 Baker Street, London.)

Membership of the Association for Business Sponsorship of the Arts (ABSA)

Established in 1976, the ABSA exists to promote and encourage partnerships between the private sector and the arts, to their mutual benefit and to that of the community at large. (Source: *The Arts Funding Guide*, ABSA, Nutmeg House, London.)

*Supplier payment time period

Scores are as follows: 0 = those who admit they have no code and vary according to the supplier; 0.5 = weak application of code; 1 = application of code. (Source: individual company reports.)

Confederation of British Industries' (CBI's) Prompt Payer Code

This comprises the Prompt Payers' Code: does the company belong to the CBI's Prompt Payer Code? (Source: CBI.)

Employee share ownership

Does the company promote a share ownership scheme, as stated in its company report? (Source: company reports.)

*Employment 1993–1996

Figures on employees in the company are obtained from several sources, including company reports and Hoover's *Handbook of World Business, 1995–1997*.[13] Some figures are average in year and others end of year. Some account as number of employees, while others use full-time equivalents. Either way, they show the trend. Mergers or break-ups can affect the results.

*Cadbury Code compliance

This is the Cadbury Code of Best Practice, recommended by the Cadbury Commission on the Financial Aspects of Corporations. Compliance was assessed by judgement after examining the company's report. (Source: LSE.)

Greenbury Code compliance

This is a financial code of best practice recommended by the Greenbury Commission. Compliance was assessed by judgement after examining the company's report. (Source: LSE.)

Two-Ticks Disability Scheme

This involves a government scheme to highlight disability-friendly companies.

Analytical body for social issues

This is limited to whether the company states if it has an analytical body for social issues in its company report. The examples so far are of directors' committees. This is far from conclusive, and only represents those companies who mention if they have some form of committee made up of directors involving environmental or social concerns. (Source: company reports.)

Pre-tax profits 1995–1997

The pre-tax profits are normally taken from company reports or the book *Company Giving*.[14] The figures in this book are based mainly on the year 1995–1996; wherever possible, the figures from the company reports were used.

*Charity giving: UK donations 1995–1997, £000

Any company giving £200,000 or more in any one year in charitable or political contributions is legally required to disclose the total of such donations in its annual report and accounts. It does not include the value of other support, such as gifts in kind or secondment. Wherever possible, the figures from the company reports were used. (Source: Directory of Social Change, www.dsc.org.uk.)

All donations

This comprises the total donations that the company has given to good causes worldwide. Wherever possible, the figures from the company reports were used. (Source: Directory of Social Change, www.dsc.org.uk.)

*Advertising Standards Authority (ASA) complaint upheld

Figures represent the number of adverts that had a complaint upheld against them. (Source: ASA, Torrington Place, London, www.asa.org.uk.)

Independent Television Commission (ITC) complaint upheld

Figures represent the number of televised adverts that had a complaint upheld against them. (Source: ITC.)

Share value 1993–1997 by end of quarter

Figures are drawn from *Financial Times* end-of-year reports. (Source: Datastream.)

*Independent audit of code of ethics?

Figures were found in the annual reports, generally reproduced in the 'board of directors' section. Here, they list the directors' responsibilities in the firm (CEO, marketing and so on) and other non-executive directorships for other firms. As part of this, they 'sometimes' list any committees that have been formed to deal with certain issues (for example, health and safety, environment and the community). There were very few who actually mentioned these committees – even fewer regarding ethics. Since these committees are normally made up of non-executive directors, it is doubtful if they can be regarded as fully independent.

*Best UK Company?

This is drawn from *The 100 Best UK Companies To Work For*. (Source: Nightingale Multimedia, UK, 1997.)

Numbers of tax haven subsidiaries

This involves the number of tax haven subsidiaries – a tax haven is defined as having low tax rates, a stable currency, banking secrecy, good communication and transport, no currency controls, and stable government. Not all tax havens are purely for tax avoidance. A company may have considerable commercial and manufacturing industries that may also attract foreign investment – for example, Ireland or Switzerland. (Source: *Ethical Consumer*, February–March 1997.)

Chapter 10

Implications of a Planetary Bargain for the Developing Countries

Introduction

This chapter focuses on two main questions about corporate social responsibility (CSR) in developing countries that must be answered if a planetary bargain is to be implemented. The first is to do with how a large transnational corporation (TNC), based in the richer world, operates in a developing country. Should such a TNC and its subsidiaries be more socially responsible than local companies? The second is what should be the response of these local companies – would the adoption of even a basic level of CSR injure their ability to compete domestically or even internationally?

Neither of these issues is a new topic for developing countries. As far back as 1982, the Asian Productivity Organization (APO) organized a conference on the issue of social responsibility in Asia; six developing countries (India, Hong Kong, Indonesia, South Korea, the Philippines and Thailand) took part and presented papers, along with Japan.[1] Indeed, one of the key questions was whether the level of social responsibility in TNCs should be higher than that of an indigenous firm in a developing country. It was observed that a TNC would often, generally, provide better pay and conditions than local enterprises, but not much better than a socially responsible indigenous enterprise (SRIE).

Multinationals' social responsibility in developing countries

The world is characterized by the emerging globalization of the economy, liberalization of trade and investments and greater interdependence. The power of single national states to control fundamental economic variables, such as interest rates, money supply and the level of domestic activity, has been massively reduced. Therefore, the effectiveness of traditional economic policy measures to sustain economic growth is being reduced, too.

The reduced autonomy of the nation state can be seen as a consequence of the rising power gained during the last decade by TNCs, who continue to play a central role in the increase of economic integration or globalization. For example, the top 300 firms make up around one quarter of the productive assets of the world.[2] Because of their often immense (quasi-national) size, decisions about the allocation of investments, production and technology by the TNCs not only influence the distribution of factor endowments – notably, capital, skilled labour and knowledge – between the less developed countries in which they run their activities, but also assume a crucial importance for their socio-economic consequences. However, the increase of power of TNCs that has reflected the corresponding decline of the role of the state is only gradually being balanced by an explicit recognition of the *new responsibilities* connected with the role of the TNCs as global actors.

Briefly, what are the *ethical and social responsibilities* of TNCs in less developed countries (LDCs)? The potential role of TNCs in promoting sustainable development or human development is a key issue. But there is no measure that can give an overall assessment of the impact of TNCs on human development.

Some of the most long-term viewing and innovative TNCs (for example, The Body Shop, Shell and British Petroleum – BP) are already being managed according to high levels of CSR, while others are increasingly recognizing (for example, Lufthansa, Toyota, Ciba and Caterpillar) the importance of a *stakeholder approach*. This values the company's product not only in economic terms, but also in more qualitative terms, such as the corporate reputation among different groups of people (employees, consumers, suppliers, investors, local communities, public authorities and the media) whose well-being is 'at stake' when talking about corporate activities.

These companies are developing different ways of disseminating information on their social initiatives, including social audit reports, environmental reports and codes of ethics. What is completely lacking, however, is a comprehensive overall system to fill the gap between 'corporate rhetoric' and identifiable contributions to human development. An analytical framework is needed to collect and process information on the compliance of TNCs with some internationally agreed standards of behaviour to conduct business in LDCs.

We have, on the one hand, the human development index (HDI) of the United Nations Development Programme's (UNDP's) *Human Development Report*, which estimates the national and mainly public-sector contribution to human development (HD). But there is no widely accepted mechanism to analyse, on the other hand, the contribution of the private sector.

There is a need, therefore to:

■ identify the key points and areas upon which there is growing agreement within the current debate on international business ethics, about global standards of CSR;

- develop a tentative list of indicators to measure levels of social responsibility of TNCs operating in LDCs; and
- test the proposed list of indicators so as to verify their applicability with existing data.

What areas, concepts and indicators could be used to define a socially responsible company in LDCs? Should they not be the same as in the developed countries? The answer is yes, eventually; but one cannot run without being able to walk first, so it is better to start slowly than to do nothing at all. A minimum list of considerations could look something like:

- observance of a core set of labour standards, suitably adapted to companies, following those suggested by the International Labour Organization (ILO) and taken up by the United Nations' (UN's) Global Compact;
- environmental protection observance by TNCs – use US or European Union (EU) existing regulation as benchmark;
- a positive relationship with the government, such as no corruption, compliance with fiscal legislation, and working with the government to ensure fair enterprise policies that are performed in a transparent manner;
- a positive relationship with the local community, such as corporate community programmes;
- good relationships with non-governmental organizations (NGOs), such as joint community ventures and direct funding; and
- an excellent level of corporate governance.

Why should TNCs care to be socially responsible in developing countries? Beyond a moral duty to behave with fairness, there are sound economic reasons that should induce corporations to consider the issue of defining and assessing their social and ethical responsibility. Being widely recognized as a 'socially and ethically responsible enterprise' can help a TNC to:

- improve corporate acceptability by its stakeholders and by new counterparts in new countries;
- enhance the corporate ability to attract new investors;
- ameliorate corporate industrial relations;
- improve customers' trust in corporate products;
- contribute to sustainable development;
- improve corporate reputation; and
- contribute to human development.

What has been the experience of CSR across the developing world? This question requires more in-depth focus than has been considered in our brief review of the continents. Since the first edition of this book, there

have been more and more discussions on CSR in ⟨
prompted by such bodies as the UN's Global Compa⟨
issues has been the question of child labour, which is lo⟨

The special case of child labour and s
responsibility

The use of child labour in developing countries is universally frowned
upon; but the story is much more complex than simply banning the
practice. In many developing countries, the observance of laws and
international conventions concerning child labour, inter alia, is an ad hoc
affair. Surprising as it may seem to Western minds – to which this is just
more evidence of widespread corruption – there is more economic sense
here than first meets the eye. For instance, in one industry – the
manufacturing of locks in India – Zafar Alam, the chairman of a large link
lock enterprise, remarks in a paper for the ILO: 'There is no doubt that
stark poverty of the lock makers is responsible for the induction of child
labour into it.'[3,4] That there is so much child labour in this particular
industry, Alam continues, is due to four main reasons: exploitation and
low contract rates; the huge labour force; perpetual indebtedness; and large
families with their attendant economic burden.

A boycott of goods from countries who are home to child labour is
normally mooted as necessary to root out the practice. Yet, this is precisely
the wrong way to go about the problem. In Nepal in 1996, the balance of
payments and national income were severely affected as exports collapsed
because of a boycott of the country's carpets (its biggest export), led by a
very strong campaign by NGOs in Germany, Nepal's main customer in
that trade. The use of children to sew carpets has long been a practice in
Nepal; however, the dyes used were causing serious health problems, which
led to the German ban. What happened in practice, though, was that dirt-
poor children from one of the poorest countries on Earth were further
deprived of any income, as were their families. No income meant no food.
Access to education and health services in the remote mountainous areas
of Nepal is almost impossible. No work for the families or their children
was just another twist in the cycle of abject poverty, increased malnutrition
and an early death. Rather than simply trying to convince a practically
helpless Nepalese government, in the face of widespread poverty, to ban
child labour, it would have been better for the German importers, NGOs
and consumers to have found out what they could do to assist the families
in gaining alternative sources of income, and to produce carpets safely and
cleanly, while encouraging a better future for the children, such as helping
them go to school.

One solution to the child labour problem was tried out by Zafar Alam
in India. He took over a school in the very thick of the lock-making

ry with the aim of halting the spiral of child labour and poverty. owever, it took him some time to persuade parents to send their children to school. They were wary and sceptical from the beginning. But they were assured that the intention was not to take away the children from their occupation. They would have to attend school from 7.00 am in the morning until 1.00 pm in the afternoon, and after that they were free to do their usual work. Slowly, they became responsive, and today the school, Luftia Higher Secondary School, has 2750 pupils, of which about 80 per cent are child labourers.

The extent of the child labour problem in developing countries is not known in any great detail, although Richard Anker of the ILO cites an old United Nations Children's Fund (UNICEF) study that there were between 13–44 million child labourers in India in 1983. Whatever the numbers, he says, the problem is large, and India is generally recognized as having a substantial number of child labourers.[5] He concurs with me that the reality of poor countries often differs from that presented by idealists in international conventions and declarations. For that reason, the ILO has developed a practical approach on how, eventually, to eliminate such labour. It recognizes that child labour is a reality that cannot be eliminated immediately. But it comes down hard, quite appropriately, on certain types of child labour that cannot (nor should be) tolerated under any circumstances – hazardous work, bonded labour, prostitution, excessive working hours and work by especially young children.[6]

Why is child labour used? Obviously, desperately poor families wish to increase their family income. But then, in terms of labour supply, is there not enough adult labour to do the work? Some reasons advanced why this may not be the case are that children have very nimble fingers, that they are cheap, that they are easy to control and that their physical size is important for some sorts of work. For instance, in Madagascar I saw children digging tunnels through rubbish dumps to collect such things as old bones, dead radio batteries, plastic and so on. The tunnels were tiny, the returns meagre. An enterprising Jesuit priest, with help from the World Food Programme, built a school right on the rubbish dump to attract the children to classes in the evening when it was too dark for them to work.

Surprisingly, Anker's research in India found that children do not have irreplaceable skills, that they are not more productive than adults and that the production cost increase would be small in many of the industries where they work. In particular, he found the argument that only children with small fingers have the ability to make fine hand-knotted carpets spurious – most children in the carpet industry work side by side with adult labourers doing the same activity.

Given that children provide no apparent monetary cost advantage to employers, are there non-pecuniary reasons, such as children being more innocent and less aware of (or able to act on) their rights? Anker found some evidence for this; he also suggested that 'tradition' was a key reason. Entrepreneurs in some industries have traditionally introduced children into the family occupation at an early age. Indeed, in many settings, employers feel that they have a social obligation to the community to provide jobs and incomes to poor people, and that they are being good citizens by providing jobs to poor children. In many places, employers actually gain social status by providing jobs to poor children.

Consequently, boycotts of goods through such activities as labelling products may do more harm than good. A label bears information that the manufacturer or marketer of a product provides to the customer at the point of sale. Social labelling is intended to inform consumers about the social conditions of production so as to assure them that the item they are about to buy was produced under fair and equitable working conditions. This puts pressure on producers to introduce such conditions. In other words, the proponents of most social-labelling initiatives concerning child labour are trying to initiate change by starting from the consumer and moving back through the marketing chain to affect modes of production and improve the lives of working children.[7]

V R Sharma, the managing director of OBETEE, the largest carpet exporter in India, with an exemplary record on child labour issues, says labelling initiatives, such as Rugmark, can cause 'serious' problems for the carpet industry if they are not done correctly.[8,9] Indeed, many just seem, instead, to concentrate negative publicity on the carpet industry. He believes that 'histrionics and theatrics' will only destroy the industry and take away the livelihood of millions of people living and working in an area where there is no other industry worth talking about. Therefore, for labelling to be successful, representatives of the carpet industry believe that a label should not be used until such time as a credible and professional system for the monitoring of looms is in place to ensure 'genuine certification of child-free carpets'.

Sharma also noted that although the best thing that could happen to the carpet industry is that children should not work in it, this is easier said than done. Child labour cannot be eliminated in the carpet industry overnight. The monitoring of carpet looms to ensure child-free carpets is almost impossible on a large scale. If children are taken out of the carpet industry, they will start working in other industries. The only solution, he says, with which I very much agree, is to provide viable alternatives to the children. Where free and compulsory education were provided, they would be paid to study in school (through stipends and free food and drink) to compensate for the loss of income from working. Some closely monitored work by these children could be done in parallel to the provision of education.

This is more or less the view of Levi Strauss of the US. It has a strict child labour policy under its global sourcing and operating guidelines, which state that the use of child labour is not permissible.[10] Their workers must be at least 14 years of age. The company has established itself as one of the corporate leaders in tackling the issue, clearly setting standards for its subcontractors to follow. However, there are certain situations where the company has seen that the economic conditions of a country deem it necessary for children to work. This is the case in Bangladesh, where young girls under the age of 14 were being employed on a full-time basis at one of the company's subcontractors. Levi Strauss established a school on the work site and paid for the girls' books and uniforms until the age of 15, while the subcontractor promised to pay the girls' salaries during this period.

What are the implications for socially responsible enterprises (SREs)? There is a dilemma. They are under pressure not to use industries with child labour. Yet, the elimination of such work undoubtedly hurts far more than it helps. Hazardous jobs should clearly be a central concern. But simply banning goods produced with such practices will not lead to the practice being eliminated. A comprehensive solution is required in which the SRE works with the local community to gradually, eliminate child labour. This would mean assisting the community in setting up alternatives for the children, such as education, training, income supplements and so on. Are SREs ready to assume these additional costs? A planetary bargain would see an agreement among major enterprises in not banning child labour, at least in the short term. We would then see SREs employing child labour, while working both to improve the socio-economic conditions of the children and, gradually, eliminating the practice. However, this is a complicated message to transmit to concerned consumers in the developed world. There is no easy solution to this; development is a complicated matter and quick fixes, more often than not, simply don't work. This is a message that must also be transmitted to the developed world.

Is there a role for large-scale corporations in alleviating poverty in developing countries?[11]

Another major CSR issue is whether large corporations should be involved in poverty alleviation over and above simply contributing to output and employment. To date, the need to address questions of low living standards, exploitation, poverty, unemployment and how to promote human development has been almost entirely the preserve of governments. Yet, the notion that the aim of business is solely business plays less well today. So, what, if anything, can corporations do in the area of poverty? Obviously, there should not be corporate poverty departments. But an emphasis on poverty alleviation may actually help a corporation to make profits – helping its own workers to avoid HIV/AIDS is just one obvious area. The profit argument is important since the argument that it is morally and ethically acceptable for corporations to be involved in poverty alleviation plays less well in the boardrooms in Dallas, Tokyo, Hong Kong and Jakarta than many of us would like.

There are both supply and demand responses where large companies can have an impact on poverty.[12] The supply response is equivalent to the development response – that is, a growing and profitable company provides a supply of jobs and incomes. Consequently, to increase this supply requires specific conditions to allow the private sector to flourish. Poverty and inequality conditions in many countries lead to instability, corruption and, therefore, much unreliability in negotiating contracts. This, in turn, leads to higher costs in doing business and a general reluctance to work and invest in poor countries. Examples abound; but Singapore, whose low corruption levels put it near the top of Transparency International's worldwide anti-corruption index, receives more than its fair share of private investment than, for instance, most sub-Saharan countries such as Nigeria, who finds itself at the bottom of the index.

Clearly, the presence (supply) of TNCs creates economic growth and employment. Large-scale TNCs may provide jobs directly; but the overall number of workers in these organizations is probably not more than 100 million worldwide out of around 2.4 billion workers in the world – that is, approximately 4 per cent of jobs.[13] There may be as many people again whose jobs and livelihoods are created indirectly by the TNCs – such as suppliers or simply those benefiting from the wealth created. However, it cannot be assumed that those who directly obtain jobs are those in poverty. Foreign investment is likely to attract and employ individuals with high skills, rather those in destitution. It is primarily the indirect effects of TNCs that will provide some benefit to the poor – these individuals will be working for the suppliers of suppliers (immediate suppliers of TNCs in developing countries will also likely be highly skilled). Of the suppliers of suppliers, it will be those in small firms or those in self-employment who will number among the poor. Consequently, foreign investment via TNCs will help the poor solely through a 'trickle-down' effect. This way of doing business is unlikely to change simply because poor people are poor and they don't have the skills necessary to help themselves out of their own poverty. Consequently, they cannot provide the skills required by TNCs.

The demand response is a little more complicated. It is what is expected, or demanded, of companies so that they can operate freely. This is a bit of an oxymoron since 'expect' and 'free' are in opposition to each other. This demand is expressed through hundreds of rules and expectations. The CSR movement is just one of many such expectations that run from initiatives such as the UK's Ethical Trading Initiative (ETI), the UN's Global Compact, the ILO conventions and standards, to legally binding ones that are enshrined in company law and that come under the heading of corporate governance. Prominent in the demand response are the stakeholders of the organization. There is no accepted definition of who these are, but they certainly include internal stakeholders such as owners, managers, shareholders and employees, while the outside stakeholders (and this is more contentious) include suppliers, local communities, families, the environment (NGO community) and the government. Each of these groups expresses 'demands' on corporations with, perhaps, only the environmental group even mentioning the issue of poverty. The TNCs' response to these demands can affect long-term profitability – hence the increasing interest by TNCs in the various stakeholder groups.

There is also a third component related to poverty which is both supply and demand and this is when private companies develop initiatives that are aimed directly at the poor. In many cases, this has come under the heading of 'business partnerships' where TNCs seek advantage through better public relations and understanding of local situations. But, normally, when one thinks of poverty alleviation, the private sector often escapes attention and the image of state-provided services is conjured up. Yet, the poor represent an enormous untapped resource for the private sector that has hardly been explored. The experience of credit programmes for the poor shows that these activities are both sustainable and profitable once the initial capacity-building and investment have begun. Awareness by the private sector of this untapped potential is a key role for international organizations and donors as facilitators in helping the poor to help themselves. Much effort is expended here. Once the poor have their feet on the first rung of the ladder, this development process needs to be sustained through, for example, the continuing supply of credit from the banking system. Moreover, when the poor have shown their credit worthiness through Grameen-type credit schemes (the pro-poor micro-credit organization started by Mohamed Younis in Bangladesh), the culture of thrift is developed and credit records can be passed on to commercial, but not exploitative, lenders.

Can CSR, therefore, have a positive effect on poverty? CSR is a good thing in itself since it leads to better treatment of stakeholders from improved codes of ethics, from better conditions for employees, from the concerns of local communities being considered, and from less damage to the environment. It also leads to increased allocations to philanthropic causes. However, the direct impact of corporations on alleviating poverty (and remember, I am talking about large TNCs and not the 'private sector') is likely to be marginal on the *supply* side. This is because:

■ Poor people don't work for TNCs and, generally, don't work for their direct suppliers either.
■ TNCs do not create many jobs – even the largest corporations only employ about 100,000–200,000 individuals, compared to a world labour force of 2–3 billion.
■ Suppliers to TNCs tend to be high tech and do not employ poor people, in general.

On the *demand* side, there is more that TNCs can do, such as:

■ Make sure that products and production processes are safe.

- Ensure a pricing policy that poor people can afford (AIDS drugs are an obvious example).
- Respect the environment.
- Have a philanthropic policy that focuses upon anti-poverty measures.
- Work with the authorities and international organizations to ensure democratic environments, peace, lack of corruption, reduced bureaucracy and anti-discrimination.

Consequently, there are a number of steps that corporations can take that will reduce poverty. However, these steps are unlikely to lead to major reductions in the number of individuals in poverty, especially since the main focus of business is business – which is where their experience lies. Few within the walls of TNCs know anything about poverty-alleviation programmes, and, unfortunately, the rationale for TNCs to employ such persons is not overwhelming. The above lists, moreover, do not suggest that there is a lot of mileage in focusing upon anti-poverty measures, with the exception of the last item. Thus, the case for a corporation to have a corporate poverty department is not strong since an emphasis on poverty alleviation is unlikely to help a corporation to make profits. It may wish to do this for public relations (PR) or philanthropic purposes; but the direct business benefit is not high.

On the other hand, the case for TNCs to have a CSR department is much stronger. There are strong benefits across the board for each stakeholder, who, generally, will not be in poverty. Consequently, even though it is certainly morally and ethically acceptable for corporations to be involved in poverty alleviation, the argument plays less well in the boardrooms across the world simply because the impact on profits is marginal.

Social responsibility within developing countries

So, what trends towards social responsibility can one see around the developing world? There is more, as will be shown in my brief review here, than convention would have us believe. Most of the new CSR activity has been concentrated either on business partnerships, whereby a TNC will assist a supplier or even small companies in setting up shop, or in straight philanthropic contributions to local NGOs and charities.

The predominant view in the developed world is that enterprises in the developing world are universally corrupt – a situation exacerbated by their renowned inefficiency. This characterization is probably not far from the truth, particularly in countries where the rule of law and democratic processes have been ignored for decades. However, the situation varies from one continent to another, and from one country to another within continents. Africa and Latin America are seen as scoring poorly on this front, while Asia has been placed higher. However, the recent collapse of business confidence in many Asian countries – in particular, Indonesia – has shown that corruption and inefficiency are not just the preserves of Africa and Latin America. All is not gloom and doom, though, as will be illustrated next.

Africa

Africa, of course, is not a continent that immediately springs to mind in terms of social responsibility. War and terrorism in the North (Algeria, Egypt, Sudan, Spanish Sahara), turbulence in the South, until recently (South Africa, Angola, Mozambique), and conflict in the East and West (Congo, Rwanda, Burundi, Somalia, Sierra Leone) make progress on the social front problematical. Widespread corruption, from Bokassa's diamonds in the Central African Republic to Mobutu's billions and the withdrawal of the International Monetary Fund (IMF) from Kenya in mid 1997, followed by the re-elections of Kenya's President Daniel Moi and Zimbabwe's President Robert Mugabe, both in dubious circumstance, is also rampant. However, there are examples of social responsibility by TNCs working in Africa and from within Africa itself, with two examples from the Congo (formerly known as Zaire) and Zimbabwe.[14]

An example of social responsibility for a whole region comes from the Congo in the diamond-mining area of Kasai before the overthrow of Mobutu's government in 1997. The public transport system in the town of Mbuji-Mayi collapsed, while hospitals and clinics ran out of medicines and suffered from cuts in power supplies. The leading diamond entrepreneurs spontaneously took on the mantle of the state. They purchased minibuses, power generators and medicines. This, in turn, stimulated the 80 per cent state-owned diamond company Société Minière de Makwanga (MIBA) to repair roads, pay soldiers, supply water and electricity to local inhabitants from its own power station, and set up a social fund of US$5 million to US$6 million a year – the equivalent of 8 per cent of its budget. The fund was used to maintain hospitals and schools, and is financing a new private university in the town. The company's chief executive officer (CEO), still technically a state employee, fought for tax exemption for the projects, arguing that MIBA should be allowed to pay its taxes by spending money locally. However, the question with a project such as this is whether it is sustainable. Should the company simply decide not to pay, then the system will collapse. What should be devised are systems that might be simple but use local resources and involve local communities. Otherwise, collapse of the system quickly ensues.

An example of a more sustainable type of system comes from Zimbabwe. Partners for Growth (PfG) was established in 1995 as a result of an initiative between more than 40 Zimbabwean business leaders. It was established to develop small- and medium-sized enterprises. The developed world is littered with such examples, some successful and some not. The aim is to create employment and sustainable businesses, because most new employment is created in small-scale enterprises in developing countries. PfG received its initial funding from the Prince of Wales Business Leaders Foundation and the UK Overseas Development Administration (ODA, now the Department for International Development (DFID)), and then received core funding from Ashanti Coalfields, BP, Coca-Cola, the Farmers' Development Trust, KPMG (one of the 'Big Four' accounting firms), Meikles, Rio Tinto Zinc (RTZ), Zimbabwe Leaf Tobacco Co, and Zimbabwe Sugar Refineries.[15] Examples of activities include subcontracting services and off-loading non-core operations to small indigenous enterprises; providing financial, technical, marketing and training support; and the launching of an enterprise education programme in partnership with one of the country's leading government schools, Prince Edward. Such initiatives work as long as existing entrepreneurs are helped to improve their business through training, exposure to new, but appropriate and affordable, technology and access to credit. New entrepreneurs can be helped, but the conditions must be even more severe for success to be assured. However, the past few years in Zimbabwe have seen increasing violence as Robert Mugabe struggles for survival as president. CSR initiatives in poorly led countries will struggle without political will – illustrating that CSR must be a planetary bargain that is not just the preserve of the industrialized countries: developing countries have their own part to play.

Thus, can there be socially responsible companies in Africa even when so many of the governments in that continent are so clearly socially irresponsible? Some hope is coming from South Africa, where many companies have adopted socially responsible policies and some have subscribed to AccountAbility and the Global Reporting Initiative (GRI) guidelines. Moreover, one of the developing world's leading lights in including ethical codes of conduct in good corporate governance is based in Johannesburg – Mervyn King. The King Commission's code of corporate governance, written for the Commonwealth countries, goes further than the Organisation for Economic Co-operation and Development (OECD) corporate governance principles in defining stakeholder groups and identifying what should be in a company's code of ethics. The King Commission's revised report was published in 2002;[16] but it is too early to judge the impact of the principles on corporate governance within Africa – many of whose countries belong to the Commonwealth.

Companies are increasingly becoming involved in HIV/AIDS prevention and cure. This is partly from pressure from activists, such as the Treat Your Workers coalition of HIV/AIDS activist groups who, in 2002, coordinated a day of action to press Coca-Cola into devoting more resources to combating the HIV/AIDS pandemic ravaging Africa. Coca-Cola, which is in partnership with the Joint United Nations Programme on HIV/AIDS (UNAIDS), argues that it, too, is at the forefront of the corporate campaign to halt the spread of HIV/AIDS. But it acknowledges that responses among its bottlers need to be accelerated. A spokesman said anti-retroviral drugs were available to families throughout Africa. The Coca-Cola foundation pays half the costs of drug treatments for workers, leaving the bottling company and the employee to pay the rest. Coca-Cola also supports HIV/AIDS care and prevention campaigns such as LoveLife and Starfish in South Africa. But activists complain that the extended health benefits are not on offer to bottlers' entire workforces.

Outside of South Africa, and with the possible exception of some companies operating out of Tunisia, African corporations undoubtedly have a poor level of social responsibility – especially those in countries where the rule of law is poorly observed and enforced by the many corrupt governments in the region. Unless governments in Africa adopt the rule of law and move toward some measure of democracy, poor governance will continue to lead to poor corporate governance, with only a few exceptions. More can be done by corporations who are based outside of Africa, yet who have operations within Africa. This is where a planetary bargain would help right across the board. Corporations who work in Africa could come together and bring pressure on governments to behave more socially responsibly. One of the UN's Global Compact working groups, under the chairmanship of Sir Mark Moody-Stuart, former chairman of Shell, has begun to think how the Global Compact could be implemented by large corporations in selected African countries.[17] As noted in Chapter 2, the Global Compact only covers part of the CSR agenda. Nevertheless, it is making a number of welcome steps in the direction of improving some aspects of CSR in Africa (the Global Compact has nine principles in the human rights, labour and environmental areas). It is now waiting for a number of companies to sign up to its programme for some selected countries in Africa.

Asia

Even in 1982, the APO symposium – held over five days in New Delhi – could announce that, irrespective of cultural and industrial differences in the APO member countries, the subject of social responsibility was becoming important for business management.[18] The symposium found clear evidence that enterprises had agreed not only to be useful economically, but socially as well. In most of the APO member countries (Bangladesh, China, Hong Kong, India, Indonesia, South Korea, Nepal, the Philippines, Sri Lanka, Thailand and Malaysia, as of 1983), there exists a foundation or legal framework laid down in such areas as physical working conditions, employment, wages and salaries, industrial relations, pollution, and so on.

The ethical aspect of social responsibility had also been put forward in some codes of ethics by business associations in some of the countries. For example, in the Philippines, increasing interest in social responsibility among employers and managers was witnessed by the participation of more than 900 chief executives of business in the workshops organized by the Bishops Businessmen's Conference for Human Development (BBC). This conference resulted in what became known as the BBC Code of Ethics for Business. A survey conducted among over 4000 businesses in the Philippines found that around 70 per cent of those who replied (65 per cent) had adopted some form of code of ethics. Furthermore, in Thailand, the Buddhist tradition of 'sharing happiness and sorrows with others' creates a form of social responsibility among people. Thus, a growing number of business leaders view corporate social investment as an attempt of finding a new way to arrange the economic order and improve the benefits of economic growth.

An even more local initiative comes from the Tata Iron and Steel Rural Development Society (TSRDS) in India. This was established during the late 1970s by the Tata Group, India's largest business, which owns some 80 diversified companies in India. TSRDS receives an annual grant from Tata, but is also free to enter into other partnerships and funding relationships. It functions as an NGO whose purpose is to focus on education and literacy; health and medical activities; agriculture and irrigation; drinking water; vocational training; and income generation in rural India. The Tata Group believes that the private sector should realize that they have a part to play in the 'spirit of trusteeship advocated by Mahatma Gandhi' because, it believes, no business success is worth while unless it serves the needs or interests of the country and its people. 'It is worthless if it is not achieved by fair and honest means.'[19]

However, there are many things that are done by the corporate sector in India, for instance, that get passed off, incorrectly, as CSR.[20] It is often the case that social service, social work and corporate philanthropy are used as synonyms for CSR. But the mutual benefit that a CSR strategy can bring back to the corporate sector is not recognized or well articulated. Work is also often ad hoc, following the whims and fancy of the CEO of the corporation, and there is little percolation of the idea down to middle or junior management.

This is the general picture, although it is not the only one. Corporations are also talking of social policies and strategies that explicitly mention mutual gains and stakeholder participation. Though the numbers of such organizations are few, the trend has started and most CSR experts are urging corporate organizations to look at CSR as a business strategy rather than as a charity option.

Social audits or reports are not normally undertaken. A few years ago TISCO (a steel-producing subsidiary of TATA) undertook a social report; but this is a very rare phenomenon. Social audits are slightly more common, but are most often carried out by organizations who are export oriented. It is not at all common for Indian organizations selling in India.

A survey conducted by the Tata Energy Research Institute (TERI) traces back the history of CSR in India and suggests that there are four models.[21] First, there is the 'ethical model', as suggested by Mahatama Gandhi, where companies voluntarily commit to public welfare and participate in nation-building. Then follows the 'statist model', post-India's independence. Propounded by Jawaharlal Nehru, this model calls for state ownership and legal requirements of CSR. The 'liberal model' by Milton Friedman talks about CSR being limited to private owners or shareholders. And the latest is the 'stakeholder model' championed by R Edward Freeman, which calls for companies to respond to all stakeholders' needs. All four models can be found working in India. A survey by Partners in Change in July 2000 showed that 85 per cent of the companies surveyed mentioned that business has a role to play in social development. The focus of most of these company activities was community development. Three-fifths of the companies polled mentioned that their activities were 'purely philanthropic' and 'no benefits were expected'. Others expected an improved image in the general public and the local areas in which they operate. Another survey in 2001, by the Centre for Social Markets (CSM), described what companies view as CSR and what they think are the main considerations in being socially and environmentally sustainable. The government was mentioned as a key barrier, with unclear policies, bureaucracy, poor monitoring, complicated tax systems and poor infrastructure. Tata Group and information technology companies InfoSys and Wipro were mentioned as the most admired companies.[22]

CSR is gaining currency in India. More and more corporations are getting involved in CSR activities – some prefer to establish in-house foundations to carry out the work, others prefer to work on their own and some work with NGOs. The NGOs and corporations are often wary of each other; hence, partnership often needs to be brokered by an intermediary organization familiar with both groups.

Much like Tata in India, the San Miguel Corporation of the Philippines is a keen proponent of social responsibility. It is the largest publicly listed food, beverage and packaging company in South-East Asia and employs over 30,000 people in the Philippines.[23] It believes that social development should be pursued because 'responsible corporate citizenship goes beyond the boundaries of philanthropy'. It carries out a number of programmes such as entrepreneurship to promote self-reliance in communities; partnerships with NGOs; partnerships with other businesses to provide health and livelihood assistance; community organizing such as a reforestation programme; training for local communities; and so on. The emphasis is on building self-reliant communities so that the company can carry out its mission, which it calls 'profit with honour'. For example, one programme to provide skills training and livelihood programmes is in place in Pampanga, benefiting 449 families who were affected by the Mount Pinatubo volcano tragedy. However, the attempt to be an SRE is not easy, and San Miguel is increasingly being accused of monopolistic practices to preserve market share. This issue (and many others) is being taken up by a very active group in the Philippines – the Philippine Business for Social Progress (PBSP).[24]

The PBSP is a private and non-profit foundation dedicated to promoting business-sector commitment to social development. It was organized in December 1970 by 50 of the country's prominent business leaders, and has since grown to become the nation's largest and most influential business-led social development foundation. From an initial membership of 50 business companies, it has grown to more than 160 members, has worked with some 2500 partner organizations, has provided over 1.6 billion pesos (US$20 million) in financial assistance, which supported over 4400 projects, and has benefited close to 2.2 million poor households.

For the past 30 years, PBSP has been the business sector's vehicle in delivering organized, professional and sustainable assistance to the Filipino poor, particularly the landless farmers, fisherfolk, rural workers, urban poor and indigenous cultural communities. An aggressive membership involvement programme continuously invites corporations from all over the country to join the PBSP membership. As member companies, corporations commit to allocate 20 per cent of 1 per cent of net income before taxes to fund the foundation's operations and programmes.

The foundation considers as its key strengths development technology, which is founded on the premise that development is about helping people to help themselves; and corporate support, in the form of financial resources, time and competencies that its member companies invest to help improve the quality of life of the Filipinos.

Turkey is an unlikely country in which to find SREs.[25] Its international reputation is poor, owing to occurrences such as the vicious treatment of prisoners, as shown in the film *Midnight Express*, and its uncompromising military reaction to the Kurds. Nevertheless, there is a mutually reinforcing tendency for groups in civil society to demand that enterprises act socially and, in turn, for enterprises to incorporate this demand within their business activities. For example, the mayor of Bursa, an industrial town in the north-western part of the country, asked the residents whether they would agree to the construction of a new Japanese car-manufacturing factory in their city. The residents' response was negative because they had already suffered from earlier industrial activities – primarily in the form of pollution and deforestation. A more striking example is that of Bergama, a small town in Central Anatolia, where a multinational company (Euro-Gold) had set up facilities for gold-mining. Since this company's extraction methods were environmentally hazardous – owing to the use of poisonous chemicals in the extraction process – the villagers themselves took the initiative to block the mining. They first protested by bringing up their complaints before public authorities and by holding demonstrations at the entrance to the facility, expressing their preference for a safe environment over job creation or a potentially profitable exploitation of natural resources. The company disregarded their concerns at first, and the villagers extended the reach of their protests to the capital Ankara and to Istanbul. The issue was widely covered in the Turkish press and television. As it stands, the company has postponed mining and is likely to suffer from closure and its already sunk costs, as well as incurring a very bad image. These two examples illustrate what can happen at the domestic level in a developing country when issues of social responsibility towards stakeholders are ignored.

Latin America

Latin America, like Africa, is known for widespread corruption, which is linked mainly to the traffic in drugs. 'Deception, bribery, dumping, fraud and dishonest negotiation between buyer and seller' increase the costs of doing business, says the Latin American Alliance.[26] However, there are signs of progress on the social responsibility front. At the end of 2002, the Inter-American Development Bank organized a well-attended conference on CSR in the Americas.[27] Many Latin American companies attended with the main purpose of finding out what CSR was all about. Most of the work, to date, has seen CSR as purely philanthropy, with the wider stakeholder model hardly apparent. Yet, there are some examples of this latter approach. For instance, in Mexico some organizations have declarations of principles and values that follow programmes promoted by the Brussels-based International Union of Christian Business Executives (UNIAPAC). Brazil abounds with activities. FIDES – Fundação Instituto de Desenvovimento Empresarial e Social – in São Paulo, has dedicated efforts to cooperate with business people in the task of defining and preparing a new executive profile. CONAR in Brazil – Conselho Nacional de Auto-Regulamentação Publicitária – has developed codes of ethics to be followed by companies, advertising agencies and the media.

A beacon for CSR in Latin America is the Ethos Institute. Its impressive website lists a multitude of activities, from social reporting to measurement.[28] It claims nearly 500 associate corporate members, as of September 2001. In Chile, CSR is still associated with philanthropy; but this is changing as interest increases in social investment.[29] This is not altogether surprising given that Ricardo Lagos, the country's president, is an ex-ILO official!

In Venezuela, the local UNDP office was approached in 1999 by Norwegian oil giant Statoil, who wished to develop its CSR image there. Lost for ideas, and not a known proponent of CSR in those days, the UNDP suggested a project to teach human rights laws to the nation's judges! That judges should need such training may come as a surprise to most readers; nevertheless, Statoil developed a very successful programme and is convinced that this example of social responsibility has helped it enormously in winning respect, and therefore approval, for a whole host of investments in Venezuelan oil fields.

The spread of interest in CSR extends to universities in Argentina, Brazil, Chile, Colombia, Mexico and Peru, who are all offering classes in business ethics. Many US companies have located their production in Mexico and other countries in Central America. This has not been without controversy, as the well-known debate between those pro- and anti-NAFTA (North American Free Trade Association) has illustrated. I noted in Chapter 4 the case of Gap, who has brought in measures to improve working conditions in the Guatemalan factories of its subcontractors. Yet, exploitation is the norm rather than the exception in Latin America. This is certainly likely to increase concern among stakeholders of large companies with operations in Latin America in the coming years. Socially responsible enterprises are still thin on the ground in that continent; but the trend is changing as stakeholder pressure continues to gather force, and enterprises themselves begin to realize that exploitation of labour and poor environmental practices are simply bad for business.

Attitudes of Egyptian businessmen to CSR

Egypt undertook a survey to see how leading businessmen, government officials, community leaders and laymen saw the future of social responsibility in their country.[30] Indeed, a reassessment of the role of the state is taking place in a large number of developing countries in response to the failure of the development models adopted during the 1960s, which has often resulted from excessive state involvement in the economy. In Egypt, there has been, and continues to be, heavy state involvement in the economy. Nevertheless, the responsibilities and modes of intervention of the state in Egypt are being redefined, with the objective of raising the overall performance of the economy along an equitable and sustainable growth path that makes better use of the country's major asset: its business persons. The challenge is to mirror the development paradigm of the successful newly industrialized countries (NICs) so as to promote the rapid growth in savings, productive investment, exports, employment, real incomes and the quality of life. The process of transition requires a major transformation so that the role of the state as arbitrator and regulator is significantly strengthened, while some of its former responsibilities are handed over to the private sector, especially those of providing employment and operating productive assets.

Consequently, now, more than ever before, the private sector is expected to carry much of the burden of future development in Egypt. The public sector is expected to ease regulations to make this process possible. However, the private sector must also lend a hand to solving problems of human development as part of the planetary bargain.

Egypt's survey was carried out in January 1995 among influential business persons (152 replied), ranking civil servants (105), community leaders (124) and citizens (132), all selected at random. A key finding of the survey was the willingness to see a larger role in Egypt's affairs for the private sector than before. When asked whether or not it is the duty of the state to perform all functions of production, services, welfare and provision of work opportunities for all Egyptians, about one fifth of the sample replied 'yes'; but more than three-quarters replied 'no'. Not surprisingly, 82 per cent of business persons said 'no'. What was surprising was the response of top state civil servants. Fewer of them (10.7 per cent) than of any other group said 'yes', while more of them (88.3 per cent) than of any other group said 'no'. If business is the *raison d'être* of business persons, the state is the *raison d'être* of civil servants – hence, it is a major surprise that an overwhelming majority of them do not want an 'imperial' state. Nevertheless, in a subsequent question, a majority of Egyptians (73 per cent) in the sample showed a preference for a moderately interventionist state that selectively takes care of the needy. By the same token, while an overwhelming majority (87 per cent) conceded the private sector's economic efficiency compared with that of the state, there was a number of reservations about allowing it a free hand in all aspects of public life.

When asked to list the major problems facing Egypt, economic problems dominated. Unemployment was cited by 68 per cent of the sample, followed by inflation (57 per cent) and 'other' economic problems (50 per cent). A distant 4, 5 and 6 on the problem list were rapid population increase (37 per cent), problems of governance (32 per cent) and illiteracy (32 per cent). Next came education (28 per cent), shortages of public utilities (19 per cent), housing (18 per cent) and health (15 per cent). Terrorism (13 per cent) was at 11 in the frequency count, followed by problems of the Egyptian bureaucracy (12 per cent) and pollution (10 per cent).

In a survey of 208 enterprises carried out by the World Bank in 1994, enterprises were asked, *inter alia*, which factors were the most burdensome in profitably operating their business.[31] The most troublesome was considered to be the high level of taxes (53 per cent of respondents), then inflation/price instability (37 per cent), followed by four more or less together – the high cost of bank finance (34 per cent); not enough demand/customers (33 per cent); bureaucratic procedures associated with tax payment (33 per cent); and competition too strong (28 per cent). Much further down the list came other bureaucratic procedures (18 per cent) and labour regulations/requirements (34 per cent). Thus, and this is surprising, businesses require a stable economic environment more than concerns about regulations!

While the increasing role of the private sector in the Egyptian economy is foreseen to generate a lot of expectations, this new role holds no obligations in terms of social objectives. Nevertheless, nearly two-thirds of the Egyptian survey believed that business persons could make profits and still fulfil social obligations to the community at large. To their credit, more of the business persons themselves (75 per cent) believed in this reconcilability than any other group in the sample.

The transformation towards a private sector-led economy means that the state should reorder its priority areas of intervention in the light of the ability of the private sector to assume the responsibility of taking over and/or deepening its existence in areas where the state is withdrawing or reducing its activities.

But the private sector can not be involved in all activities. The Ibn Khaldoun survey asked for opinions on education and health. A very small percentage (around 5 per cent) of the sample would concede monopoly to the private sector in educational services. The rest were almost evenly divided between state monopoly and mixed competition. A majority of business persons (55 per cent) and top civil servants (53 per cent) would like to see university education provided by both. In this respect, they were twice as keen as laypersons (26 per cent).

With regard to health, more than two-thirds of the sample wanted both public and private sectors providing the service, while fewer laypersons felt this way than business persons (72 per cent), community leaders (71 per cent) and civil servants (71 per cent). One important symbol of state control of civil society is the mass media. Respondents were asked who should control the 'printed media' as well as the 'air media', and were given three options: state only, private sector only or both. A majority (64 per cent) of the sample opted for a mixed participation of state and private sector in issuing printed media, as did a smaller majority for the air media (54 per cent). Nevertheless, more than half of every single group was willing to see the private sector share in the electronic mass-media market.

Members of the sample were also asked a number of questions about private-sector performance. An overwhelming majority (87 per cent) believed that the private sector is more efficient than the state and/or its public sector. As would be expected, the business persons were more adamant in this respect (90 per cent) than all others, especially laypersons (85 per cent). However, valuing the private sector's efficiency does not seem to extend to other attributes. In the simple but blatant question as to whether the 'private sector was all good', only one third said 'yes' and more (40 per cent) said 'no', with the rest (26 per cent) uncertain.

Finally, altruism remains high in Egypt. When asked whether the success of business persons 'should oblige them to do more public service for society', an overwhelming majority of 89 per cent agreed, including 90 per cent of the businesspersons themselves!

Small enterprises and social responsibility

This book has concentrated upon large-scale TNCs. But what is the likely impact upon small enterprises where most of the employment is being generated in the developing countries? Clearly, one impact is that as TNCs become more socially responsible, they will need to ensure that their suppliers and subcontractors are also observing the same rules of the game.

Many small enterprises deal, not directly with the TNC but, more likely, with a supplier to the TNC's subsidiary. Will the concern of social responsibility make it more difficult and costly for small enterprises to operate?

The main issue in contention is likely to be whether the small business has, and acts by, a code of ethics. But what should be in such a code? This was discussed in Chapter 2, where the move toward a core set of labour standards was raised. It could be expected that for small firms it may well be easier to comply with a core set of labour standards than for larger firms. This is because the owners usually know their workers well and subject themselves to the same conditions. The level of trust is also high in smaller firms, particularly in family firms, and is something normally missing in larger companies.

However, satisfying economic standards might be much more of a problem for a small enterprise than for a larger one. This is especially so where wages are concerned. In most developing countries, the government sets a minimum wage, which – if it is less than the market wage – is not of much concern. The problem comes when the minimum wage is higher than the market wage to the extent that its application will throw the small enterprise into difficulties. As an example, I came across such a case in a recent evaluation of ILO Employment Intensive Programmes (EIPs).[32] The EIP has tried to establish domestic industry capacities by developing small enterprises able to apply employment-intensive construction and maintenance methods. Since employment-intensive public or community works projects provide a unique opportunity to introduce a number of ILO's fundamental standards, they potentially contribute to the improvement of working and living conditions among target groups. However, the shift to private-sector execution of public works has increased the risks of workers' exploitation and non-respect of basic labour standards as related to minimum wage, minimum age, non-discrimination, workers' compensation for work accidents, safety and health, and conditions of work for casual labour. The main instrument for minimizing these risks is the inclusion of social clauses in the contract documents. The EIP has, in a number of countries, assisted governments in drawing up contract documents, including clauses related to improved conditions of work for the largely casual workforce. While experiences have not yet reached that stage, the next step would be to enforce the respect of these clauses by keeping short-listed only those companies who actually apply the clauses. The incorporation of elements relating to labour standards and social dialogue into training materials for both government staff and small contractors is another, softer, means of promoting the welfare of the workers. An economic argument is the importance of labour productivity in labour-based projects, which can only be optimal if the workers enjoy good working conditions and, of course, appropriate tools.

My observations of this in action illustrate the dilemma. In Chipata, in eastern Zambia, at the end of 1997, I met a tobacco grower who complained that when the road rehabilitation project passed near his tobacco grading and collecting shed, he lost many of his labourers to the project. He was paying Kwacha 800 per day, while the project's contractors were paying Kwacha 2000 (approximately US$1.50). In a discussion with a representative from the provincial labour office, we took this up and discovered that the labour office was not particularly clear in its advice on what labour laws applied to the project's quasi-casual labourers (they normally work from two to three months). If considered as casual labour, they should receive Kwacha 245 per hour, plus travel (if more than 3 kilometres away), and lunch allowance. This, for an eight-hour day, came to between Kwacha 1950 and Kwacha 2400 a day. If the labourers worked for more than three months, they then had another set of regulations that applied to them. The tobacco grower was clearly paying below the minimum wage set for the country as a whole, and the project was just about legal; yet it seemed that the minimum wage was set at above the market wage for the area (the tobacco grower was presumably paying the market wage). There is a dilemma. The EIP/ILO clearly wishes to abide by labour legislation; but this pushes costs up above the market costs, leading, eventually, to increased unemployment with better living conditions for those who are employed. This was illustrated by the labour officer's experience with shopkeepers whom she had visited. Where she found shop workers receiving less than the minimum wage, she advised the shopkeeper to fire some of his other employees so as to be able to offer one employee adequate conditions of work as proscribed under Zambia's labour law! Those fired, because they had been employed for more than three months, should receive adequate redundancy compensation, as also proscribed by the labour law. The result is likely to be that when shopkeepers see the labour inspector walking up the road, they will shut up shop and hide, or else (the more unlikely case where enforcement of regulations is poor, as in most developing countries) they will adhere to the labour law and pass on their increased costs to consumers. This is inflationary, creates unemployment, will increase the poverty of the consumers and could potentially drive the shopkeeper out of business, thereby concentrating the retail market in the hands of a few. There is, of course, substantial agreement that workers should not be exploited; but the lesson learned is not entirely straightforward. Labour codes must take account of local conditions so as to prevent exploitation; but, equally, they must not be so severe as to ruin employment and development prospects.

The human development enterprise (HDE)

I first thought of creating an index to rank the Fortune 500 companies on the basis of social responsibility – a human development index for *enterprises* – after attending a workshop at the end of 1992 in New York on the UNDP's HDI for *countries*. During the nearly ten years since then,

I have not been able to achieve this aim, but am moving in this direction with the socially responsible enterprise index (SREI) for companies in the UK and my Corporate Responsibility Index through Internet Consultation of Stakeholders (CRITICS) questionnaire and index that I described in Chapter 9. My interest in doing this was also stimulated by an ILO economist, Guy Standing, in a paper he published at the end of 1992.[33] He developed a set of indicators for what he called the 'human resource enterprise' (HRE) and set about examining the issue with a random sample survey of 1311 industrial establishments in the Philippines in 1990. Standing's HRE had to have five main characteristics:

1   It should provide those entering the establishment with training, either directly or by paying for its provision.
2   It should have an objective, non-discriminatory recruitment policy.
3   It should provide regular employment for all or the great majority of the workforce.
4   It should include internal working conditions.
5   A good HRE should operate a system of labour relations that gives workers a 'voice' in the production and work process.

The HRE contained the following 12 indicators:

1   Training is usually provided to newly recruited workers.
2   Initial training is not merely informal and on the job.
3   Retraining is provided to improve job performance or enable workers to switch between jobs.
4   Retraining under (3) is formal.
5   Retraining to upgrade workers is provided.
6   Retraining under (5) is formal.
7   The workforce is unionized.
8   The union is an independent, industrial one.
9   Fewer than 10 per cent of the workforce have a non-regular employment status.
10   A labour–management cooperation is operated.
11   A job-rotation policy exists.
12   Recruitment policy is non-discriminatory on sex grounds.

The difference between my set of indicators and those of Standing's is clear. He concentrates on labour within the firm, while I include this as only one of my seven stakeholders.

When applying these indicators in the Philippines, Standing found that there was no evidence that labour costs were higher as a proportion of total production costs in firms with high HRE scores. Nor did he find any evidence that employment growth was inversely related to HRE scores as, he says, might be expected by economists who argue that high non-wage labour costs act as a brake upon employment. Firms with high HRE scores were also more likely to have carried out work reorganizations and to have introduced technological changes, both signs of dynamic enterprises.

In a more recent paper, Standing asks what is a good enterprise for the 21st century.[34] He revises his HRE concept and now calls it a 'human development enterprise' (HDE), which is a type of firm that, in the late 1990s, could be regarded as having 'exemplary labour and employment practices and mechanisms to ensure development in terms of skill reproduction security, social equity, work security, economic equity and democracy'. The indicators he uses for applying the concept both in South Africa and in Russia are similar to the ones used in the Philippines, at least for the composite indicator he calls HDE1 – that is, it focuses primarily on worker training issues. In different variants of the same indicators, he adds such elements as accidents at work; how many workers are women; disabilities; wages compared with society norms; unionization; share ownership by workers; profit-sharing elements; and methods of appointment of senior managers.

Again, he focuses on internal aspects of the firm, although he widens his choice to consider more than training indicators. He finds for Russia that labour costs as a share of total production costs were lower in firms with high values of HDE. He tackles the vexed question, in Russia, of whether those enterprises who treat their employees well are, nonetheless, unresponsive to market pressures. His results are inconclusive because he, indeed, finds that higher HDE firms had cut employment by less than those with lower HDEs. But what is interesting and important in Standing's work is that he is one of the few people, if not the only one, to have tried to quantify what is meant by a responsible enterprise in a developing country. To do this he conducted his own survey, and this must be the future even in industrialized countries. I found for myself, even in the UK, that the published data does not give a broad enough view to analyse what is actually meant by a socially responsible enterprise in practice – nor what are the consequences of being socially responsible in terms of profitability, equity and longevity.

Chapter 11
Conclusion: The Next Millennium

The future

The future within which companies will operate will be entirely different from what we see today. This future will be created, partly, by the private sector and, increasingly, by the visions that socially responsible companies have and will have. The future is not just being created by enterprises, although these are having a bigger influence than ever before. Think tanks, universities, governments, non-governmental organizations (NGOs), communities and inspired individuals all play their part. Reflections on this future are, of course, pure speculation based upon perceived trends of the moment.

One of the most interesting views in recent years has come from the report *Tomorrow's Company*, which raised a major debate in the UK when it was published in the late 1990s. In interviews with 48 company leaders, six major forces for change were identified. First, these were the technological developments that are transforming markets, revolutionizing information and communications, and creating new possibilities for what, how and where work is done. Second, the globalization of markets, supply chains, work and capital is racing ahead faster than ever before, demanding new sensitivity and a more rapid response from business. Global competition is producing changes in cost and quality on an unprecedented scale. Third, new employment patterns have emerged with the rise in importance of the knowledge worker, the growing numbers of self-employed people and small businesses, the erosion of the traditional concept of the job as being full time, permanent and male-only, and the consequent changes in the role and outlook of trade unions. Fourth, new organizational structures are emerging, with the introduction of the networked organization, the reduction and streamlining of corporate centres, the subcontracting of whole functions and the growing use of independent specialists. Fifth, environmental issues are becoming of critical importance for business, not only because of the rising threshold of public concern and expectations, but also because of the need for business to fulfil a significant role in helping to solve global environmental problems. Sixth, the death of deference means pressure on companies from more demanding employees, customers and communities who expect their individual needs and values to be respected. To these I add a seventh, the decline in government and the need for large-scale enterprises to take on more of the responsibilities formerly seen as the sole preserve of governments. It has only been a decade since the notion was entrenched that government should run the railways, the telecommunication network, the airlines, the postal service and so on. That notion seems very old fashioned today.

What could companies do next?

Social forces both within and without a company will have an impact on future profitability that is no less important than competitive conditions or technological developments.[1] Corporate social policy needs, therefore, to be part of any large company's strategic considerations. The main questions before the chief executive are:

- What is the company currently doing that is socially irresponsible, and what is it doing that is socially responsible?
- Specifically, on what new issues, if any, should the company seek to lead social expectations?
- What more, if anything, should the company be doing to include social responsibility in its strategy?
- What are the likely costs and benefits in the short and medium term that are likely to arise from including more items of social responsibility in the company's strategy?

Some managers, of course, will choose to ignore the problem in the belief that all parties will eventually follow an equal path as it is forced upon them by local or international regulations. But legislation will always be behind companies who have a global footing and who, anyway, may just decide to move to the location that offers the most favourable environment. Yet, as noted repeatedly elsewhere in this book, a planetary bargain in which all parties agree to follow certain socially responsible guidelines is beneficial for everyone in the medium to long term.

Looking ahead pays off. Ackerman and Bauer noted, for example, that a sensitive understanding during the mid 1960s of the social issue life cycle, as it applied to ecology, would have prompted the prediction that expenditures for pollution control in some industries were likely to become a significant part of capital budgets.[2] For the firm who gave strategic significance to this prediction, future benefits were possible from the then current decisions on plant location and manufacturing process design. Early efforts to work with the issue may have produced subsequent cost savings that were not available to those other firms who held back until action was forced by legislation.

Box 11.1 Suggested memo from CEO to create/review the company's CSR[3]

To: Senior staff
From: CEO
Re: 15-point programme for corporate social responsibility (CSR)

As a result of our recent decision to review our social responsibilities, I would like you to commence work on the following items:

- Identify our business goals and decide upon the purpose of our social responsibility programme. How does our long-term vision match up with our business goals?
- Identify problem areas or areas of opportunity to enhance our CSR.
- Research: what are the latest business standards? Check out Social Accountability 8000 (SA8000), AccountAbility 1000 (AA1000), the Global Reporting Initiative (GRI), the International Labour Organization (ILO) conventions, World Trade Organization (WTO) discussions, the Caux Principles and so on. What are the key issues for us as a business and why?
- What are our competitors doing on CSR? Who is producing the best social report?
- Identify our key stakeholders and check what we are currently doing with them.
- Identify the key indicators to measure our progress as a socially responsible enterprise.
- Ensure that our code of ethics has been distributed and discussed with all stakeholders and indicate how that has been done. The quality of this process is essential for an effective outcome.
- Verify that our suppliers have adopted a code of ethics in dealing with us.
- Identify and brainstorm programmes on what more, if anything, we can do.
- Make a recommendation on what NGOs and/or business networks we should contribute to (for instance, conservation, charity, community associations, sporting associations, and so on).
- Prepare a list of suggestions on how our products might be made more socially responsible. Ideas could be gleaned from all stakeholders who should be canvassed accordingly. For instance, could we be more cost effective, more environmentally friendly, more truthful in marketing and sales, improve our external communications?
- Identify the costs and benefits of the proposals.
- Implement the activity or programme, ensuring that it relates well to other proposals in the pipeline.
- Research and develop a series of advertisements to show what we are doing in the area of CSR and market the programme accordingly. Ensure that we can back this up with internal, consistent practices since this is a dangerous pitfall if that is not the case.
- Evaluate the social responsibility proposals against cost/benefits.

In all of these projects, remember that the most economical proposals have the greatest chance of acceptance. We must, of course, ensure that our bottom line is kept in mind.

Assuming that all of this has been taken on board by the chief executive officer (CEO) of a large transnational corporation (TNC), what sort of memorandum could be imagined for him or her to write? It might look something like what is presented in Box 11.1.

What will businesses look like in a new 'CSR' world?

As we begin a new century, what sort of socially responsible business can we expect to see? Of course, this will depend upon what sort of world we can expect, and with change occurring very rapidly it is not completely possible to separate changes in the social arena from the technological or economic ones. Technology increasingly requires less natural resources for the same products, which, in turn, are more and more efficient. The replacement of copper wiring by glass fibre made out of abundant silicon (which is sand) is just one example of this. In the future, too, we shall see less and less the need to travel to a place of work. Production will be more or less entirely carried out by machines, and the main jobs will be in the service sectors – communication, care and social delivery. It is facile to say it, but there is no need for unemployment when the world is crying out for teachers, when the old require increasing amounts of care and so on. Production will pay for this through a more efficient distribution system than we have now. Not only will there be less travel to work, but many services will be carried out in people's own backyards. This will lead to increased fulfilment in work. There will also be less of today's pressures, where we see those in employment working under tremendous stress and long hours, while others cannot get jobs and, despite their inherent skills, are resigned to long hours of leisure that are ruined by the lack of income.

The planet cannot support the consumption and rate of natural resource use for everyone at today's levels in the US, where the highest level of consumption per capita in the world is found. The US will change. Signs of this are already evident – for instance, the move towards healthier foods; towards greater vegetable consumption, which requires less land than meat; towards smaller cars and more energy-efficient homes; and so on. Some will say that the change is far too slow, and that catastrophe is just around the corner. Indeed, for some, the catastrophe is already with us, as a walk in the streets of Calcutta or a kilometre from the White House in Washington, DC, will illustrate. There will be an equilibrium point at which the world will settle – the poorer countries will become richer, while the richer countries may have to give up those social provisions that destroy incentives, as we see today in France and Germany. But this does not mean impoverishment and less caring. Many social services can be delivered more efficiently and cheaply than they are today, and socially responsible business will contribute to the large voluntary efforts that already deliver many social services.

The existence of dozens of billionaires in a world of extreme mass poverty is not sustainable. The remarkable offer of US$1 billion by Ted Turner to the United Nations (UN) a few years ago is an excellent example of what is likely to be the new mood.

As this new world takes shape, large enterprises will be more socially responsible than many governments. The startling social responsiveness of Levi Strauss to its suppliers and employees, for example, exceeds that in many nation states. And 'compassion will be one of the most important characteristics business leaders will need for success a decade from now', according to executives of Fortune 1000 companies, surveyed by Cornell's Johnson Graduate School of Management.[4] Companies such as Levi Strauss and The Body Shop will be the rule, not the exception. The socially responsible companies in this new world will care for its stakeholders; there will be a code of ethics monitored by an independent group and it will be part of a planetary bargain where rogue companies are punished by consumers and governments alike. Work in these new companies for employees will be a pleasure, with a caring company and flexible work practices. The workers, who are also consumers, will see a new world of environmentally socially responsible products. Those left behind by society, for whatever reason, will be cared for by the 'haves', in so far as the 'have-nots' also work to help themselves. Owners and investors will be socially responsible while making profits, and these profits will be closely shadowed by social and ethical investment funds.

The future, then, will not be one where each company vies to outdo its competitors through beggar-thy-neighbour policies. There will be competition between companies; but there will be a level playing field brought about by increased global cooperation. And the conflict between government and governed, where the former spends and the latter pays, will gradually draw out to new social arrangements where the private sector becomes kinder and gentler in its own and society's interest – the 'acceptable' face of capitalism within a new planetary bargain. CSR does matter, and will matter in the future more than ever before.

Notes and References

Preface

1　Michael Hopkins (1998) *The Planetary Bargain: Corporate Social Responsibility Comes of Age*, Macmillan, Basingstoke
2　Thanks to Laurel Dryden, indefatigable head librarian of the ILO in Geneva, for suggesting the new title

Chapter 1

1　James W McKie (ed) (1974) *Social Responsibility and the Business Predicament*, Brookings Institution, Washington, DC
2　Gary von Stange (1994) 'Corporate Social Responsibility through Constituency Statutes: Legend or lie?', *Hofstra Labor Law Journal*, vol 11 (2), spring, pp461–467
3　See President Bush's speech in early 2002 and again in July 2002: www.whitehouse.gov/news/releases/2002/03/20020307.html
4　See www.nytimes.com
5　Charles Handy (1997) 'Will Your Company Become a Democracy?' in *The World in 1997*, published by *The Economist* (cited in Marcello Palazzi and George Starcher (eds) (1997) 'Corporate Social Responsibility and Business Success', The European Baha'i Business Forum, Northill, UK)
6　Social Investment Forum (1997) 'Responsible Investing in the US Tops the Trillion Dollar Mark', Washington, DC, 5 November, p1. (Note: 1 trillion is 1000 billion)
7　*Ethical Investor Newsletter*, no 41, 10–16 September 2001: www.ethicalinvestor.com.au/default.asp
8　*Financial Times*, London, 11 July 2001
9　See, for example, Eric Kolodner (1994) 'Transnational Corporations: Impediments or catalysts of social development?', UNRISD, Geneva, Occasional Paper No 5, World Summit for Social Development, November
10　Meryl Davids (1990) 'The Champion of Corporate Social Responsibility', *Business and Society Review*, vol 74, pp 40–43
11　See www.library.fandm.edu
12　The Malcolm Baldrige National Quality Award is given to US organizations that have exemplary achievements in seven areas: leadership; strategic planning; customer and market focus; information and analysis; human resource focus; process management; and business results

13 Barbara Ettorre (1992) 'The Winner Is...', *Management Review*, vol 81, pp16–20
14 See www.business-ethics.com/100best.htm#Chart
15 See www.accaglobal.com
16 See www.bitc.org.uk/index.html
17 The rankings are based on data from Kinder, Lydenberg & Domini (KLD) (see Chapter 7); but *Business Ethics* notes on its website (see endnote 14) that what KLD looks at in each area 'will vary by company. There is no set formula.'
18 See *Business Horizons* (July–August 1991)
19 OECD (1999) 'Principles of Corporate Governance', May, OECD, Paris
20 CACG Guidelines, 'Principles for Corporate Governance in the Commonwealth', Commonwealth Association for Corporate Governance (CACG), PO Box 34, Havelock, Marlborough, New Zealand, November 1999; see www.cbcglobal.org
21 See Chapter 4 on the Caux Principles. It is also noteworthy that Riva Krut of Benchmark, a Maine-based environmental consulting organization, maintains a database of 'codes of ethics' as a guide to best practice in the industry. See also the Vancouver-based Centre for Applied Ethics website for a list of companies, primarily in the US, with codes of ethics – www.ethics.ubc.ca/resources/business
22 Robert Ackerman and Raymond Bauer (1976) *Corporate Social Responsiveness: The Modern Dilemma*, Reston Publishing, Prentice-Hall, Reston, VA
23 These are drawn from the website www.mhcinternational.com which is updated as definitions and concepts harden or improve. Readers are invited to place their own views on the site. Simon Zadek with Niels Hojensgard and Peter Raynard (2000) 'The new economy of corporate citizenship', The Copenhagen Centre, Copenhagen; Stephanie Draper (2000) *Corporate Nirvana: Is the Future Socially Responsible?*, The Industrial Society, London; Ackerman and Bauer (1976), see endnote 22; Sir Adrian Cadbury (2000), in 'Global Corporate Governance Forum', World Bank, Washington, DC; John Rosthorn (2000) 'Business Ethics Auditing: More than a stakeholder's toy', *Journal of Business Ethics*, vol 27 (1), pp9–19
24 Toby Webb (2002) 'Editor's Notes', *Ethical Corporation Magazine*, March–April, p3
25 Michael Hopkins (2002) 'Letters', *Ethical Corporation Magazine*, May, p15
26 Milton Friedman (1970) 'The Social Responsibility of Business Is to Increase Its Profit', *New York Times Magazine*, 13 September, pp32–33, 122–126
27 John Plender (1997) *A Stake in the Future: The Stakeholding Solution*, Nicholas Brealey Publishing, London and Sonoma
28 Howard R Bowen (1953) *Social Responsibilities of Business*, Harper, New York; Albert O Elbing and Carol J Elbing (1964) *The Value Issue in Business*, McGraw-Hill, New York; Morrell Healt (1970) *The Social Responsibility of Business: Company and Community, 1900–1960*, Case Western Reserve University Press, Cleveland, OH
29 D F Linowes (1974) *The Corporate Conscience*, Hawthorn Books, New York
30 See endnote 22
31 See endnote 22
32 See endnote 22

33 Young-Chul Kang and Donna J Wood (1995) 'Before-profit Social Responsibility: Turning the economic paradigm upside down' in Douglas Nigh and Denis Collins (eds) *International Association for Business and Society*, Conference Proceedings, Vienna, June

34 See endnote 33

35 See Martin Wolf in www.ft.com

36 See James C Collins and Jerry I Porras (2002) *Built to Last: Successful Habits of Visionary Companies*, HarperBusiness, New York

37 L E Preston (1990) 'Stakeholder Management and Corporate Performance', *Journal of Behavioural Economics*, vol 19 (4), pp361–375

38 R E Freeman (1994) *Strategic Management: A Stakeholder Approach*, Pitman, Boston (cited in R K Mitchell, B R Agle and D J Wood (1997) 'Toward a Theory of Stakeholder Identification and Salience: Defining the Principle of who and what really counts', *Academy of Management Review*, October)

39 M B E Clarkson (1995) 'A Stakeholder Framework for Analyzing and Evaluating Corporate Social Performance', *Academy of Management Review*, vol 20 (1), pp 92–117

40 Royal Society of Arts (1995) *Tomorrow's Company: The Role of Business in a Changing World*, Royal Society of Arts, London, 6 June

41 David Wheeler and Maria Sillanpää (1997) *The Stakeholder Corporation: A Blueprint for Maximizing Stakeholder Value*, Pitman, London

42 John Plender (1997) *A Stake in the Future: The Stakeholding Solution*, Nicholas Brealey Publishing, London and Sonoma

43 Will Hutton (1995) *The State We're In*, Jonathan Cape, London

44 Cited in Plender (1997), see endnote 42

45 Will Hutton (1997) *The State to Come*, Vintage, London

46 Samuel Brittan (1997) 'Cheat in Moderation', *Financial Times*, 5 June

47 See endnote 36

48 Christopher Lorenz (1995) 'Why Some Companies Live to a Ripe Old Age While Others Suffer Long-term Decline', *Financial Times*, 4 August

49 As cited in Collins and Porras (1994), see endnote 36

50 Bruce Lloyd (1996) Letter, 'Narrow Interest That Leads to Conflict', *Financial Times*, 9 February

51 Arie de Geus (1997) 'The Living Company', *Harvard Business Review*, March– April, pp51–9

52 See endnote 43

53 Francis Fukuyama (1995) *Trust: The Social Virtues and the Creation of Prosperity*, Free Press, New York

54 See www.friendsprovident.co.uk

55 See, for example, *Meeting the Energy Challenge: The Shell Report 2002*; *People, Planets and Profits: The Shell Report 2001*; *People, Planet and Profits: The Shell Report 2000*; *People, Planet and Profits – An Act of Commitment: The Shell Report 1999*, Shell International, London, available at www.shell.com

56 See endnote 53

57 Samuel Brittan (1997) 'Cheat in Moderation', *Financial Times*, 5 June

58 Rob Harrison (1997) 'Bare-faced Cheek', *New Internationalist*, April

59 George Chryssides and John Kaler (1996) *Essentials of Business Ethics*, McGraw-Hill, Maidenhead, UK

60 Since the first edition of this book, courses on CSR are proliferating. For instance, in July 2002, CSR network organized a conference at the renowned

business school INSEAD (Institut Européen d'Administration des Affaires) in Fontainebleau, France, to raise the profile of CSR in business education. Over 250 particpants took part, including myself – over half from business schools. INSEAD is to sponsor work on 'business in society', its name for CSR

Chapter 2

1   John Rawls (1971) *A Theory of Justice*, Oxford University Press, Oxford, p11
2   The Global Reporting Initiative (GRI) has mounted a major effort to develop such indicators. During the period January–December 2001, the GRI convened a Measurement Working Group, with myself as an adviser; see www.globalreporting.org/workgroup/measurement.asp
3   According to Minister for International Development Claire Short, reported by Sarah Ryle in the *Guardian*, 8 July 1997
4   It is, however, excessively ambitious to believe in the elimination of poverty through any means, let alone a combination of private- and public-sector support. Major inroads can be made; but to 'eliminate' poverty in the world is difficult if not impossible – see Michael Hopkins and William Bartsch (1996) *Poverty in Sub-Saharan Africa*, UNDP, New York
5   *Financial Times*, 19 September 1997
6   Cited in Ryle (1997), see endnote 3
7   I am grateful to Henry Jackelen, head of UNDP's private-sector programme, and Elkyn Chaparro, head of the World Bank's corporate citizenship initiative, for information and discussions on their work
8   He was Republican chairman of the senate's powerful foreign relations committee until replaced by Democrat Joseph Biden in early 2001
9   Lloyd Garrison (1997) 'Money Matters to Marshall Carter: So does the developing world', *Choices* (UNDP), vol 6 (3), pp4–9
10 Eric Kolodner (1994) 'Transnational Corporations: Impediments or catalysts of social development?', United Nations Research Institute for Social Development (UNRISD), Geneva, Occasional Paper No 5, World Summit for Social Development, November
11 Commission of the European Communities (2002) 'Communication from the Commission Concerning Corporate Social Responsibility: A business contribution to sustainable development', Brussels, 2 July 2002, COM (2002) 347 final, p3
12 I am grateful to an unknown reviewer for pointing this out to me in comments on an earlier version of this manuscript
13 Alan S Blinder (2002) 'A time for government action', *International Herald Tribune*, Monday 22 July 2002, p8
14 John Plender (1997) *A Stake in the Future: The Stakeholding Solution*, Nicholas Brealey Publishing, London and Sonoma
15 See, for example, Gus Edgren (1979) 'Fair Labor Standards and Trade Liberalisation', *International Labor Review*, vol 118, p523
16 It has been argued that without such a clause, increased international competition might lead to 'a destructive downward spiral in the conditions of work and life of working people all over the world', International Confederation of Trade Unions (ICFTU) (cited in Van Liemt (1989) 'Minimum Labor Standards: Would a social clause work?' *International Labor Review*, vol 123, p4)

17 The ILO's international standards consist of conventions and recommendations. The basic difference between these two forms of labour standard is that a convention is intended to be ratified, like an international treaty; a ratifying state undertakes to discharge certain binding legal obligations and there is regular international supervision of the way in which these obligations are observed. A recommendation, on the other hand, gives rise to no binding obligations, but provides guidelines for national policies and action

18 Some halting steps were announced in the ILO director general's report to the 85th session (1997), when he said there was a need for 'an overall evaluation of the impact of instruments in terms of legal, economic and social effects, which would attempt [...] to measure the success achieved in fulfilling the specific objective set forth in the convention or recommendation', p25; see www.ilo.org

19 Gijsbert van Liemt (1989) 'Minimum Labor Standards: Would a social clause work?', International Labor Review, vol 128 (4)

20 OECD (2000) International Trade and Core Labour Standards, OECD, Paris

21 Cited in OECD (2000) International Trade and Core Labour Standards, Policy Brief, OECD, Paris, October 2000, p2

22 See Stephen S Golub (1997) 'Are International Standards Needed to Prevent Social Dumping?', Guest Article, Finance and Development, vol 34 (4), December, pp20–23

23 The ILO has sponsored a web page to capture developments in this area – see http://oracle02.ilo.org/vpi/welcome

24 Michel Hansenne (1997) 'The ILO, Standard Setting and Globalisation', International Labour Conference, Report of the Director-General, 85th Session, p11

25 From an article by Roger Crowe in the Guardian, 15 June 1997

26 I am grateful to Masaru Ishida of the ILO for his insightful comments on this point in his review of the first edition of this book – see M Ishida (1999) 'Books', International Labour Review, vol 138, no 4, pp468–471

27 Janus (2002) 'Comment', Ethical Corporation Magazine, July

28 'Guest Column', Ethical Corporation Magazine, March 2002

29 Bernard Avishai (1994) 'What Is Business's Social Compact?', Harvard Business Review, January–February, pp38–48

30 Karl Marx (1967) Capital, vol 3, International Publishers, New York, Part III

31 Jerome Rothenburg (1974) 'The Physical Environment' in James W McKie (ed) Social Responsibility and the Business Predicament, Brookings Institution, Washington, DC

32 'Guest Column', Ethical Corporation Magazine, March 2002

33 Samuel Brittan (1997) 'Cheat in Moderation', Financial Times, 5 June

34 OECD (1994) The OECD Guidelines for Multinational Enterprises, OECD, Paris; ILO (1977) Tripartite Declaration of Principles Concerning Multinational Enterprises and Social Policy, International Labour Organization, Geneva

35 ILO (1977, p3), see endnote 34

36 See www.globalsullivanprinciples.org

37 In 'The New CEP Overseas Labor Auditing Process', Business Ethics, vol 11 (4), July/August 1997, p6

38 CEP (1997) 'Social Accountability 8000', mimeo, October, Council on Economic Priorities, New York

39 See www.cepaa.org
40 For a fuller brief on employment theories, see Michael Hopkins (2002) *Employment Planning Revisited*, Palgrave, Basingstoke and St Martin's Press, New York
41 Will Hutton (1995) *The State We're In*, Jonathan Cape, London
42 Among many other places, this is set out forcefully in Nobel Laureate L R Klein's (1961) *The Keynesian Revolution*, Macmillan, New York (first published 1947)
43 John Maynard Keynes (1936) *The General Theory of Employment, Interest and Money*, Macmillan, London and St Martin's Press, New York
44 See, for example, P Sweezy (1946) 'What Has Keynes Contributed to the Analysis of Capitalism?', *Science and Society* (New York), October
45 See Peter Kenway (1980) 'Marx, Keynes and the Possibility of Crisis', *Cambridge Journal of Economics*, vol 4 (1), March, pp23–36
46 V V Bhatt (1974) *Sterility of Equilibrium Economics*, Economic Development Institute, World Bank, Washington, DC
47 A Berry and R Sabot (1978) 'Labour Market Performance in Developing Countries: A survey', *World Development* (Oxford), November–December
48 Todd G Buchholz (1999) *New Ideas from Dead Economists*, Penguin Books, London, p226
49 Angus Maddison (2001) *The World Economy*, OECD, Paris, p18
50 Maddison (2001, p23), see endnote 49
51 I am grateful for discussions on this point with David Henderson, former chief economist of the OECD, despite the fact that in his own book on CSR he characterizes my CSR argument erroneously when he accuses me of saying in the earlier version of this book 'that the key to economic progress in developing countries and, indeed, to ending world poverty is easily found: big international companies should pay people well'. This 'straw man' is nonsense as can be seen by my writing above; but see David Henderson (2001) *Misguided Virtue: False Notions of Corporate Social Responsibility*, Institute of Economic Affairs, London, p75
52 Drawn from my visit to the Maldives in 1995 at the invitation of the UNDP

Chapter 3

1 R K Mitchell, B R Agle and D J Wood (1997) 'Toward a Theory of Stakeholder Identification and Salience: Defining the principle of who and what really counts', *Academy of Management Review*, October
2 Anne Svendsen (1998) *The Stakeholder Strategy: Profiting from Collaborative Business Relationships*,Berrett-Koehler Publishers Inc, San Francisco, p49
3 Marcello Palazzi and George Starcher (1997) in 'Corporate Social Responsibility and Business Success', *Via Europa*, pp42–47, have a similar list for 'six dimensions of corporate social responsibility'. I have a similar set of groups, with the exception that I split managers off from employees
4 Rob Harrison (1997) 'Bare-Faced Cheek: Can we as consumers really make business more ethical?', *New Internationalist*, April, pp26–27
5 See endnote 4
6 *Business Ethics*, September–October 1997, p20

7   *Financial Times*, 23 August 1997, p5
8   Students for Responsible Business (1997) 'Executives call for compassion in corporate America', www.srb.org
9   20 March 1997; cited in Marcello Palazzi and George Starcher (1997) in 'Corporate Social Responsibility and Business Success', *Via Europa*, p46
10 'News from Campus', *Financial Times*, Monday, 24 September 2001
11 Gabriel Hawawini, Dean of INSEAD, in a speech at the launch of the European Academy of Business in Society, to which I was invited, on 5 July 2002, Fontainebleau, France
12 *Business Week*, 15 September 1997, p116
13 *Business Week*, 15 September 1997, p109
14 In an amusing swipe at dot.coms bordering on the truth, Dave Barry, a syndicated columnist with the *Miami Herald*, wrote that any company with a capital letter in the middle of its corporate name could not be trusted!
15 John Cole (2002) Conference on CSR and Business Performance, University of Middlesex, Centre for Corporate Responsibility and Business Performance, London, 14 April
16 Drawn from Michael Hopkins (2002) 'CSR: 5 minutes with the CEO', *Monthly Feature*, March, www.mhcinternational.com/CEOandCSR.htm
17 James C Collins and Jerry I Porras (2002) *Built to Last: Successful Habits of Visionary Companies*, HarperBusiness, New York
18 It is also getting increasing recognition for this role – its 2000 social report was nominated the winner of those producing social reports in the UK in 2000 by the Institute of Social and Ethical Accountability (ISEA), London
19 *Guardian*, July 1997
20 Cited in *Guardian*, July 1997
21 Katherine Adams (1996) 'Making Capital out of Investors in People', *Employee Development Bulletin*, vol 84, p11
22 HMSO (1989) 'Training in Britain: A study of funding, activity and attitudes', Training Agency, HMSO, London
23 J Hillage and J Moralee (1996) 'The Return on Investors', IES Report 314, September, Institute of Employment Studies, Brighton, UK
24 See endnote 23; based on responses from 535 employers in the IES's 1995 survey who were either recognized as, or committed to, becoming Investors in People, and whose business performance had improved over the previous year
25 Cited in Marcello Palazzi and George Starcher (1997) in 'Corporate Social Responsibility and Business Success', *Via Europa*, p9
26 See endnote 4
27 This subject is treated in depth in United Nations Development Programme (UNDP) (1998) *Human Development Report 1998: Consumption for Human Development*, Oxford University Press, Oxford
28 Alison Thomas (2000) 'Banking on Favourable Terms', Working Paper No 00/490, Department of Economics, University of Bristol, July, p35
29 Mark Suzman (1996) 'Measuring Up to Expectations', *Financial Times* Surveys, London, December
30 The Conference Board, cited in Mark Suzman (1996, p7), see endnote 29
31 See for example Patricia James (1979) *Population Malthus: His Life and Times*, Routledge and Kegan Paul, London
32 I Burton, and R W Kates (1964) 'Slaying the Malthusian Dragon', *Economic Geography*, vol 40, pp82–89

33   Rachel Carson (1962) *Silent Spring*, Houghton Mifflin, Boston
34   Donella H Meadows, Dennis L Meadows, Jorgen Randers and William W Behrens (1972) *The Limits to Growth: A Report for the Club of Rome's Project on the Predicament of Mankind*, Universe Books, New York
35   Sam Cole (1972) *Thinking About the Future: A Critique of the Limits to Growth*, Chatto and Windus Press, UK
36   WCED (1989) *Our Common Future*, Oxford University Press, Oxford
37   See www.wbcsd.ch
38   Sara Parkin (1991) *Green Futures*, HarperCollins, London
39   H E Daly and J B Cobb (1989) *For the Common Good: Redirecting the Economy towards Community, the Environment and a Sustainable Future*, Beacon Press, Boston, MA
40   R Goodland, and H H Daly (1992) 'Three Steps Towards Global Environmental Sustainability', *Development* (Journal of the Society for International Development), p2
41   *The Green Business Letter*, October 1996, cited in Marcello Palazzi and George Starcher (1997) in 'Corporate Social Responsibility and Business Success', *Via Europa*, p15
42   *Business Ethics* (1996) 'The 100 Best Corporate Citizens', vol 10 (3), May–June 1996
43   Julie Hill (1992) *Towards Good Environmental Practice*, Institute of Business Ethics, London
44   See www.hays-plc.co.org
45   James C Collins and Jerry I Porras (2002) *Built to Last: Successful Habits of Visionary Companies*, HarperBusiness, New York
46   Simon Zadek (2001) *The Civil Corporation: The New Economy of Corporate Citizenship*, Earthscan, London, p122
47   See Chapter 2 for my suggestions for government intervention in social responsibility
48   Business in the Community (1997) London, handout
49   See endnote 48
50   See Chapter 5 for a more detailed discussion on GrandMet's *Report on Corporate Citizenship, 1997*
51   See endnote 48
52   According to Marcello Palazzi and George Starcher (1997) in 'Corporate Social Responsibility and Business Success', *Via Europa*, p14
53   This subject is discussed further in Chapter 10, with the focus on small enterprises in developing countries
54   Johann Graf Lambsdorff (2000) 'The Precision and Regional Comparison of Perceived Levels of Corruption: Interpreting the results', Transparency International and Gottingen University, Germany, September. The index is based on perceptions of business people who participated in a survey for the 90 countries covered (up from 52 in 1997). See also www.transparency.com

Chapter 4

1   King Committee on Corporate Governance (2002) *King Report on Corporate Governance for South Africa 2002*, Institute of Directors in Southern Africa, Johannesburg, p220, www.iodsa.co.za

2   N Harris (1989) *Professional Codes of Conduct in the UK: A Directory*, Mansell, London (cited in Alan Kitson and Robert Campbell (1996) *The Ethical Organisation: Ethical Theory and Corporate Behaviour*, Macmillan, Basingstoke)

3   Emeritus Professor Alan Stainer and I have set up an International Centre for Business Performance and Corporate Responsibility at Middlesex University's Business School in London; see www.mdx.ac.uk/www/icbpcr

4   See www.eti.org and Rhys Jenkins, Ruth Pearson and Gill Seyfang (2002) *Corporate Responsibility and Labour Rights: Codes of Conduct in the Global Economy*, Earthscan, London

5   L Nash (1992) 'American and European Corporate Ethics Practice: A 1991 survey' in J Mahoney and E Vallance (eds) *Business Ethics in a New Europe*, Kluwer, Dordrecht

6   Cited in Alan Kitson and Robert Campbell (1996) *The Ethical Organisation: Ethical Theory and Corporate Behaviour*, Macmillan, Basingstoke

7   Jean-Paul Sajhau (1997) 'Business Ethics in the Textile, Clothing and Footwear (TCF) Industries: Codes of conduct', Working Paper, Industrial Activities Branch, Sectoral Activities Programme, SAP 2.60/WP.110, International Labour Organization, Geneva

8   G R Weaver (1993) 'Corporate Codes of Ethics: Purpose, process and content issues', *Business and Society*, vol 33 (1), p46

9   This is drawn from Sajhau (1997, p17), see endnote 7

10 See www.globalexchange.org/economy/corporations/gap/overview.html

11 Sajhau (1997), see endnote 7

12 According to *Hoover's Handbook of World Business* (1997) William Snyder Publishing, Oxford

13 Marjorie Kelly (2002) 'Building Economic Democracy', *Business Ethics Magazine*, July. See also BizEthicsBuzz online via BizEthics@aol.com

14 This issue is partly covered in this book; for a longer version see Michael Hopkins (2002) *CSR: Is There a Business Case?*, Association of Chartered Certified Accountants (ACCA), London

15 See www.globalsullivan.com

16 'Codes of Conduct', *Futures*, vol 27 (2), March 1995, p265

17 See www.caux.ch

18 Summarized from www.caux.ch

19 *Business Ethics*, vol 11 (4), July–August 1997, p15

20 Bob Massie (1997) 'Environmental Reporting Takes Off', *Business Ethics*, vol 11 (4), July–August, p10

21 Simon Webley (1992) *Business Ethics and Company Codes: Current Best Practices in the UK*, Institute of Business Ethics, London

22 C Langlois and B Schlegelmilch (1990) 'Do Corporate Codes of Ethics Reflect National Characteristics? Evidence from Europe and the United States', *Journal of International Business Studies*, pp519–39

23 Andrew Marshall (1997) 'The Principles People Pull out of Burma', *Independent*, 4 July. See also Jubilee Campaign (1999) 'Burma: Briefing Paper', September, Jubilee Campaign, Guildford, available at www.jubileecampaign. co.uk/world/burll.htm

24 Neither Burma nor El Salvador appears in Transparency International's list (given in Chapter 3), apparently because of lack of data

25 See *The Economist*, 26 July 2002

26 Ernst & Young (1997) 'Reviewing the Effectiveness of the System of Internal Financial Control', www.ey.com
27 Confederation of British Industry (1996) 'CBI at Work', *CBI News*, January
28 Alan Kitson and Robert Campbell (1996) *The Ethical Organisation: Ethical Theory and Corporate Behaviour*, Macmillan, Basingstoke, p115
29 Clare Short (1997) 'Development and the Private Sector: A partnership for change', the Institute of Directors, 8 July, DFID, London, p13
30 *Internal Control: Guidance for Directors on the Combined Code*, September 1999
31 Drawn from ACCA (2000) *Turnbull: Internal Control and Wider Aspects of Risk,* Association of Chartered Certified Accountants, London, p5
32 Chris Tuppen (2000) 'The Implications of Turnbull: A corporate view' in *Turnbull: Internal Control and Wider Aspects of Risk,* Association of Chartered Certified Accountants (ACCA), London, p10
33 ETI (2001) *Purpose, Principles, Programme and Membership Information*, Ethical Trading Initiative, London, available at www.ethicaltrade.org/pub/publications/purprinc/en/index.shtml
34 See www.ethicaltrade.org
35 See Chapter 5
36 David Clutterbuck with Dez Dearlove and Deborah Snow (1992) *Actions Speak Louder: A Management Guide To Corporate Social Responsibility*, Kingfisher/Kogan Page, London, p303 (cited in Alan Kitson and Robert Campbell (1996) *The Ethical Organisation: Ethical Theory and Corporate Behaviour*, Macmillan, Basingstoke, p122)
37 Simon Webley (1992) *Business Ethics and Company Codes: Current Best Practices in the UK*, Institute of Business Ethics, London
38 W Manley (1992) *The Handbook of Good Business Practice*, Routledge, London, 1992 (cited in Alan Kitson and Robert Campbell (1996) *The Ethical Organisation: Ethical Theory and Corporate Behaviour*, Macmillan, Basingstoke, p129)
39 Alan Kitson and Robert Campbell (1996) *The Ethical Organisation: Ethical Theory and Corporate Behaviour*, Macmillan, Basingstoke
40 OFT (1996) 'Voluntary Codes of Practice: A Consultation Paper', December, Office of Fair Trading, London, p8; see also www.oft.gov.uk/Business/Codes/default.htm
41 See Michael Hopkins and Simone de Colle (2001) 'Measurement and training issues in ethics and human resources', Fourth Conference on Ethical Issues in Contemporary Human Resource, Middlesex University Business School, 19–20 April
42 John Rawls (1971) *A Theory of Justice*, Oxford University Press, Oxford
43 See endnote 11
44 The full report is available at www.calbaptist.edu/dskubik/young.htm
45 Bob Herbert (1997) 'Mr Young Gets It Wrong', *New York Times*, 27 June, available at www.citinv.it/associazioni/CNMS/archivio/multinazionali/young.html

Chapter 5

1   Drawn from The Body Shop (1995) *Measuring Up: A Summary of The Body Shop Values Report* and the four volumes by the company: *Environment Statement 95* (1995); *Ethical Auditing* (1996); *Animal Protection Statement 95* (1995); and *Social Statement 95* (1995), The Body Shop, Littlehampton, UK; www.thebodyshop.com

2   Anita Roddick (1991) *Body and Soul*, Crown Publishers, New York

3   The report was repeated in 1997 (see www.thebodyshop.com); but The Body Shop has since branched out into supporting human rights and fair trading initiatives. Anita Roddick left day-to-day running of the company a few years ago but still retains 25 per cent of shares

4   David Wheeler and Maria Sillanpää (1997) *The Stakeholder Corporation*, Pitman, London, p189

5   See endnote 4

6   The Body Shop (1995) *Measuring Up: A Summary of The Body Shop Values Report*, The Body Shop, Littlehampton, UK

7   See www.thebodyshop.com

8   See www.thebodyshop.com

9   Jon Entine (1994) 'Shattered Image', *Business Ethics*, September; see also Jon Entine (1995) 'The Messy Reality of Socially Responsible Business', *BWZ (Better World 'Zine)*, issue 1, available at www.betterworld.com/BWZ/9512/cover2.htm

10 Jon Entine (1998) 'Squandering the Integrity Premium: An analysis of the Body Shop's use of social marketing', runjonrun@earthlink.net, 15 February, p3

11 Wheeler and Sillanpää (1997, pvii), see endnote 4

12 Reported in *Evening Standard*, London, 25 August 2001

13 This section draws upon CEP (undated) 'Levi Strauss & Co and the Global Sourcing Guidelines', mimeo, Council on Economic Priorities, New York

14 Jon Entine (undated, presumed 1996) 'The Curse of Good Intentions', www.mngt.waikato.ac.nz

15 See my remarks on child labour in Chapter 10, where I differ from Levi Strauss's code

16 *The Economist* (1997) 'The Quiet American', 8 November, p84

17 Karl Schoenberger (2000) *Levi's Children: Coming to Terms with Human Rights in the Global Marketplace*, Grove Press, New York, p181

18 The full report is available at www.calbaptist.edu/dskubik/young.htm; see also Bob Herbert (1997) 'Mr Young Gets It Wrong', *New York Times*, 27 June, available at www.citinv.it/associazioni/CNMS/archivio/multinazionali/young.html

19 Cited in Herbert (1997), see endnote 18

20 Andrew Young (1997) Letter, *New York Times*, 11 July

21 See endnote 20

22 For a continuing analysis of Nike's CSR credentials, see www.globalexchange.org/economy/corporations/nike/stillwaiting.html

23 B&Q (1998) *How Green is My Patio? B&Q's Third Environmental Review*, B&Q, Eastleigh, UK. See also B&Q (1995) *How Green Is My Front Door? B&Q's Second Environmental Review*, Quality and Environmental

Department, B&Q, Eastleigh, UK; B&Q (forthcoming 2003) *Social Responsibility Update: January 2001–December 2002*; www.diy.com

24 Claire Finch, Social Responsibility Co-ordinator, B&Q, personal communication, 2 April 2003

25 UNEP/Sustainability (1997) *The 1997 Benchmark Survey: The Third International Progress Report on Company Environmental Reporting*, UNEP, Paris

26 The Co-operative Bank (2001) *Our Impact: Partnership Report 2001*, The Co-operative Bank, Manchester, available at www.co-operativebank.co.uk/partnership2001; see also *Making Our Mark: The Partnership Report 2000*, www.co-operativebank.co.uk/partnership2000

27 See www.camelotplc.com

28 The attraction of a lottery as 'well, someone has to win' even in my family goes against the logic that the average return is a negative 50 per cent after costs and allocations to 'good causes' are subtracted and you lose your stake. An alternative investment scheme run by the UK government, the Premium Bonds, is unsurprisingly less publicized since an average payout of 3 per cent can be obtained and you get your money back!

29 Van City (1997) *Social Report 1997*, Vancouver, Canada

30 Its latest is *Meeting the Energy Challenge: The Shell Report 2002*, Shell International, London, available at www.shell.com

31 See www.groupbt.com/betterworld

32 The full report is available from www.groupbt.com/betterworld; this precis is based upon *Ethical Performance*, vol 3, issue 10, March 2002

33 The BT definition of social responsibility is limited and applies mainly to its 'external stakeholders'

34 Chris Tuppen (2000) 'The Implications of Turnbull: A corporate view' in *Turnbull: Internal Control and Wider Aspects of Risk,* Association of Chartered Certified Accountants (ACCA), London

35 *Ethical Performance*, vol 3, issue 10, March 2002

36 John Elkington (1997) *Cannibals with Forks: The Triple Bottom Line of 21st Century Business,* Capstone Publishing, Oxford

37 See www.globalreporting.org

38 This example is drawn from *The Economist*, 2 August, 1997, pp52–53

39 See endnote 38

40 See endnote 38

41 For a survey of ethical and green investments available, see Holden Meehan 'The Survey', www.holden-meehan.co.uk

42 See David Lewis (2000), 'Promoting Socially Responsible Business, Ethical Trade and Acceptable Labour Standards', SD SCOPE Paper no 8, available at www.globalmarch.org/virtuallibrary/dfid/promoting-socially-responsible-business.pdf

43 According to Jon Entine (1996) 'Ethical Investing', September–October, in *At Work*, Berrett-Koehler Publishers, San Francisco, CA

44 Cited in *Ethical Performance*, vol 3, issue 6, November 2001, p1

45 Marshall Glickman (1997) 'Banking Where Your Values Are', *Business Ethics*, vol 11 (4), July–August, p20

46 Cited in Entine (1996), see endnote 43

47 According to a report in the *Financial Times*, 23 August 1997

48 Jean Eaglesham (1997) 'Bad Guys Smoked Out', *Financial Times*, 19–20 July

49 Entine (1996), see endnote 43
50 'SEC Goes after Parnassus Fund', *Business Ethics*, vol 11 (4), July–August, p22
51 Doug Fleer (1997) 'Social Investing gets Diluted', *Business Ethics*, 11(4), July–August, p10
52 Cited in Entine (1995), see endnote 9
53 See www.ftse4good.com
54 *Financial Times*, 'Letters', 11 July 2001
55 *Financial Times*, 'Letters', 14 July 2001
56 See endnote 55
57 A report on the results from the first year's application of CRITICS is available for a small charge from ijhopkins@mhcinternational.com
58 See www.mhcinternational.com
59 See www.mhcinternational.com/jcurve.htm
60 I am grateful to Stewart Lewis, a director of MORI, for allowing me access to some of the basic data from the 1996 survey
61 In 1997, an investigation by *World in Action*, a documentary series of the ITV in the UK, revealed that former British SAS soldiers had trained paramilitaries in Columbia; see John Pilger (1999) 'Phoney war', *Guardian*, 19 October, available at www.guardian.co.uk/comment/story/0,3604,256625,00.html

Chapter 6

1   Of course this could change, should consumers start to look for something different
2   The main source for this section is Daisuke Okamato (1995) 'Social Responsiveness as a Corporate Objective: From the viewpoint of an evaluation of corporations', *Japanese Economic Studies*, ME Sharpe, Armonk, NY, vol 23 (2), March–April
3   Karl Schoenberger (2000) *Levi's Children: Coming to Terms with Human Rights in the Global Marketplace*, Grove Press, New York, p102
4   For this section, I draw heavily from Britta Rudolph (1997) 'Enterprises and Social Policy in Germany', New Partnership for Social Cohesion, Working Paper No 8, Socialforskningsinstituttet, Copenhagen
5   The Economist Intelligence Unit's (EIU's) index measures the relative cost in doing business relating to wages, costs for expatriate staff, air travel and subsistence, corporation taxes, perceived corruption levels, office and industrial rents, and road transport (cited in *The Economist*, 24 January 1998, p126)
6   Kim Moller and Erik Rasmussen (1995) *Partnership for New Social Development*, Mandag Morgen for the Social Summit, Copenhagen
7   See Siemens (2000) *Corporate Citizenship Report 2000*, Siemens AG, Berlin and Munich. See also www.siemens.com/corporate_citizenship
8   These figures have reduced slightly since the first edition of this book in 1998; see, for example, recent issues of *The Economist*
9   The measurement of unemployment is fraught with difficulties; the data here is taken from the standardized definitions of the OECD quoted in *The Economist*, 31 January 1998, p108

10 *Financial Times*, 29 October 1993
11 Brian Groom (1997) 'Attractions of Relocation Lure French Groups', *Financial Times*, 18 September
12 In 'Globalisation through French eyes', *The Economist*, 4–10 August 2001, p25
13 *The Economist*, 6 September 1997, p54
14 Thanks to Simone de Colle for a first draft of this section on Italy
15 Drawn from Hans Bach and Anne-Birte Kylling (1997) 'The Danish Partnership Concept', New Partnership for Social Cohesion, Working Paper No 4, Socialforskningsinstituttet, Copenhagen
16 Development Division, Ministry of Social Affairs (1996) 'A New Partnership for Social Cohesion', Copenhagen, May, p21
17 See www.copenhagencentre.org
18 Socialforskningsinstituttet (1997) 'New Partnership for Social Cohesion', 19 June, Copenhagen; prepared for International Think Tank on New Partnership for Social Cohesion under the auspices of Ms Karel Jespersen, Minister for Social Affairs, Denmark, p50
19 Drawn from Marcel Einerhand (1997) 'Social Responsibility of Enterprises: Country report for the Netherlands', New Partnership for Social Cohesion, Working Paper No 9, Socialforskningsinstituttet, Copenhagen
20 Moller and Rasmussen (1995, p44), see endnote 6
21 Moller and Rasmussen (1995, p56), see endnote 6
22 Moller and Rasmussen (1995, p46), see endnote 6
23 Nestlé (2001) *Nestlé in the Community*, Nestlé SA, Public Affairs, Vevey, Switzerland, and www.nestle.co.uk
24 Swiss Infocentre (1994) 'Focus on Sandoz: An economic, ecological and social analysis', Swiss Infocentre, Fribourg, September
25 I am grateful to Catherine Voutsinas, a Swiss lawyer, for pointing these facts out to me
26 For this section I draw from J S O'Connor (1997) 'Social Partnership for Social Cohesion in Ireland', New Partnership for Social Cohesion, Working Paper No 10, Socialforskningsinstituttet, Copenhagen

Chapter 7

1 See www.AccountAbility.org.uk
2 See www.globalreporting.org
3 Peter Pruzan and Ole Thyssen (1994) 'The Renaissance of Ethics and the Ethical Accounting Statement', *Educational Technology*, January, pp23–28
4 Simon Zadek and Peter Raynard (undated, presumed 1996) 'Accounting for Change: The practice of social auditing', mimeo, New Economics Foundation, London
5 Robert Ackerman and Raymond Bauer (1976) *Corporate Social Responsiveness: The Modern Dilemma*, Reston Publishing, Prentice-Hall, Reston, VA, p15
6 The matrix of indicators given in Chapter 8 for each stakeholder, as well as for other areas, is a basis for a social audit. Use of this framework would ensure a certain amount of comparability between companies. I used the framework to

produce an index of CSR. This one number allows a quick, rough-and-ready approach to the problem of comparison. But given the multidimensionality of companies in different settings, it is not uncontroversial

7   This was the Measurement Working Group of the GRI, held in London in September 2001, at which I was present as an adviser; see www.globalreporting.org/workgroup/measurement.asp

8   See, for example, Mallen Baker (2002) 'The Global Reporting Initiative: Raising the Bar too high?' at www.mallenbaker.net

9   See www.mallenbaker.net/csr/nl/index.html

10 See endnote 9

11 For a fuller description, see www.mhcinternational.com/measurement.htm

12 John Elkington (1997) *Cannibals with Forks: The Triple Bottom Line of 21st Century Business*, Capstone Publishing, Oxford

13 See www.cepaa.org

14 I am grateful to Shareen Hertel of CEP for providing me with an early draft of CEP (1997) 'CEPAA Framework', Council on Economic Priorities, New York, September

15 See Ralph Estes (1996) 'The Sunshine Standards for Corporate Reporting to Stakeholders', *Business Ethics Insider's Report on Responsible Business*, Special Report No 1, December

16 Ingeborg Wick (2001) *Workers' Tool or PR Ploy? A Guide to Codes of International Labour Practice*, SÜDWIND Institute, Siegburg, Germany

17 It is, possible to create 'one indicator' of social responsibility, as I have done through my CRITICS questionnaire; see www.mhcinternational.com

18 It is difficult to quantify the human and social elements in the social capital of a firm that combine together with the physical and financial capital to bring about the firm's dynamics and eventual profit stream

19 This matrix is drawn from Michael Hopkins (2002) 'Sustainability in the Internal Operations of Companies', *Corporate Environmental Strategy*, vol 9, no 2, pp1–11

20 International Centre for Business Performance and Corporate Responsibility (ICRBP), Middlesex University Business School, London, UK; see www.mdx.ac.uk/www/icbpcr

21 Note: indicators are instruments chosen to measure social and economic phenomena and come in a wide variety of forms. The 'strongest' indicators, in a mathematical sense, are those on an interval scale, followed by an ordinal scale (ie 1 = very good; 2 = good; 3 = poor) and then by a nominal scale (1 = yes; 0 = no). Indicators can be mainly (a) input or process, such as 'number of people in a training course'; or (b) output or outcomes, such as 'number of people who can create a web page'

22 KLD (1994) *Social Screens, KLD COMPANY REVIEWS: Key to Ratings: Analysis Year 1993–1994*, KLD

23 Peter Kinder, Steven Lydenberg and Amy Domini (1993) *Investing for Good*, Kinder, HarperBusiness, New York

24 For a more extended discussion on KLD indicators, see Sandra Waddock (2002) *Leading Corporate Citizens: Vision, Values, Value Added*, McGraw-Hill Irwin, New York, pp200–209

25 Personal communication, August 2002

26 Dale Kurschner (1996) 'The 100 Best Corporate Citizens', *Business Ethics*, May–June, pp24–35

27 Anne Fisher (1998) *The 100 Best Companies to Work for in America*, Fortune, New York. See also www.fortune.com/fortune/bestcompanies
28 See www.sustainability-index.com

Chapter 8

1   Lee E Preston and J E Post (1975) *Private Management and Public Policy: The Principle of Public Responsibility*, Prentice-Hall, Englewood Cliffs, NJ, p3
2   Archie B Carroll (1979) 'A Three-Dimensional Conceptual Model of Corporate Social Performance', *Academy of Management Review*, vol 4, pp497–505
3   Donna Wood and Raymond Jones (1995) 'Stakeholder Mismatching: A theoretical problem in empirical research on corporate social performance', *International Journal of Organizational Analysis*, vol 3 (3), July, pp229–267
4   Wood and Jones (1995), see endnote 3
5   Donna J Wood (1994) *Business and Society*, 2nd edition, HarperCollins, New York
6   William C Frederick (1978) 'From CSR1 to CSR2: The Maturing of Business-and-Society Thought', Working Paper, Katz Graduate School of Business, University of Pittsburgh
7   Robert Ackerman and Raymond Bauer (1976) *Corporate Social Responsiveness: The Modern Dilemma*, Reston Publishing, Prentice-Hall, Reston VA
8   Steven L Wartick and Phillip L Cochran (1985) 'The Evolution of the Corporate Social Performance Model', *Academy of Management Review*, vol 10, pp758–769
9   See K Davis (1973) 'The Case for and Against Business Assumptions of Social Responsibilities', *Academy of Business Management*, vol 16, pp312–322
10 Wood (1994, p155), see endnote 5
11 Robert Levering, and Milton Moskowitz (1993) *The Best 100 Companies to Work for in America*, Penguin, New York, pp45–47
12 The original research for this chapter was done by Alton Strachan and myself – see Michael Hopkins and Alan Strachan (1995) *Defining Indicators to Assess SREs*, MH Consulting Report, Geneva. I have since updated the work with the aid of generous email communications from Donna Wood

Chapter 9

1   See www.mhcinternational.com and follow the link to 'Rate your company'
2   Peter Kinder, Steven Lydenberg and Amy Domini (1993) *Investing for Good*, Kinder, HarperBusiness, New York
3   *The Guardian*, London, July 1997
4   See www.foe.co.uk
5   This was suggested by Michael Nisbet, personal communication, 9 April 1998, after he read an earlier version of this chapter
6   See www.diageo.com
7   *The Observer*, London, 2 August 1997

8   New Consumer (1991) *Shopping for A Better World*, Kogan Page, London
9   Financial Times (FT) Guide (1997) *Business in the Community*, FT Surveys, London
10 I have written about this elsewhere; see Michael Hopkins (1999) *A Planetary Bargain and the Bottom Line: Corporate Citizenship, Financial Performance and Staying Power*, ILO Enterprise Forum, International Labour Organization, Geneva
11 Personal communication, 16 September 1997
12 All of these indicators for the 100 largest UK companies can be obtained in machine-readable form on request from the author at www.mhc international.com
13 Hoover's (1997) *Hoover's Handbook of World Business 1995–1997*, William Snyder Publishing, Oxford. For the latest figures for 300 non-US based companies, see Hoover's (2003) *Hoover's Handbook of World Business 2003*, Hoover's Business Press, Austin, TX
14 Paul Brown and John Smith (1998) *A Guide to Company Giving, 1997–1998*, Directory of Social Change, London

Chapter 10

1   Asian Productivity Organization (1982) *Social Responsibility of Business*, Asian Productivity Organization, Minato-ku, Tokyo 107
2   Colin Hines and Tim Lang (1995) 'Employment and the Culture of Insecurity', *Economic Report*, July, Employment Policy Institute, London, p3
3   I am grateful to Richard Anker, my former colleague in the ILO, for discussions and for providing me with pre-publication material from his book Richard Anker (ed) (1997) *The Economics of Child Labour in Selected Industries*, Himalaya Press, New Delhi
4   Zafar Alam (1997) 'Problem of Child Labour in the Lock Making Industry of Aligarh', in Anker (1997, pp167–171), see endnote 3
5   Other numbers of child labour are given by Christaan Grootaert and Ravi Kanbur (1995) 'Child Labor: A review', Policy Research Working Paper No 1454, May, World Bank, Washington, DC
6   See International Programme for the Elimination of Child Labour (1997) *Child Labour: Targeting the Intolerable*, International Labour Organization, Geneva; and also at www.ilo.org
7   Janet Hilowitz (1997) *Labeling Child Labour Products: A Preliminary Study*, International Labour Organization, Geneva, p3
8   V R Sharma (1997) 'Economics of Child Labour in the Carpet Industry', in Anker (1997, p131), see endnote 3
9   One of the best-known of all social labelling initiatives with reference to child labour, it arose after European consumer groups became aware of the extent and conditions of child labour in the production of hand-knotted carpets in South Asia, chiefly India, Nepal and Pakistan
10 Danish National Institute of Social Research (1997) 'New Partnership for Social Cohesion', mimeo, 19 June, Danish National Institute of Social Research, Copenhagen, p97

11 Drawn from Michael Hopkins (2001) 'Is There a Role for Large-Scale Corporations in Alleviating Poverty in Developing Countries?', Paper presented at Corporate Social Responsibility Working Group, Development Studies Association, University of Manchester, 11 September

12 There are no objective measures to define who are poor and non-poor in developing countries. The World Bank has a rule of thumb that defines poor people as those who gain less than US$1 a day or who fall in the bottom 30 per cent of income earners. When I talk about poor people in this section, my 'mental' image is of those at the bottom of the income distribution, not *all* people in a poor developing country. But this is a far more complicated subject than these few words can convey. It is also something that I have written about extensively elsewhere; see, for example, Michael Hopkins and William Bartsch (1997) *Alternatives to Poverty in Sub-Saharan Africa*, UNDP, Regional Bureau for Africa, New York

13 Assuming that there are around 1000 TNCs with 100,000 employees, this gives 100 million employees. With a world population of 6 billion, and assuming that about 40 per cent are in the labour force, this gives 2.4 billion workers

14 The examples for Zaire, Zimbabwe and India are drawn from Danish National Institute of Social Research (1997, pp94–96), see endnote 10

15 See Jane Nelson (1996) *Business as Partners in Development*, The Prince of Wales Business Leaders Forum, London, p120

16 King Committee on Corporate Governance (2002) *King Report on Corporate Governance for South Africa 2002*, Institute of Directors in Southern Africa, Johannesburg, www.iodsa.co.za

17 This was agreed in a UN- and UNEP-sponsored meeting of the Global Compact, to which I was invited, in Paris, 17–18 June 2002

18 Asian Productivity Organization (1982, p1), see endnote 1

19 Danish National Institute of Social Research (1997, p96), see endnote 10

20 I am grateful to a personal communication on 17 September 2001 for this section on India from Dr Vikas Goswami, director general, Business and Community Foundation, 1 Jai Singh Road, New Delhi – 110001

21 TERI (2001) 'Altered Images: The 2001 state of corporate responsibility in India poll' (cited in www.sustainability.com/news/articles/core-team-and-network/kavita-pr)

22 Cited in www.sustainability.com/news/articles/core-team-and-network/kavita-pr

23 San Miguel Corporation (1996) *Social Development: A Corporate Commitment*, Manila, the Philippines

24 See www.pbsp.org.ph

25 I am grateful to Serra Ayal for contributing a first draft of this section

26 See http://enviropa.envirolink.org/resource.html?itemid=892&catid=5

27 See papers from the conference on www.csramericas.org

28 See www.ethos.org.br

29 See 'Filantropia y Responsabilidad Social en Chile', *Prohumana*, Revista Trimestrial, Ano 2/No 6, June 2001

30 These results were originally reported in Institute of National Planning (1995) *Egypt: 1995 Human Development Report*, Institute of National Planning, Cairo, Egypt. The two principal writers of that report were Osman M Osman, now Minister of Planning, Eygpt, and myself

31 World Bank (1994) *Private Sector Development in Egypt*, World Bank, Washington, DC
32 Michael Hopkins (1998) 'An Independent Thematic Evaluation of ILO's Employment Intensive Programme', POLDEV, January, International Labour Organization, Geneva
33 Guy Standing (1992) 'Identifying the "Human Resource Enterprise": A Southeast Asian example', *International Labour Review*, vol 131 (3)
34 Guy Standing (1996) 'The Human Development Enterprise: Seeking flexibility, security and efficiency', mimeo, November, ILO Enterprise Forum, International Labour Organization, Geneva

Chapter 11

1 This is stated in Robert Ackerman and Raymond Bauer (1976) *Corporate Social Responsiveness: The Modern Dilemma*, Reston Publishing, Prentice-Hall, Reston, VA, p41, along with several examples of CSR actions to take. I draw and expand on their recommendations in this concluding chapter
2 Ackerman and Bauer (1976), see endnote 1
3 Thanks to Patrice Van Riemsdijk of the Institute of Social and Ethical Accountability (ISEA), UK, for useful comments on an earlier version of this memo
4 See www.srb.org

Index